A.J.A. Symons was born in 1900. His short literary career has left *The Quest for Corvo* as its most permanent legacy, though in another field he will be long remembered as co-founder of the Wine and Food Society by the grateful members. Symons' many interests included the collecting of musical boxes, the inventing of elaborate games, and the study and practice of forgery; these eccentric pursuits left him time to edit an anthology of the verse of the nineties, to write brilliant studies of the explorers Stanley and Emin Pasha, and to compile a history of the Nonesuch Press. He died at Finchingfield in Essex in 1941.

THE QUEST for Corvo

AN EXPERIMENT IN BIOGRAPHY

A.J.A. SYMONS

With a Memoir by Sir Shane Leslie

QUARTET BOOKS

Published by Quartet Books Limited 1993
A member of the Namara Group
27/29 Goodge Street
London W1P 1FD

Originally published by Cassell & Co. Ltd 1934

This edition copyright © by Quartet Books Ltd 1993

A catalogue record for this title is available from the
British Library

ISBN 0 7043 0197 0
Printed and bound in Great Britain by
Cox & Wyman, Reading, Berks.

TO SHANE LESLIE

CONTENTS

A Memoir

Out of the present darkening days I am asked to write about A.J.A. Symons. Certainly there were moments when we were as close as literary minds could be. That is to say, our intellects clicked pleasantly, humorously and almost absorbingly on certain subjects. We saw each other seldom, but always on an intense plane of conversation. We enjoyed each other's conversation very much, and I can truly say neither found the other dull for a moment. I think we kept each other like a kind of rare liqueur for the mind: not for daily consumption or prandial potations – but occasionally when rarely so disposed.

It hardly seems so long ago since the First Edition Club was started – more than a quarter of a century ago.

It was an admirable idea, and made an easy halt for refreshments near the British Museum. There was a palatial house in Bedford Square, which was seldom full, for England is not a literary country in the way that France or Germany is – in fact I hardly met a soul there, and only A.J. striding about with incessant conversation and exhibiting brilliant shows of books – foreign bindings and first editions – kept any life in the building at all.

It was a great pity that it could never succeed, and that only a handful of people took up subscriptions. As a club it lacked the importance of the Olympian Athenaeum where the greatest literati could lunch and browse and meet their fellows, and on the other hand was too imposing for the pale and haggard hordes of 'literary ghosts' and research-agents who haunted the British Museum. In any other country it would have drawn from all literary categories, but in England it drew neither the writers nor the collectors, and of course to invite the intellectuals to Bloomsbury was drawing coals to Newcastle.

A.J. lived a shadowy life but one of considerable refinement. He was beautifully tailored. His evening clothes hung gracefully to his elegant figure and were the subject of theft by the envious. He moved like a kind of messenger of the gods, a Hermes of letters chiefly in the underworld of the writing and bookselling community. If that underworld had not been so limited in England he would have found scope to make money, collections and friends on a larger and sufficient scale. In Paris, Rome, Vienna, such a life could have been lived; and he would have established himself as a character and moved from salon to salon.

But England – London – knows no salons where all manner of literary lions and adventurers can meet under the wand of some presiding blue-stockinged lady. A.J. essayed the next best thing – a literary club. That would have succeeded abroad in the form of a high-class café. But clubs in England are not for the Arts. They are for the Philistine and the Philathletic, and it would be inconceivable for a genius to be elected to any St. James's club as such. So the First Edition Club was bound for many reasons to fail and to disappear together with the guarantees of a few sanguine benefactors. A.J.A. Symons became more shadowy, though he retired to somewhat dark and crabbed lines under the aegis of Blooms-bury Church. The Front Line of Letters was not for him to hold.

He was a character in search of a patron, and would have done better in the eighteenth century, especially under some opulent member of the Roxburghe Club. He could have made an admirable attendant to the Spencer or Sunderland libraries and would have been happy planning their cata-logues and exhibitions. But the great patrons are no more found in English life, and he fell across the strangest and rather sinister Maecenas possible, the late Maundy Gregory, whom no novelist could have accurately characterized. Judg-ing from his bookplate Maundy Gregory inherited a succes-sion of noble bloods. Without a title himself, others he jauntily and amazingly set upon the titular way. It was Maundy Gregory who patronized and subsidized the research necessary for the biography of Corvo.

Of the three occasions which brought our minds together, flicking and flashing in the manner through which Victorian and Edwardian conversation sometimes reflects itself in a book of memoirs, the most notable was A.J.'s scintillating *Quest for Corvo*. From the moment that he discovered Corvo his efforts were directed in search and research of a character as shadowy and brilliant as himself. Corvo of course was different, being an outcast from every literary and social circle. It was his utter loneliness and impossibility which made his posthumous charm. During his life he was mordant and unpleasant enough: but even those who suffered most from his libels and aberrations never ceased to enjoy talking about him, living or dead.

Corvo's unhappy figure had so dwindled in the memory and estimation of men that doubts were freely expressed whether he had ever existed. Certainly the Complete Peerage can be searched in vain for the Barony of Corvo. But A.J. set out in high spirits and began to recover quantities of letters and lost books and MSS. Maundy Gregory, who belongs rather to Symons's life than to Corvo's, was so fascinated that he provided the annual fantastic dinner given at the Ambassador Club in Corvo's memory. On these occasions A.J. was vastly in his element, and the diners enjoyed a marvellous menu variated by exciting brands of wine and elaborately printed programmes. This kind of literary amusement came to an end, but the book survived, beautifully printed and produced – *The Quest for Corvo*.

A.J. came to me self-introduced, which was quite right, for he was self-made. I think his dandyism and his literary preciousness were entirely his own ideas. I never had time to inquire his origins, his old school tie, or his more respectable claims on society. All that interested me was his mercurial career in and out of Bloomsbury. Even the Bloomsbury set were not aware of him, and he played his lonely hand of double dummy by himself. The dummies (only so called because they were down among the dead men) were of course Baron Corvo and Oscar Wilde, both of whose biographies he worked on with pellucid humour and unwearied research. The fourth chair was alternately occupied by Maundy

Gregory and myself. Gregory was a social adventurer. So, in another sense, was Symons. I would gladly have been in that underworld or *demi-monde* of letters in which I understood both were interested. But I was tied down to a life of respectable paternity in Paddington: a destiny I accepted with one or two dashes into literary scandal. Symons was fascinated by literary scandal and relived Lives in the memories of Corvo and Wilde, about both of whom I am convinced no man ever accumulated such detail. He often reminded me of a frail phantom of either, according to mood. He haunted the Nineties, and they haunted him.

It was a literary tragedy that Symons died before the Wilde biography was complete. What I read of the manuscript impressed me deeply, but there are many unborn who will write Lives of Oscar. I doubt if any will write a second Life of Corvo. It is by his *Quest for Corvo* that Symons will live in the twilight of English letters. I am proud every time I make my annual reading of that master quest that my name stands on the page of dedication.

Symons exhausted the sources of Corvine information, even if he did not print all that passed into his ken. Oscar has never ceased to find biographers, from Sherard and Frank Harris onwards. Harris was a superlative cad, whom I last met in his final American phase. He was also a pure journalistic adventurer, but robust and unscrupulously successful. He was a grandoise liar. He seemed to me to have achieved the position which Symons would have graced had Society welcomed his gentlemanly converse and amity, but he had not the brazen power of the social thruster. Both talked immeasurably about Oscar, but how utterly different the two men were.

I was always forcibly reminded that Symons was a generation behind his time. He belonged entirely to the Nineties and he should have been held at the inky font by Beardsley and christened out of the *Yellow Book*. No one better than he knew the period or better remembered the many forgotten minor writers who sang or smirked in the vivid light of the Green Carnation. He produced a Catalogue of the Nineties for which I wrote a Ballad, and for which Beardsley had unknowingly limned a posthumous sketch. He was the first who collected the whole *Yellow Book* school, distinguishing carefully between editions, cancels and covers, all of which he carefully folded in coloured papers. George Moore amongst the collected still lived, and Symons proceeded to Ebury Street to discuss dates and occasions of early works. Moore was immensely flattered and enjoyed being dissected in his own lifetime. Certainly he signed elaborately all the first editions he was shown, including the *Pagan Poems* he had disowned with a great prosarian's horror of his wild oats in verse. Symons had a whimsical way which won him all my store of Corviana as soon as he told me he intended to write Corvo's Life.

I had long regarded this as an impossibility, though I collected any stray Corviana that came my way, for the mysterious Baron had deeply interested me since Cambridge days. He was amusingly wicked, though not as terribly wicked as he liked to believe.

It is an old story now, but inadequately told in Father Martindale's life of Monsignor Robert Hugh Benson, how that impressionable priest became fascinated by Corvo's *Hadrian the Seventh* and so much so that he was willing that his style as well as his script should become Corvine. Corvo, who was in unusually shallow water at the time, responded eagerly. It was not only food and money that he was in need of, but of rehabilitation in the world of bourgeois respectability, which he had certainly flouted on every possible occasion. He hoped by associating his name with Benson's in a book concerning the blissful Martyr, St. Thomas of Canterbury, that he would become less an outcast among writers and less reviled among publishers. This scheme, alas, was foiled from Llandaff House, where Benson was living in refuge with Monsignor Arthur Barnes, before Cardinal Bourne would permit him to take up regular work in the Archdiocese of Westminster.

Monsignor Barnes felt alarmed at this prospect and, taking counsel with Arthur Benson, then Master of Magdalene, they decided to break the literary combination. Robert Hugh Benson proved obedient, sad and apologetic. Corvo became intractable and unforgiving. His genius was welcomed, but not his name.

Corvo's contact with Cambridge brought him or his works into touch with a number of undergraduates to whom his style showed an amusing escape from the rather bourgeois manner in which the English language was written for tutors and examinations. Like Benson, we were all astonished by his literary brilliance. He seemed to be able to produce the sparks and scintillations with single words and phrases that Macaulay could only produce with whole sentences.

Hugh Benson had become a focus for a circle of young men like Ronald Firbank, Vyvyan Holland, Jack Collins, and there was no knowing how far Corvo's influence would be able to spread. Jack Collins passed to the teaching staff of Downside Abbey, and Ronald Firbank, after vainly endeavouring to reconcile a life of advanced mysticism with rowing conditions at Trinity Hall, passed temporarily into the ranks of the Papal Guard in Rome. Though Corvo was frowned upon by the Colleges, I do not remember that he proposed to add anything more dangerous than Astrology to academical life. Like all mediaevalists, Corvo was intensely interested in the influences of the stars. What has since become a newspaper vogue suitable to all tastes and all classes was then a study reserved to arcane circles.

Life at Cambridge was tremendously brisk and bright in the sense that studies and athletics impinged on each other. Muscular Christianity was still a vogue. Visitors, speakers, new characters and famous people arrived at all times, and shadowy creatures like Corvo were quickly forgotten. His books stayed on our shelves, but after his fierce quarrel with Benson he himself disappeared, as we learnt later, to become an amateur gondolier in Venice where he could follow his tastes literary, historical, swimming, yachting, to the utmost. Benson himself had taken up the life of vagabondish popular preacher in which he lived his remaining years to his own perfect satisfaction. There were preaching trips to America to come, more successful books and the glory of the Roman Purple. But Corvo he never saw again. Unfortunately Corvo would not allow him to forget his derelict friend. Correspondence was all on Corvo's side, and it was as virulent as the inks in which it was written. Even his insults Corvo wrote in a script more beautiful than is used in Papal Briefs.

The story of his Venetian life has been collected as well as possible in the *Quest*. Like so much of his life, much could never be told, but no doubt he felt it was better to perish miserably as an outcast free of pen and philosophy (ghastly as it was) than to live affluently as a bourgeois in England amid the Philistines, the Protestants and those whom he had come to consider worse – the English Catholics. How he loathed them, as he insisted, for their lack of charity, lack of real Faith, lack of superstition, lack of the whole Renaissance spirit, lack of all love of beauty and art! He sank and sank, but, alas, not into the pure waters of the lagoon. He lived for what ignoble pleasure he could collect. But he could hardly have been as diabolical as he described himself in unprintable letters. His last writings were terrible, and must be attributed to a stained imagination rather than to autobiography. He still wrote books in that indeflectible handwriting. He still libelled the living and the dead and betrayed every vestige of friendship that was offered to him, and bit as deeply as he could every hand that was lifted to feed or help him. He became a kind of fuming solitary, an *Athanasius contra mundum* in his own mind, but the world, which had so scarcely noticed him, now forgot he had ever existed. Stripped of all things that soothe the fitful fever, he died in Venice in October 1913. By his side was a glass of water. Was it an overdose that sped him? Was it the infamous Borgia venom, the secret of which he claimed he had discovered? The poison which alone of poisons leaves no trace?

Possibly, and possibly not, for he had received the last overwhelming Absolution and Sacrament from the Franciscans which the Church administers to Emperor or vagrant, to Baron or beggar. It does not appear that he received the Eucharist, but Extreme Unction must have pleased him as a ceremony, as well as gathered him for his last journey. He asked for prayers for his soul (he was so tired) but he did not specify from whom. From one at least he received piteous assistance at the Altar. Robert Hugh Benson, in agony that he did not know whether Corvo had committed the suicide he had so often threatened or not, offered the Mass of Requiem for his incomprehensible friend. In exactly a year he was destined to follow him.

Benson was immeasurably distressed, for he felt that Corvo's wayward soul was somewhat his responsibility, and he had allowed his advisers to persuade him to cast him off. To break friendship deliberately is like breaking a glass bowl with one's own hands. Benson felt he had cast out a drifting soul and left him to drown. Great indeed are the claims of respectability, and Church and family had prevailed.

Benson was an instance of the absorbing interest Corvo could wield on the impressionable. He certainly altered his life, confirming him as a littérateur and a mediaeval adventurer, rather than letting him become a dull forgotten curate, the usual fate of convert clergymen. It must be remembered that Corvo was also a convert, but not on grounds of piety or antiquarian research (like Monsignor Barnes). Out of the very Protestant and prosaic oystershell of Grantham Grammar School he had plucked the pearl of Faith. His reasons began with a historical hatred of Henry VIII, the bogey of all English history teachers, and flowered into an adoration for the Borgias, Popes, criminals or Saints.

The key to Corvo's life was that he imagined he was a Borgia reborn and was therefore capable of their splendid depths or their hidden heights. His trend was certainly toward their depths in preference to the sanctity which one at least achieved, but he recognized their immense powers affecting the welfare of the world. So he came to write his *Chronicles of the Borgias* without any education in historical methods, without an inkling of research or knowledge of authorities. But the passionate will lead the way and his good angel reappeared in the head of Jesus College, at Oxford, who had been his kindly but bewildered headmaster at Grantham.

It had been obvious that Corvo was not a proper instructor to let loose on the tender grammar-boys of Grantham, but Dr. Hardy felt no scruples in accepting him as his private secretary at Oxford as a means of giving him hours of research in the Bodleian, one of those corners of the world where the history of the Western World is undoubtedly confined if it can be dissected by the living eye of an Acton or the dead finger of a Bury.

Corvo was far from being either. He had set up for himself the majestic outlines of the Borgia Popes and proceeded to paint them with the most brilliant and lurid colours. The high ceremonial style and manufactured words which he employed added immensely to the vigour of the book and even to the prestige of the Holy See. If the wicked Popes, so called, could be so magnificent and prodigious of achievement, what could not be adduced in praise of the institution which made their background? For Corvo a Borgia Pope, drunk with power, was worth any number of milksop Victorian Archbishops.

The book was published in worthy format. In these days it is a handsome volume which collectors are glad to cherish. The edition passed out of print and almost out of mind. Only the ecclesiastically-minded really fed upon its rich paragraphs.

There was a long list of charitable Catholics to whom Rolfe had applied for help at different times, from Archbishop Smith and the Marquess of Bute downwards. Most of these had found themselves disappointed and even dismayed by the experience. Corvo demanded alms as a right and sympathy as a convert. Unfortunately there was little gratitude in his scintillating make-up. I think it is important to realize that he entirely lacked the gifts of humour and gratitude. This may explain much.

The *Chronicles of the Borgias* was Corvo's self-projection on the past. But *Hadrian the Seventh* was his splendid shadow in the present surrounding world which had so inconceivably rejected him. This was the book which arrested Benson, and in which he became eventually part, for he became one of the rejectors. One explanation of Corvo's callousness to others may have been that from the beginning he visualized them as literary phantoms and puppets ready to be energized and galvanized in his future books. However much he tried to mortify them, the only person he succeeded in making thoroughly miserable was himself.

His literary acclaim was posthumous and limited. His personality as revealed in the *Quest* has always proved more interesting than his books: and what generation could ever become engrossed in reading *Hadrian the Seventh*?

But his fame grew between the two Wars, and he would have greatly appreciated the Corvine dinners which were brilliantly arranged by Symons, and provided at the Ambassador Club. It was a collection of publishers, patrons, and all who were interested in Corvo generally. There was a Corvine grace recited to the effect that the Lord feedeth the ravens, *Deus pascit corvos*, and, amongst the many fine wines, glasses of *Corvo Spumante* were filled in which to drink the health of the namesake. The menus were works of art, and True Recitals of the speeches were printed. On one occasion copies were distributed of an unpublished Excommunication of Lord Northcliffe as the Enemy of the whole Anglican race! On these occasions the superb Pedigree and genealogical descent of the Borgias was exhibited, in which the insignia and heraldry of the family were cunningly emblazoned. The only fly in the ointment was the sad fact, which had to be revealed, showing that the last of the Borgias had extinguished his Papal blood as a Methodist!

Such banquets are not likely to be revived, but sufficient reprints of the Works and of the *Quest* will give Frederick Rolfe Baron Corvo that literary acceptance and quasi-fame which he sought so avidly and so vainly during his lifetime. Corvo owned more to A.J.A. Symons than Johnson owned to Boswell.

The early thirties, when *The Quest for Corvo* was published, must have been the happiest period of A.J.'s life. He felt his feet well up on the rung of letters. The *Quest* was an astonishing success. So many picked it up to jest but read and read until they could almost pray for the soul of its unhappy subject. The Corvine myth was odd enough in the mouths of publishers and creditors, but the real Corvo, exhumed from the most unexpected quarters and quarries, was stranger still. A.J. found himself in the highly appreciated gallery of snapshot biographers – all crowding down the Lytton Strachey path – and his next immediate ambition was to write the full and final life of Oscar Wilde, the great figure surviving from the welter of the Nineties. About this he set with confident zeal and all his persuasiveness. It was clear that certain chapters would be illuminated as never before. New material was found for the Irish years and schooling of Wilde, and most important of all, A.J. was able to win the confidence and assistance of both Lord Alfred Douglas and the representatives of Oscar.

The First Edition Club was followed in his life by the Wine and Food Society, a last Lucullan memory before the sea of Austerity broke upon our civilization. A.J. had retired to Finchingfield, in Essex. He was no longer seen in Bloomsbury. He was reputed mysteriously ill, and the illness proved fatal. The life of Oscar Wilde was never completed. The period between wars, in which alone A.J. could have flourished, was telescoped, and when he died the things for which he had lived had become ruined, endangered, or at least postponed until times return worthy of the dandy and the dilettante to move again upon this earth.

SHANE LESLIE

PREFATORY NOTE

It will be apparent to any reader of the following pages that I am under heavy obligations to many friends and correspondents. Most of these debts are acknowledged, explicitly or by inference, in the course of my narrative; a certain number, however, require separate statement, and accordingly I take this opportunity to offer thanks to Messrs. Vyvyan Holland and Vincent Ranger, whose careful reading of the proofs of this book have saved it from many errors; to Mr. Shane Leslie, Mr. Desmond MacCarthy, and Sir John Squire, who have for many years recognized Baron Corvo's powers as a writer, and encouraged me in my task; to Mr. D. Churton Taylor, who has spared no pains in ransacking both his office files and his memory; to Mr. Stephen Gaselee, by whose kindness I was permitted to examine certain papers referring to Corvo contained in the Foreign Office files and in the Consulate at Venice; to Mr. E. F. Benson for permission to print letters written by his brother; to Miss Kathleen Rolfe for permission to print letters written by her father; to Mr. John Holden for a letter which had the length and merits of an independent essay; to my wife, always my most patient listener; to Trevor Haddon for his interesting 'intermission'; to Mr. J. Maundy Gregory for many favours and his share in the Quest; to Mr. and Mrs. Philip Gosse, in whose garden the last chapter was written; to Mr. Brian Hill and Dr. Geoffrey Keynes, by whose assent I had access to the Corvo papers of the late A. T. Bartholomew; to Dr. G. C. Williamson and Mr. R. H. Cust for suggestions and the loan of material; to Mr. G. Campbell, formerly Consul at Venice; to Mr. Grant Richards, Professor R. M. Dawkins, Mrs. van Someren, Mr. Sholto Douglas, Canon Ragg and the many others who have supplied me with personal reminiscences, particularly Mr. Harry Pirie-Gordon; and finally to Mr. Ian Black, without whose practical assistance the writing of this book would have been delayed at least a year. Alone among the characters the Rev. Stephen Justin is presented under a fictitious name.

I have ventured to call *The Quest for Corvo* 'an experiment in Biography' to signify that it is an attempt to fulfil those standards which I endeavoured to set up in an essay on biographical tradition published by the Oxford University Press in 1929.*

* *Tradition and Experiment in Present-day Literature* (by various authors). O. U. P. 1929.

LIST OF ILLUSTRATIONS

Fr. Rolfe during his period of training
at the Scots College

I

THE PROBLEM

MY quest for Corvo was started by accident one summer
afternoon in 1925, in the company of Christopher Millard.
We were sitting lazily in his little garden, talking of books
that miss their just reward of praise and influence. I mentioned *Wylder's Hand,* by Le Fanu, a masterpiece of plot,
and the *Fantastic Fables* of Ambrose Bierce. After a pause,
without commenting on my examples, Millard asked:
'Have you read *Hadrian the Seventh?*' I confessed that I never
had; and to my surprise he offered to lend me his copy—to
my surprise, for my companion lent his books seldom and
reluctantly. But, knowing the range of his knowledge of
out-of-the-way literature, I accepted without hesitating;
and by doing so took the first step on a trail that led into
very strange places.

Millard comes into this story more than once; and a short
digression regarding him will not be out of place. I am glad,
indeed, to pay his memory the tribute of these words, for
to me at that time, living in the country by preference, in
London by profession, he was one of the compensations of
town, as he must have been to many others. His queer
character and odd way of living offered unending contra-
dictions and problems for an intelligent observer: nevertheless I could rely on him to provide literary conversation,
and a glass of Val de Peñas, at almost any hour of the day or
night. Contrariety was perhaps his most consistent attribute.
At Oxford he flouted the authorities in acts of noisy
folly; in early manhood he became an enthusiastic Jacobite,
ostentatiously laying his white rose at King Charles the
First's feet every year, and acknowledging Prince Rupert of
Bavaria as his rightful sovereign; in later years he became

an ardent Socialist, wore flaming ties, and (to the astonishment of yokels) sang 'The Red Flag' very loudly in quiet
country inns. Yet, despite his Oxford antics, he took a good
degree; despite his Jacobite feelings he fought very loyally
for King George; and his Socialist views did not prevent him
from incarnating most of the Conservative virtues.

His history was a sad one, though he never obtruded it.
He had filled many posts with ability. Turn by turn he was
schoolmaster, assistant-editor of the *Burlington Magazine*,
secretary to Robert Ross, record-clerk in the War Office.
Under the pen-name of Stuart Mason he compiled a biblio-
graphy of the writings of Oscar Wilde, under his own a
catalogue of the work of Lovat Fraser; and each remains a
model of its kind. But what had been folly at Oxford became criminal misdemeanour in later life, and he felt the
lash of the law; it was, indeed, his imprisonment that taught
him Socialism and sympathy with the working man. After
the War he became a dealer, in a small way, in rare and
unusual books; and by this means, a small pension, and a
legacy of £100 a year which his friend Ross had left him, he
lived. Nevertheless he was (for such a man) painfully poor.
He lived entirely alone (unless the tits he fed counted for
company) in a small bungalow hidden behind a Victorian
villa in Abercorn Place, reached by descending area steps
and walking round the side of the house. His establishment
consisted of a sitting-room (with bookshelves modelled on
those of Aubrey Beardsley) in which he kept his stock, a small
bedroom, also lined with books, a tiny kitchen-bathroom,
and a shed or shelter in which, during fine weather, he slept
in open air.

If Millard could have maintained this bungalow without
financial cares he would have been completely happy; but
though his tastes were simple, his simplicity was of the sort
that is satisfied only with good things. He would buy salmon
for his supper, carry it home in greased paper, and cook it
himself; but it must be Scotch, and a prime cut. Bread and
cheese would suffice for his lunch, but the cheese must be a

choice Stilton. Modern beer was his despair; and he abhorred
in equal measure imported meat, and credit accounts. In
the matter of wine he was less exacting: he relied upon a
reasonable Val de Peñas, which he bought cheaply from a
shipper friend, and drank at any hour that pleased him.
Indeed, despite his cramping poverty, he contrived to live
almost entirely as he pleased. He rose early or late, and idled
or worked, according to his mood. When the successful
sale of a book brought him a profit, he would live in perfect
contentment until the money was gone; not till then would
he look about for more. Much of his time he spent in
correspondence with literary Americans on points of biblio-
graphical research: he had an eighteenth-century appetite
and aptitude for that pastime. But he would instantly
interrupt any work in favour of conversation with a
friend; and his love of poetry and close acquaintance with
nineteenth-century English literature made his conversation
particularly agreeable to me.

In person this natural philosopher was a striking figure.
More than six feet tall, always hatless, dressed in dark blue
shirt, grey flannel trousers, and green jacket (all of which
he mended and patched with his own hands when necessary),
he had an air and dignity which never left him. A deep
voice and abundant, greying, curling hair, set off this confident carriage; he was perhaps the most self-possessed man
I have ever known. He was certainly the most self-sufficient:
not only did he live alone, he made his own bed, washed
his own dishes, cooked his own meals, and even, I believe,
sometimes made his own clothes. A queer character in
modern London; but such was the man to whom I owe my
first knowledge of the life and work of Baron Corvo. Alas,
that he did not live to learn the end of the story.

*   *   *

The title-page of *Hadrian the Seventh*, dated 1904, proclaimed it to be the work of Fr. Rolfe, of whom I had never
heard. I began to read it filled with curiosity as to Millard's

reason for departing from his principle that a man who wants
to read a book should buy it; but before I had turned twenty
pages my curiosity deepened into gratitude for his recommendation: I felt that interior stir with which we all recognize
a transforming new experience. As soon as I had finished the
story I read it through again, only to find my first impression
enhanced. It seemed to me then, it seems to me still, one
of the most extraordinary achievements in English literature:
a minor achievement, doubtless, but nevertheless a feat of
writing difficult to parallel; original, witty, obviously the
work of a born man of letters, full of masterly phrases and
scenes, almost flabbergasting in its revelation of a vivid and
profoundly unusual personality.

From the absence of any indication to the contrary on the
title-page of the tattered first edition that Millard had lent
me, I inferred that this remarkable experiment in fiction
was its author's first book: first novel, at least. The plot,
though well conceived and executed, gives evidence, in
some details, of inexperience and an unpractised hand.
Nevertheless the story is astonishing in its depth and force,
and survives the summarization which is necessary to display
its effect on me when I first read it.

The 'Prooimion' reveals George Arthur Rose vainly
endeavouring to work while almost prostrate from the
pain of an arm on the tenth day of vaccination. His work is
writing; and from the detailed description of his possessions
and surroundings which follows, it becomes credible as well
as clear that this poor, lonely and misanthropic sufferer in
a suburban bed-sitting-room is a remarkable man as well
as a struggling author. There are many characters in literature intended to impress such a conviction on the reader's
mind; very few succeed. But George Arthur Rose, suffering
from pain as from a personal affront, sitting in his low,
shabby brocade armchair with a drawing-board tilted on
his knee, and his little yellow cat asleep on the tilted board;
with two publisher's dummies at his hand, one a compendium
of phrases transcribed in his archaic script, the other a

private dictionary compiled by forming Greek and Latin compounds to enrich his English vocabulary (which includes such 'simple but pregnant' formations as 'hybrist' and 'gingilism'); who counts the split infinitives in the day's newspaper while he dines on soup, haricot beans, and a baked apple; who carefully preserves the ends of his cigarettes so that he may break them up and make a fresh cigarette when he has a sufficient quantity; whose mantelpiece holds, with other queer things, the cards of five literary agents, and another inscribed *Verro precipitevolissemevolmente;* whose garret windows are always open to the full; who exists in terrified anticipation of the postman's knock; this man starts to instant life in Fr. Rolfe's pages, for the best of all reasons (as I discovered later): because he was Fr. Rolfe himself.

The action opens with an unexpected visit to this impoverished eccentric from a Cardinal and a Bishop. In the long, electric conversation that follows, many things become apparent. George Arthur Rose is a Catholic, and a rejected candidate for priesthood, still smarting from the bitter injustice done him twenty years before, when his superiors decided against his vocation. Nevertheless Rose has never wavered in his personal confidence in that Call which his fellow-Catholics have neither recognized nor tolerated. After leaving the theological college under a cloud, he has contrived to keep himself alive by shift after shift, though time and again betrayed by friends of his own faith. Still, after twenty years, he holds an undiminished belief that he has a Divine Vocation to the priesthood, an unswerving resolution to attain it. All this is implied to the reader in the course of Rose's verbal fencing with the two priests, which is conducted by the author with a skill not far short of Meredith's at his best. The feline figure of Rose, sore, suspicious, ready to take offence at any slighting word, immovably convinced of the justice of his cause, moves alive in front of us; we can hear his voice.

The motive for the ecclesiastical visit is disclosed. A tardily penitent friend of George Arthur Rose, aware of the shameful treatment that has been meted to him, has urged a reconsideration of his case. Thus prompted to an examination of this forgotten matter, the Cardinal in turn has been struck by Rose's long faithfulness to his Call, and has in turn become convinced that a great wrong was committed twenty years before, when Holy Orders were refused to one who has since signally shown by his devotion that he deserved them. And so he has come to make belated amends, and to invite the outcast to prepare himself for reception into the ranks of the clergy.

Rose, who has been the dominating figure throughout the long interview, treats the proposal with magnificent coolness. He makes conditions. He must have a written admission of the wrongs that have been done him, and a sum of money equal to that which he has lost by his unpaid labours for Catholics who have defrauded him. The Cardinal is prepared; both points are conceded. And then Rose is at last moved from his chill reserve. He casts the acknowledgement of his injuries into the flames, not wishing, as he says, to preserve a record of his superior's humiliation; and he gives back to charity half the sum presented in restitution. And he agrees to attend next day to receive from his Eminence's hands the four Minor Orders. 'Meanwhile, I will go and have a Turkish bath, and buy a Roman collar, and think myself back into my new—no—my *old* life.' So ends one of the most unusual interviews in fiction.

The conclusion of the chapter is not less unusual. We stand behind the scenes and witness the admission of the candidate to priesthood. Word by word we hear his confession and examination. We hear his inner thoughts expressed, his avowal of belief; and with him we receive the blessing: 'ego te absolvo ✠ in nomine patris et filii et spiritus sancti. Amen. Go in peace and pray for me.' The preliminaries are passed through without hitch, and the novice is to say his first mass in the private chapel, with the Bishop as his assistant and the Cardinal to serve him. After storm, this is indeed calm and peace for the man of wrongs.

*   *   *

The scene shifts abruptly to Rome, where the Papal Conclave is sitting to select a Pope. Here, too, we have a description which, though not unique, is rare in English literature. The method of procedure is carefully described, Scrutiny by Scrutiny; the Cardinals taking part are named, and the voting given. Unacquainted though I was with modern religious history, I guessed as I read, rightly, that many of the skilfully-sketched figures were portraits of real men.

After many vain attempts, there is still a deadlock: no member of the Sacred College can secure the necessary majority. The Way of Scrutiny having failed, the Way of Compromise is adopted: nine Cardinals are chosen by lot as compromissaries and invested with 'absolute power and faculty to make provision of a pastor for the Holy Roman Church'. Still they are confronted by a clash of interests which prevents decision; still no certainty is felt of the suitability of any of the remaining Cardinals (the nine compromissaries have relinquished their own chances by accepting office). Providence intervenes. Struck by Rose's likeness to one of the compromissaries, the English Cardinal tells the story of his amazing persistence in his vocation despite the hardships and trials of twenty years. The story makes a deep impression: far deeper than its narrator anticipates. Rose seems, to those who hear the tale of his tribulations and steadfastness, more than mortal clay. 'You owe it to that man to propose him for the Paparchy', says one of the listeners; and so it comes about that he who was for so long rejected is taken to be the corner stone: George Arthur Rose is chosen as Pope.

There may seem, in this summary, to be more improbability in that turn of the story than there is as Rolfe presents it. He handles the problem of making anything so unlikely

seem probable with skill. When Rose, attending the Cardinal
in Rome, not knowing what is in store for him, learns with
amazement that the choice has fallen on him, the reader
also is agreeably astonished; for though he has been shown
the breakdown of the Way of Scrutiny, and the necessity
of Compromise, the secret of the selection is kept from him
—as it is from Rose, until, in the Sistine Chapel, he hears
an intense voice from the gloom reciting (in Latin) the
question: 'Reverend Lord, the Sacred College has elected
thee to be the successor of St. Peter. Wilt thou accept
pontificality?'

Now the fun begins. Unexpected though the transfor-
mation is, Rose instantly adjusts himself, and shows his will
to rule. He is not in the least abashed by the extraordinary
dignity conferred upon him, and carries himself with enig-
matical equanimity all through the long ceremony of
consecration. At the conferring of the episcopal ring he
annoys the Cardinals by demanding an amethyst instead of
the proffered emerald. When asked what pontifical name
he would choose:

'Hadrian the Seventh': the response came unhesitatingly,
undemonstratively.

'Your Holiness would perhaps prefer to be called Leo, or Pius,
or Gregory, as is the modern manner?' the Cardinal-Dean
inquired with imperious suavity.

'The previous English pontiff was Hadrian the Fourth; the
present English pontiff is Hadrian the Seventh. It pleases Us;
and so, by Our Own impulse, We command.'

Then there was no more to be said.

Hadrian's next act is to require the opening of a blocked
window looking out over the city, one of those blocked up
in 1870 in the dispute between the Papal and temporal
powers, and not opened since. And, despite the protests of
the Cardinals, opened it is, and from it a tiny-seeming
figure in silver and gold, radiant in the sun, gives the
Apostolic Benediction to the City and the World.

It is not necessary to follow the story in detail through all its convolutions to the end. During his two decades of wandering misery, George Arthur Rose, driven in upon himself, has had plenty of time in which to clarify his theories and wishes; now he has the chance to give them effect, and he does. He breaks the self-imposed Papal obligation of remaining within the Vatican walls by walking in procession to his coronation. He astonishes the world by an *Epistle to all Christians,* and by a Bull in which, on the text that 'My Kingdom is not of this World', he makes formal and unconditional renunciation of all claim to temporal sovereignty. He denounces Socialism and the principle of equality in an *Epistle to the English;* and in further demonstration of the unworldliness which should be the mark of God's minister, sells the Vatican treasures for a vast sum, which he gives to the poor. Not the least interesting part of this section of the book is the interview which he gives to the Italian ambassador for the discussion of the world's political future. Some of Fr. Rolfe's guesses were very far from the fact, but looking back at them, as I did, after twenty years, the real shrewdness of his observation was very clear.

Such a story is obviously a difficult one to bring to a conclusion; and Fr. Rolfe, with less plausibility than in other parts of his fantasy, relies upon the machinations of a disappointed woman and a corrupt Socialist agitator. The conspiracy between them, with blackmail based on a knowledge of Hadrian's early life as its main object, is frustrated; and the baffled Comrade, in a fit of rage, shoots the Pope as he is returning to the Vatican. 'How bright the sunlight was, on the warm grey stones, on the ripe Roman skins, on vermilion and lavender and blue and ermine and green and gold, on the indecent grotesque blackness of two blotches, on Apostolic whiteness and the rose of blood.' The final words are worthy of their author: 'Pray for the repose of his soul. He was so tired.'

*   *   *

The style in which *Hadrian the Seventh* is written is hardly less remarkable than the story it tells. Fr. Rolfe shares his hero's liking for compound words; and his pages are studded with such inventions or adaptations as 'tolutiloquence', 'contortuplicate', 'incoronation', 'noncurant', 'occession', and 'digladiator'. In constructing his sentences he sets his adverbs as far before both parts of the verb as he can; and though he often lapses into learning and Latin, the most homely expressions are not disdained in his elaborate paragraphs. But these peculiarities do not rob him of a real eloquence; as, for instance, when describing Hadrian's private visit to St. Peter's:

They passed through innumerable passages and descended stairs, emerging in a chapel where lights burned about a tabernacle of gilded bronze and lapis lazuli. Here He paused while His escort unlocked the gates of the screen. Once through that, He sent-back the guard to his station; but He Himself went-on into the vast obscurity of the basilica. He walked very slowly: it was as though His eyes were wrapped in clear black velvet, so intense and so immense was the darkness. Then, very far away to the right, He saw as it were a coronal of dim stars glimmering—on the floor, they seemed to be. He was in the mighty nave; and the stars were the ever-burning lamps surrounding the Confession. He slowly approached them. As He passed within them, He took one from its golden branch, and descended the marble steps. Here, He spread the cloak on the floor; placed the lamp beside it; and fell to prayer. Outside, in the City and the World, men played, or worked, or sinned, or slept. Inside, at the very tomb of the Apostle, the Apostle prayed.

And Fr. Rolfe also has the secret of a staccato brilliance, of phrases that tell as much as the paragraphs of others; of such expressions as 'that cold white candent voice which was more caustic than silver nitrate and more thrilling than a scream'; 'miscellaneous multitudes paved the spaces with tumultuous eyes'; 'they mean well; but their whole aim and object seems to be to serve God by conciliating Mammon.'

Perhaps above all the astonishments of *Hadrian the Seventh*
I ought to put its revelation of a temperament. Hadrian, as
he is presented by his creator, is a superman in whom we are
compelled to believe. The felinity of his retort, his ready
command over words, the breadth of his vision, the noble
unworldliness of his beliefs and bearing, his mixture of pride
and humility, of gentle charity and ruthless reproof for
error, his sensitiveness to form and hatred of ugliness, his
steadfast and touching confidence in God and in himself; all
these things unite to create a character as difficult to match
as the story of his exploits.

*   *   *

Those who are susceptible to literary influence will have no
difficulty in imagining the effect of *Hadrian the Seventh* upon
my imagination and my interest. Other occupations seemed
colourless by contrast with the necessity of learning more
about Fr. Rolfe. Was he alive or dead? What else had he
written? How was it that I had never heard of a man who
had it in his power to write such a book as *Hadrian the
Seventh*? Many years before (though I was, of course,
unaware of the circumstance) a similar enthusiasm over-
came Robert Hugh Benson after he had thrice read *Hadrian*.
Benson's admiration moved him to write a glowing letter
to the author, which brought the two together in hectic
friendship and enmity. Some such step occurred to me; but
first I went to see Millard.

Millard was pleased by my pleasure, and began to talk in
his discursive fashion. Had I realized that the book was
really an autobiography, that Rose was Rolfe himself, that
half the incidents were based on his experiences, and most
of the characters drawn from living men? Actually I had
not; but, with that duplicity which we practise even to our
oldest friends, I disguised my blindness. We talked round
and round. I gathered that Rolfe was dead, that he was a
spoiled priest, and that, rather mysteriously, he had written
other books under the title or pseudonym of Baron Corvo.

The news that Rolfe was Baron Corvo struck a chord of
remembrance: vaguely I recalled having read a short story
by that author which had seemed to me so excellent that I
had intended, but forgotten, to seek out more of his work.
Then from one of his tin boxes (Millard was a great man
for files and cases, and could put his hand at a moment on
any scrap or book, despite the seeming disorder of his
shelves and floor) my friend produced a morocco-bound
quarto. 'Since you are becoming interested in Rolfe you had
better read these too', was his comment. The few sentences
that caught my eye as I turned the pages were arresting; and
I would have begun my reading then and there; but in his
gently autocratic way Millard insisted upon my paying
attention to his remarks, and not to the book, which
I could read at leisure. I left the bungalow half-stifled with
curiosity.

How well I remember that midnight when, alone in my
tiny study, I sat down to read Millard's mysterious book.
It contained, I found, typescripts of twenty-three long
letters and two telegrams, forming a series addressed from
Venice in the years 1909–10 to an unnamed correspondent;
and as I read my hair began to rise. Here, described with the
frank felicity of *Hadrian the Seventh*, was an unwitting
account, step by step, of the destruction of a soul. The
idealism of George Arthur Rose, the generous sentiments
and hopes for man and the world which distinguish *Hadrian*,
were not to be found in these pages. On the contrary, they
gave an account, in language that omitted nothing, of the
criminal delights that waited for the ignoble sensualist to
whom they were addressed, in the Italian city from which
his correspondent wrote. Only lack of money, it appeared,
prevented the writer from enjoying an existence compared
with which Nero's was innocent, praiseworthy, and un-
exciting: indeed, it seemed that even without money he had
successfully descended to depths from which he could
hardly hope to rise. Throughout all the letters one purpose
was visible: they were an entreaty to their recipient to bring

his wealth to a market where it would buy full value. Rolfe could answer for the wares he offered: he had tested them, and he would willingly be guide to this earthly paradise. An undercurrent of appeals for immediate aid, for money, money, money, ran through the series, mixed with odd fragments of beautiful description, and sudden, bitter attacks on individuals with whom Fr. Rolfe had been concerned in one way or another. It would have seemed impossible that this could be the private correspondence of the author of *Hadrian the Seventh* had not the signature of his style rung in every sentence. What shocked me about these letters was not the confession they made of perverse sexual indulgence: that phenomenon surprises no historian. But that a man of education, ideas, something near genius, should have enjoyed without remorse the destruction of the innocence of youth; that he should have been willing for a price to traffic in his knowledge of the dark byways of that Italian city; that he could have pursued the paths of lust with such frenzied tenacity: these things shocked me into anger and pity. Pity; for behind the ugliness of their boasts and offers, these letters told a harrowing story of a man sliding desperately downhill, unable to pay for clothes, light or food; living like a rat in the bottom of an empty boat, slinking along side streets in misery at frustrated talents and missed chances, with no money in his pocket or meat in his belly, who had come at last to convince himself that every man's hand was against him. With the letters were two telegrams, one of them from the English consul to say 'Fr. Rolfe in hospital dangerously ill asks you wire ten pounds urgent necessities'. The errant Catholic was given the last Sacrament, but recovered from that illness brought on by exposure and lack of food. The last of all the letters in point of date was perhaps the saddest. As despair deepened in the heart of the lost Englishman in Venice, his demands decreased; and in the end he subdued all his persuasiveness to plead for five pounds. 'For God's sake send me five pounds', concluded the concluding letter. Five pounds. . . . A slip in Millard's hand ended the story: 'Rolfe died two years later, 1913, *ætat* 53.'

It took me two hours to read those extraordinary letters; and when I had, I was unable to sleep. I could not banish from my mind the thought of that gifted and intellectual man dragged down by his kink of temperament to perish in shame, want and exile. Horrible though the letters were, they possessed all the graces of the book that had so charmed me: the spirit and the content differed, not the style. As I lay restlessly turning from side to side, I realized suddenly that my curiosity was still unslaked. What was the course and cause of this tragic decline? In *Hadrian* and the letters I had (what I took to be) the opening and the close of a career. What story lay in between? The desire to know swelled in me so urgently that I almost rose from bed to telephone to Millard that I was coming back; only the certainty of being roundly and rightly cursed in his heavy voice deterred me. But I went next morning.

II

THE CLUES

MILLARD was very willing to tell what he knew about Fr. Rolfe, whose life and books had formed one of his main amusements for many years. But he warned me that his information was not extensive, and that it had already been used by Mr. Shane Leslie for a biographical account in the *London Mercury*. First he produced the originals of the Venice letters, which I had read in typescript. They were hardly less surprising in their physical form than in their content: written on paper of the oddest shapes and sizes, in the most beautiful handwriting I had ever seen, in red, blue, green, purple, and black inks, presumably chosen as occasion chanced. So far as appearance went, they were not unworthy of the author of *Hadrian;* but I could not resist a shudder at the sight of those cries from the depths. Next Millard handed me a proof of Mr. Leslie's account of Rolfe; and, finally, a batch of letters and press-cuttings which it had evoked. My friend assured me that when I had mastered these documents I should know as much as he did, and probably as much as anyone living, of the man who had so signally roused my curiosity. He was wrong in that belief: there was much more to be learned; but I shall always be grateful to him for giving me the first clues.

I lost no time in examining the dossier. Earliest in point of date came a cutting from the *Star* newspaper of October 29, 1913, which read:

A curiously interesting and almost mysterious character has passed away in the person of Mr. Frederick Rolfe, who was found dead in his bed at Venice a few mornings since. Mr. Rolfe was the author, under his own name, of various novels in which an extraordinary amount of very ill-assimilated learning was displayed, and the life of the Italian priesthood, rural as well as at the Curia, was portrayed with an insight and appearance of exact knowledge which impressed the critics.

Under the name of Baron Corvo, an Italian title which he claimed to have acquired through the gift of some estates by a former Duchess of Cesarini-Sforza, he wrote verses and controversial articles on Catholic ritual and Italian politics. He used to state that he had been at one time in priest's orders, but this, we believe, was denied by the authorities of his Church.

A devout Catholic in doctrine, he was at issue with the hierarchy over Italian matters, being a strong opponent of the temporal power. He compiled an elaborate genealogical table to show that the King of Italy was the legitimate King of England, and fantastic as the idea may appear, the scholarship and research involved were frankly acknowledged by antiquarian and heraldic criticism.

Mr. Rolfe resided for some years as Baron Corvo at Christchurch, Hampshire, where he was noted for outbursts of elaborate expenditure, alternating with an extreme asceticism. Latterly, at Venice, he had led a life of the latter character exclusively. He will, perhaps, chiefly be remembered for his *Stories Toto Told Me,* a volume of *contes* which is remarkably illustrative of Italian peasant life.

Next I turned to Mr. Leslie's article, which I read with close attention. Again I was astonished; and an underlying note of sarcasm which I had half felt in the *Star* report was explained. 'Curiously interesting' and 'almost mysterious' were understatements when applied to Rolfe. His career was at least as extraordinary as his book; his adventures matched those of Gil Blas. I began to see why his name was not remembered: apparently he had passed through life in a state of opposition and exasperation, giving and taking offence without cause or scruple, until even his friends feared and avoided him. Despite Mr. Leslie's epigrammatic sparkle and amusing verve, the tale of Rolfe's

THE CLUES

17

tribulations, self-caused though they largely were, made
very melancholy reading. Here was indeed a tragic comedy,
more sombre and fantastic than I had expected or hoped.
From the beginning, it seemed, this unfortunate man's
temperament and circumstances had warred with his talent.
Frustration and poverty had been the condition of his early
years as of his last; tutorships, odd jobs, and charity were
the actual lot of the dreamer who (in his dreams) had ruled
the world. It was not in Venice only that he had starved.
Such hardships and disappointments would have turned
most men crazy; small wonder that in the end friendship
with Rolfe became 'a minor experiment in demonology'.
I concurred, as I read, in Mr. Leslie's verdict: 'A self-tortured
and defeated soul, who might have done much, had he been
born in the proper era or surroundings.' But though I concurred in his verdict, there were a dozen tantalizing gaps
in his narrative which left my curiosity rampant. What was
Rolfe's lineage or upbringing? How had he come to be so
strangely stranded in Venice? Could nothing more have
been done to help a man whose talent must have been
obvious? Obstinate, indeed, as well as obvious; for in the
course of a life which can have had few equals for uncertainty
and discomfort, Fr. Rolfe had somehow contrived to produce
at least four books beside *Hadrian*: books which sounded,
in Mr. Leslie's descriptions, hardly less interesting than the
one I already knew. There was, for example, *Don Tarquinio*,
an account of twenty-four hours in the life of a young
nobleman in the company of the Borgia, A.D. 1495: a tale
composed, so I gathered, in language even more elaborate
and mannered than that of *Hadrian*, and with a plot very
little less striking. Evidently Rolfe was a profound mediæval-
ist, for he had also written *Chronicles of the House of Borgia*,
an historical work packed with obscure learning and tart
epigrams. More attractive still sounded that volume of
Stories Toto Told Me mentioned in the *Star* obituary,
described as 'the most amazing, fantastical, whimsical,
bizarre, erratic and hare-brained of books', written in an

'orchidaceous' vocabulary full of fancy coinages and indi-
vidualistic spelling. Rolfe had even translated *Omar Khayyam*
(from Nicolas' French text, not from the Persian) into
so-called 'diaphotick' verse designed to emphasize the
humour and sarcasm of the original.

My appetite had been whetted by *Hadrian;* these hints
of pleasures to come were a fresh incitement to my unsatis-
fied zest. I turned to the final cuttings of Millard's little
collection for further light. The most substantial was an
extremely ably written *Times Literary Supplement* review
of a new edition of Rolfe's *Toto* stories, to which Mr. Leslie's
article had been prefixed as introduction. The critic praised
Rolfe's work, in which, he predicted, 'the unhappy Catholic
vagabond will live, and perhaps increase in fame. Caviare,
like Huysmans, he must always be, but so rich a dish will
not be left untasted. A man who can lay bare his soul as
Rolfe did in the opening chapters of *Hadrian the Seventh*
need not fear for readers'. This article, evoked by Mr.
Leslie's introduction, had in its turn provoked correspondence, which Millard, in his usual methodical manner,
had kept. On December 25, 1924, Mr. Harry Pirie-Gordon
wrote to the editor:

Sir,

In last week's review of *In His Own Image*, by Frederick Baron
Corvo, mention is made of some of that writer's other books.
There are, however, two more to be added to the list, books which
he wrote in collaboration. One of these, called *The Weird of the
Wanderer*, was published in 1912 as being by 'Prospero and
Caliban'; the other, called *Hubert's Arthur*, dealing with a wholly
imaginary career ascribed to Arthur, Duke of Brittany, was in
manuscript at the time of Rolfe's death. It was entrusted to the
kindly Anglican clergyman who befriended him during the last
weeks of his life in Venice; and it is in the hope of getting into
touch with this last of the many who tried to be benefactors to
Frederick Rolfe that I ask you to publish this.

Harry Pirie-Gordon

A week later another letter appeared in *The Times*, this time from Mr. Frank Swinnerton:

Sir,

Mr. Harry Pirie-Gordon refers to an unpublished novel by Frederick Rolfe entitled *Hubert's Arthur*. I at one time saw the manuscript of this piece of virtuosity; and I also saw a complete novel (written earlier) which had the title *A Romance of Modern Venice; or the Desire and Pursuit of the Whole*. The latter work was in the hands of Mr. Ongania, the bookseller, of Venice. It was a very beautiful and absorbing story. Unfortunately, according to my memory, which is vague after the ten or more years which have elapsed since I read the book, this *Romance of Modern Venice* contained a good deal of matter that was possibly libellous, regarding persons whose books Frederick Rolfe claimed to have written for them. But if there is to be any research into the unpublished manuscripts of Rolfe, it would be well that this book should not be overlooked.

Yours faithfully
Frank Swinnerton

When I had read these letters, a resolution which had been latent in my mind ever since my introduction to *Hadrian* took definite shape. I would find these lost manuscripts, and write a Life of Frederick Rolfe.

*   *   *

At once I began to write letters in all directions. I wrote to Mr. Swinnerton, enclosing a letter for transmission to Ongania, to Millard, asking him to procure me Rolfe's other books, to Mr. Leslie, to Mr. Pirie-Gordon, and to Mr. Charles Kains-Jackson (this last, according to Millard, one of Rolfe's personal friends). Then, quite happy, I sat down to await events. The first of my correspondents to answer was Mr. Swinnerton:

Dear Sir,

I wish very much that I could help you; but I'm afraid I can't do
so. In the first place, I do not know the present address of Mr.
Ongania, the Venetian bookseller. I am therefore compelled to
return to you the letter which you addressed to him. My impression is that Mr. Ongania is dead; but I am not sure. Further,
I ought to explain how it came about that I ever saw any manuscripts by Fr. Rolfe, and why I wrote to *The Times Literary
Supplement*. I will do so.

I acted from 1910 until 1925 as 'reader' to the firm of Chatto
and Windus. During the early part of that period, two manuscripts at least by Fr. Rolfe were submitted to Chatto and Windus, and declined by them. It is my *belief* that these manuscripts
(they were actually in the author's handwriting) were both sent
to the firm by Mr. Ongania, with whom they had been lodged
by Fr. Rolfe as security for money lent. The first of these, unless
I am mistaken, was *The Desire and Pursuit of the Whole*: a beautiful
but very lengthy and libellous book (libellous, at least, in my
opinion, because Rolfe described his central male character as
having written the work for which several lightly-described
persons had received credit—as a 'ghost', in fact). It could not
be published because of this implication. The second was a
pseudo-historical novel called *Hubert's Arthur*, which purported
to tell the true story of the pretended blinding of Arthur by
Hubert. The manuscript of this book was sent, I understood, by
the author's authority, to an American gentleman, in whose
possession it presumably still is. That was the extent of my
knowledge, and it was merely with the wish to place upon record
that these manuscripts had at one time existed that I wrote to
The Times Literary Supplement.

Subsequent to the publication of my letter, I received a post-
card from an Italian gentleman who informed me that he believed some of Rolfe's manuscripts had been in the possession
of a lady now dead. He asked for further information, which
I could not give. I also had a long letter from a brother of Fr.
Rolfe—an Australian schoolmaster—who said that when Rolfe

died he was unable to execute the will owing, I believe, to the fact that to do so was to accept debts which he found himself unable to liquidate. He invited me to do anything possible to discover the manuscripts of Rolfe, in order that he might now benefit under the will. Messrs. Chatto and Windus, at my instigation, made further inquiries, and it was discovered that other rights, specific or implied, existed. It proved impossible—or seemed to be impossible—to ascertain exactly who owned the rights in Rolfe's unpublished works; and the matter was thereupon allowed to drop. I no longer have the Australian Mr. Rolfe's letter. I believe that in addition to this Mr. Rolfe there is another brother, a barrister, who is at present in England. But just how you could get into touch with either brother, and what useful purpose would be served supposing you succeeded in doing so, I am unable to suggest. You might possibly ask Chatto and Windus if they could assist you at all; but that is the only course which occurs to me.

I knew nothing personally of Fr. Rolfe. I once caught a glimpse of him, but no more. Nor do I know of anybody who had any acquaintance with him. Messrs. Chatto and Windus published two of his novels—*Don Tarquinio* and *Hadrian the Seventh*—but this was before I began to 'read' for them. All I can tell you is that *The Desire and Pursuit of the Whole* and *Hubert's Arthur* have existed in manuscript; and this, from my letter to *The Times Literary Supplement*, if not otherwise, you already knew. It would have been a great pleasure to me to place at your disposal any information which might have helped in the making of what I am sure will be a valuable and interesting book, and I greatly regret that I cannot do so.

With regrets, therefore, that I should be so helpless

I am, Yours faithfully,

Frank Swinnerton

This letter, it will be seen, gave me several new lines of exploration. It seemed fairly clear that Messrs. Chatto and Windus must know something; and I therefore called upon

Mr. C. H. C. Prentice, a partner, with whom I had a slight but agreeable acquaintance. Mr. Prentice was disposed to help, though dubious of his power. The firm's correspondence with Rolfe had long before been destroyed, and none of the present members had ever met him. On the other hand, I learned, to my great astonishment, that the manuscript of *The Desire and Pursuit of the Whole* lay at that moment in Messrs. Chatto's safe; had lain there forgotten, in fact, since the time of Rolfe's death. All eagerness, I asked to be allowed to read it; but here the traditional caution of the publisher stood in my way. Prentice, too, had observed Mr. Swinnerton's letter to *The Times,* with its references to libels; and he was in consequence unwilling to show the manuscript without authority. *What* authority he would accept was not clear. Rolfe's barrister brother, he told me, was alive and in London; but there was great uncertainty as to whether he or that Anglican clergyman to whom Mr. Pirie-Gordon had referred owned the rights of the long-forgotten book. He advised me, and I determined, to seek Mr. Herbert Rolfe. I wrote at once; and the passage of a few posts brought me the following:

Dear Sir,

I am not unwilling to give you facts relating to my brother Frederick William Rolfe, but I fear I cannot spare much time for the purpose. I am certainly anxious that whatever may be written about him may be correct. You might perhaps send me a list of the facts you require. Or would you prefer to see me in chambers here? If so please come before term begins. An appointment could be arranged by telephone. I shall probably be in from about 11.30 to 4.0 p.m. most ensuing days. I presume you would let me see a proof of whatever you may write. Did you know my brother personally?

I should warn you that I may not be able to furnish you with precise dates for each of his movements.

Yours faithfully,
Herbert Rolfe

Before I could reply to Mr. Rolfe's guarded offer, however, another letter arrived:

Dear Sir,

My brother opened your letter by mistake, and has only just forwarded it. I put all I could collect about Baron Corvo into a *Mercury* article illustrated by his writings. His novel *Hadrian the Seventh* was discovered by R. H. Benson, and had a great influence on us at Cambridge twenty years ago. I was entirely carried away by his tyrianthine style. Grant Richards had a book of letters of Corvo. After the failure of his firm it passed to More and Co., who showed me stacks of coloured script. Apply to Grant Richards, who published the Borgia book for Rolfe. You will have to get his leave to use the letters.

Yours sincerely

Shane Leslie

I wrote forthwith to 'More and Co.', whom I had no difficulty in identifying as the De la More Press, publishers of a series of *King's Classics* which had been very familiar to my boyhood. While I was waiting for a reply, yet another avenue was disclosed to me:

Dear Sir,

If you will let me know what day will suit, I will call upon you at 5 p.m. on that day to talk about Baron Corvo.

Yours faithfully

Harry Pirie-Gordon

Looking back, I find in each of these letters a reflection of its writer, from the legal caution of Mr. Rolfe, the ready helpfulness of Mr. Swinnerton, Mr. Leslie's use of the word 'tyrianthine', Mr. Pirie-Gordon's brevity. The most urgent letter seemed to be Mr. Rolfe's; and, obeying his instruction, I telephoned to fix an appointment next day. But meanwhile a new woodcock fell to my springe: Mr. Kains-Jackson was announced. He had answered my letter promptly and in person.

* * *

My white-haired visitor had a very interesting story to tell; for he had known Rolfe intimately, and, as I found later, nearly everyone who knew Rolfe thought him the most remarkable man of their acquaintance. This particular connection came about by chance in the very early 'nineties, when Mr. Jackson, then a City solicitor, was taking a customary holiday at Christchurch in Hampshire, at that time a quiet village quite separated from Bournemouth, much patronized in the summer by the artistic. For both personal and business reasons Mr. Jackson had called on a local client, the late Gleeson White, then well known as an art critic; and in Gleeson White's house he encountered a slim, clean-shaven, slightly clerical man who was introduced as the Baron Corvo. Baron Corvo, despite his foreign name, did not affect Italian blood. He proclaimed himself an Englishman and an artist. On closer knowledge he proved to have many gifts: to be an excellent sculler, swimmer and fisherman, a skilful musician, photographer and scribe, a man of taste with a pleasant turn of the tongue. Gleeson White was a good talker, even for those days, when conversation was practised as an amusement; but when he fell silent the Baron was always ready with a topic, and he could hold the company with tales of Italy and England, even better than his host's. Corvo owed his title, or said that he owed it, to an elderly English lady, the Duchess Sforza-Cesarini, like himself a convert to Catholicism, who had met him in Italy, more or less adopted him as a grandson, and bestowed on him a small estate carrying the baronial title much as certain English properties carry the privilege of being Lord of the Manor. There seemed no reason to doubt his claims. He certainly received remittances from the Duchess in Italy, for Mr. Jackson could remember cashing her lira cheques, which the Baron received more or less monthly. Corvo was living in a house let out in apartments by a retired butler; he had made a studio on the first floor, and was usually busily engaged with his art. The local Catholic church had been liberally adorned by his brush in a fresco of figures still to be seen by the curious, and it was said that churches elsewhere also rejoiced in his work. Perhaps the oddest thing about the Baron as he lived and worked at Christchurch was his method of painting. Conscious of a weakness in figure drawing, it was his custom to photograph his models, make lantern slides from the photographs, and then project the image on to the painting area so that he could sketch in an outline. The Byzantine eikon was his ideal, and some of his oil-paintings were enhanced with needlework, and spangled with sequins. Corvo appeared to be a very pious Catholic, who required his brushes to be blessed before he used them. His subjects were almost invariably ecclesiastical, and Mr. Jackson delighted and diverted me with a reproduction of one of Rolfe's more ambitious pictures. Some years afterwards I showed a head of St. William of Norwich, painted by Corvo, to Ricketts and Shannon, who thought it showed an interesting touch. The fresco at St. Michael's, Christchurch, though damaged by damp, is still, in its way, impressive.

I was surprised to find that in these early days Rolfe was not in the least regarded as a writer: he gave himself out, and was accepted, as a painter; indeed, it was his promise in that art which had persuaded the Duchess to support him. He did, however, write occasional verses, mostly inspired by his own pictures.

The Baron continued for some time to enjoy the pleasures of local society, to take part in the picnics of others, and to return this modest form of hospitality. But his growing friendship with Mr. Jackson, who found the companionship more and more inspiring, was broken off by an unfortunate transaction which ended Corvo's Christchurch stay. Gleeson White was the owner of a stationers' business and lending

library, occupying two freehold premises known as Caxton
House; and these the Baron proposed to buy. It became
Mr. Jackson's duty to act for White; and in his professional
capacity he could not help becoming aware that Baron
Corvo's finances were overstrained.

Rolfe also was represented by a solicitor, whom he summoned in unusual fashion. Hearing that John Withers was
a good lawyer, he despatched a telegram to the effect:
'Please come to Christchurch Hampshire immediately for
important conveyancing transaction. You will be met at
station by barouche with white horse. Baron Corvo.' The
young solicitor hurried off with visions of an important
client, but his illusions were dispelled when he found that
the 'barouche with white horse' was only the station fly
drawn by a fleabitten grey hack.

Corvo had proposed to complete the purchase by the sale
of his own properties at Bristol and Oxford; but these
proved to be already mortgaged to the hilt; and so the deal
was off. Moreover, rumour began to be busy with the
Baron's name. His debts to local tradesmen were mounting
skywards; the Duchess's allowance ceased; and it was said
that Baron Corvo was not a Baron at all, but only Frederick
Rolfe. The gossip thickened; and some time between
December 1891 and June 1892 'Baron Corvo' vanished
from Hampshire, leaving his paintings, his brushes, and his
debts to look after themselves.

Nevertheless the Baron regarded himself as the injured
party. The last that Mr. Jackson heard of him was an extract
from a letter to a friend, written by Rolfe ten years later:

If you are writing to K-J, you should say this: he made a ghastly
blunder; and there is no evidence before me that he ever has
attempted or desired to set it right. Were I aware of any such
disposition on his part, I hope I am not ungenerous enough to
withstand him. But at present he appears to me as an avoidable
person, expressing opinions based on no sure warranty and
obviously false to facts. I much regret it; for, though I owe my

ten years' hell to him, I like his personality. Please do not give him the slightest unnecessary information about me or my doings.

This Christchurch story was disturbing in its implications. Mr. Jackson seemed to have no doubt that Rolfe's plan had not been an honest one; and mentioned that he had thought it necessary to warn his friends against any financial dealings with 'the Baron'. Still, I had heard one side of the story only; I needed further material for any judgement. The material was at hand. From the file in which he had kept Corvo's letters, Mr. Jackson produced two long newspaper cuttings, dated 1898, taken from the *Aberdeen Free Press*. He had noticed them at the time of their appearance, and kept them as curiosities. To me they were almost as engrossing as Millard's Venice letters: a wonderful piece of luck at the outset of my labours. Here was a detailed account, seen through the eyes of an enemy, of the early adventures of the erratic being whose life I had set myself to trace. As I read it, I began to understand Rolfe's embittered later years, to glimpse the inner misery of his life.

III

THE NEWSPAPER ATTACK

THE ostensible cause of the articles which Mr. Jackson left with me for study was a pseudo-reminiscence by Rolfe, published in the *Wide World Magazine,* a monthly that for a short time, and very rashly, guaranteed the veracity of its contributors. The tall stories of Louis de Rougemont which appeared in its pages brought, however, so much ridicule upon its assertion that it provided nothing but the truth that the claim was speedily withdrawn. In the last number to carry the short-lived guarantee there appeared the harmless and entertaining fiction, to which I shall refer later, which afforded Rolfe's enemy his opening point.

The first part of the attack is headed

BARON CORVO

MORE 'WIDE WORLD' ADVENTURES

EXTRAORDINARY STORY

A NOBLEMAN FROM ABERDEEN

and opens thus:

The world was recently startled by the discovery by the *Wide World Magazine*—a new periodical devoted to the promulgation of true statements of thrilling adventure—of a greater than Robinson Crusoe in the person of M. Rougemont, and a little later the public was equally amused when it was shown what manner of man that great explorer and anthropologist really is. Being about done with the Rougemont affair, the *Wide World Magazine* has discovered another personage. This time it is a nobleman, and in this month's issue of the magazine he is presented with the customary editorial flourish which, at the head of an article, is understood to give a keener relish to the tale. The new writer tells a story of his experiences with great minuteness, but there are many experiences of his much more striking than the statements of the *Wide World Magazine*, which it would be well for the world to know. The article in question is entitled *How I was Buried Alive* and is 'By Baron Corvo'—though no quotation marks will be found beside his name anywhere in the Magazine to indicate that he is not the real quality. And the patent of nobility is further endorsed in the serious editorial statement already mentioned, in which the story is described as 'Baron Corvo's fearful experience described in minute detail by himself and illustrated with drawings done under his own supervision'. A picture of a youngish man is given in the front of the article as a photo of Baron Corvo. It may be said that it is a very good photo, and has been recognized by many people in Aberdeen and neighbourhood, who can tell something regarding him vastly more interesting than what appears in the *Wide World Magazine* under His Excellency's signature. . . . The merit of [that] story lies in its being an actual experience of this nobleman, and . . . it will be well, for many reasons, to indicate how far His Excellency the Baron Corvo is to be taken *au sérieux*.

And first as to title. People will look in vain in the peerage of this or any other country for the lineage of Baron Corvo. But 'the Baron' has not now used the title for the first time; nor does he use it without being well warned by those with whom he was acquainted as to the complications likely to result if he persisted in doing so. It was all right so long as he employed the title to those who knew what value to put upon it, but he has been fond of subscribing himself in formal communications 'very truly, Corvo', and even as 'Frederick Baron Corvo'. Those who knew him pointed out the folly, to say the least of it, of this kind of thing.

So far the attack had proceeded with menacing restraint. Now, however, the author opened his hand. Evidently he was well informed; for he turns to the Christchurch incident, and relates in detail how 'the Baron' had attempted to purchase Gleeson White's property and was 'treated seriously in the negotiations—for a while'. He gives, too, the text of a taunting and sarcastic letter written to Rolfe by Mrs. White which concludes:

'As regards your persistence in maintaining that you could buy our property, I can only hope you were self-deceived. No other excuse can justify the extreme and unnecessary worry you have caused us both. Are you leaving on Saturday? An absurd report has reached me that you are to be sold up then and are going to the workhouse. Under the circumstances I hope your old friend Mr. T. and your priest will come to the rescue—but how about that £100 you have told us repeatedly you have still at your London bank under your real name Rolfe? which let me advise you to re-adopt for the future, for the very fact of your assuming a new and foreign title has, I find now, given rise from the first to suspicions here and elsewhere. . . . Deeply regretting that you have made it impossible for us to assist you further, I am, etc. etc.'

This [continues the article] shows something of the nature of the Baron, and it may simply be added that the title Baron Corvo, as His Excellency told on various occasions to those who knew him, is 'a distinction I picked up in Italy'.

Having (it must be admitted, quite skilfully) thus thrown cold water on 'His Excellency's' rank, the unknown commentator asks 'Who, then, is Baron Corvo?', a rhetorical question which he proceeds to answer:

This gentleman is Frederick William Rolfe, and his history prior to his emergence in Aberdeen may be briefly told. While an undermaster at Grantham School he became a Roman Catholic and had to leave his mastership. This was in 1886. At times, as he himself put it, he 'starved in London', alternated with short periods of tutorship. At one time the Marquess of Bute, having founded a school for outcast boys at Oban, appointed Rolfe the master. There were two priest chaplains, and among the three matters did not move smoothly. In a month or two Rolfe was out again. After a while he decided to go in for the priesthood.

The Bishop of Shrewsbury was induced to look into his case, with the result that in the end of 1887, as an ecclesiastical subject of the prelate, he went to Oscott (Roman Catholic) College, but in a few months was discharged.

After more 'starving in London' he came across Mr. Ogilvie-Forbes, of Boyndlie in Aberdeenshire, and stayed at Boyndlie for three or four months. Another temporary tutorship and then the late Archbishop Smith of Edinburgh, well known for his softness of heart in such cases, was induced to take him up, and sent him to the Scots College in Rome, to be trained for the priesthood. After five months he was expelled. It was owing to his lack of Vocation . . . [and] because—as is averred on authority which the Baron is not likely to challenge—he was regarded as a general nuisance in the place, to say the least of it. Even there he contracted large debts, which he said the Lord Archibald Douglas had agreed to pay, but which Lord Archibald would have nothing to do with. However, Mr. Rolfe has always been characterized with a polished manner, backed up by such accomplishments as a little music, some capacity for art, and a considerable expertness as an amateur photographer. As a student he contrived to make himself very agreeable to a Roman Catholic old English lady with an Italian title, the Duchess Carolina Sforza, from whom he got considerable sums of money; and by her he was maintained for some time after his expulsion from the Scots College. However, that, like many another kindness to Mr. Rolfe, came to an end. He returned to England towards the end of 1890, and, maintaining that he had been promised by the Duchess an income—which he variously stated as from £150 to £300 a year—for two years to enable him to prosecute his art studies, he went to Christchurch.

There follows a further dig at the Gleeson White episode, with a conclusion that amplifies Mr. Jackson's recollection:

The Duchess declined, however, to rise to the occasion in the matter of the promised income, though Rolfe continued for years to write to her begging her aid, until the letters were either

not answered or were replied to by communications on which
there was neither the prefix 'Mr.' nor the affix 'Esq.', to say
nothing of the lordly title of 'Baron', which he soon came to be
constantly using. It may just be noted in passing that the title
which the Baron selected is of the following signification—
Latin, corvus; Italian, corvo; French, corbeau; Scotch, corbie;
English, crow.[1]

Even this well-informed critic was unaware, it appeared,
of Rolfe's ancestry. I found his story intensely interesting;
not the less so because as I went on I found that this press
attack had been very largely Mr. Leslie's authority on
Corvo's early years.

And now we come to 1892, when this gentleman began to
honour with his residence the Northern city of Aberdeen. Sold
out at Christchurch, he did the 'starving' again for some months
—or was charitably maintained by the Fathers of the Roman
Catholic Church, Ely Place, London. About the middle of that
year, however, and continuing to look about among well-to-do
Roman Catholic families for aid, he was given the post of tutor
to the young Laird of Seaton, at Seaton Old House, Aberdeen.
For a brief space he lived in clover, driving out and in to the city,
being able to invite his friends to lunch and so forth, all as
becometh one with lordly aspirations; though here it ought to
be said that for a time he followed Mrs. White's sensible advice,
and went under his own name of Frederick William Rolfe. . . .
However, he had to depart from Seaton, and a curious story may
be told as showing the light in which he was regarded after his
departure. A few months afterwards he found his way into the
Seaton grounds. Nobody saw him enter; but as he was coming
out again by a different gateway, he found the gate locked.
'Gate', he shouted to the old woman in the lodge. The old body
looked out, inquiring who it was, and, on being told, 'Well,'
she drily observed, 'I suppose I may let you out, though I have
orders not to let you in.'

[1] This gibe is inaccurate; *corvus* is raven, not crow; and it was the
raven that Baron Corvo took as his emblem.

Mr. Rolfe, looking about for a friend in need, found one in the Rev. Fr. Gerry, Roman Catholic priest of Strichen (now Dufftown), who kept him for some weeks. Father Gerry found it extremely hard to get rid of him—as did many another—for on the day fixed for his departure the guest usually fell sick and was unable to go.

About . . . the beginning of November 1892 Mr. Rolfe made application to Messrs. G. W. Wilson and Co., photographers, to be taken on their staff. He did not care a pin for money. All he desired was opportunity to improve and perfect himself in the photographic art. He was told that no improvers were taken on there; but he persisted, and ultimately on being told that there was a boy's place vacant, which he might have if he cared to take it, and be subject to the ordinary rules of the works, he accepted. For fully three months he was in Messrs. Wilson's works at 12s. 6d. a week, but merely messing about, coming and going when he liked, pretty much doing what he liked, telling enormous yarns to his fellow-workers of his father's property in England and abroad—for by this time he was reverting to the use of the baronial title. . . . At length the firm could endure His Excellency no longer and he received his notice. But again the difficulty was to get rid of him. After being told not to come back, he would return and start work smilingly as usual. It was thought advisable, therefore, to send him a formal intimation to his lodgings (which he had not paid for months) that the thing could go on no longer, and he must go. He immediately sent back to Messrs. Wilson a letter, of which the following is an extract: 'Dear Sir, It is a curious thing that at the moment I received your note I was about to carry out an intention I have been forming for some time past, viz. to ask you whether one would be allowed to invest a small sum, say £1000, in your business, and to secure a permanent and congenial appointment suited to my capacities. Perhaps it is inopportune now, but I think I had better mention it.' Even after this he turned up at the works, and had ultimately to be threatened with ejection by the police if he did not clear out. Then Mr.

Rolfe proposed to sue the firm. He went to one of the principal legal firms in Aberdeen and got them to write to Messrs. G. W. Wilson intimating a claim of about £300 for the retention, he said, of certain property of his, and for breach of contract. A single communication from Messrs. Wilson showed the lawyers the kind of man with whom they had to deal, and they dropped the case. Mr. Rolfe tried to get another to take up the case 'on spec', as he put it, but failed, and so that matter passed away.

The expression 'passed away' was much favoured by whomsoever wrote the attack on Rolfe; indeed, there are many repeated turns of phrase which must have revealed to the victim the identity of his enemy.

The Baron chiefly occupied himself in what he called 'beating up' all the well-to-do Catholics, from the Duke of Norfolk downwards, for money to aid him in carrying out schemes which he put forward of colour-photography, submarine photography, new light for instantaneous photography, and all the rest. But he did not confine his attention to Catholics. . . . He did not hesitate to attempt even the highest flights, as the following communication will show: 'Baron Corvo presents compliments to Sir Henry Ponsonby, and is desirous to offer Her Majesty the Queen a small picture of the Nativity at Christmas. It is his own work, and is quite unique, being photographed from the living model by magnesium light. He would be very grateful to Sir Henry Ponsonby for directions as to the necessary form to be observed on these occasions.'

But, after all, it was to Roman Catholics that [Corvo] chiefly made his epistolary appeals. One of those upon whom he bestowed unsleeping attention was the late Roman Catholic Bishop of Aberdeen, Hugh Macdonald. Writing to the Bishop on one occasion acknowledging the loan of £1, which the kind-hearted Bishop had sent him, Rolfe wrote: 'My Lord Bishop— I regret that I have made a mistake as to the funds at your Lordship's disposal, but I was informed . . . that a sum of £4,600 had been inherited by the Catholic Cathedral clergy "for the relief of the Catholic poor". I repeat my apologies for having troubled your Lordship about a matter on which I was misinformed.' The note from the Bishop in reference to this matter was pointed and not without a touch of ecclesiastical humour: 'My dear Mr. Rolfe, As I told you on Saturday, I have no funds at my disposal for the relief of the Catholic poor. No such sums have been left lately, so that you must have been misinformed. May our Lord help you out of your difficulties, for I have no faith in submarine photography. Hugh C. SS. R. Bishop of Aberdeen.'

But the further adventures of Baron Corvo must wait for another day.

Not, however, for long. One article did not satisfy the spleen of Rolfe's first biographer. He returned to the attack in the next issue of the *Aberdeen Free Press*, pleading, in the fashion that I recognized, that 'It will be well' to give some further particulars of the Baron's residence in Aberdeen. It is unnecessary to repeat in full all the instances he gives of the ways in which Rolfe struggled to keep his head above water. He appealed all round for aid to finance inventions of which there is no longer any record. Perhaps a hint of one can be gleaned from the letter to Sir Henry Ponsonby quoted above, and another to Mr. W. Astor in which Rolfe claims to have 'invented a portable light by which I can dispense with the sun'. His reference is to photography by magnesium light, at that time (the early 'nineties) still a novelty. It is charitable, and reasonable, to suppose that Rolfe, who, even in the admission of the Aberdeen writer, was an 'expert' photographer, had stumbled upon some advance, or improvement, on the methods then employed. Even his other inventions, so called, seem to have had at least *prima-facie* claims. They so far impressed Commander Littledale, then in charge of H.M.S. *Clyde,* that the Commander undertook to bring some of Rolfe's submarine schemes before the United Service Institution; though even that minor triumph brings its sting, for

this [news] was, of course, instantly communicated to friends, with the additional information that [Rolfe] wanted funds 'to conduct the experiments before the experts, which will mean two if not three fortunes to me'. But that matter also passed away.

He made a similar hit in approaching Lord Charles Beresford, who gave him an appointment, but

immediately a shoal of letters was sent out—one to the Bishop of Shrewsbury, another to the Bishop of Aberdeen, others to the Duke of Norfolk, to Mr. W. T. Stead, to Mr. Gleeson White, etc. etc., intimating that Lord Charles Beresford had expressed his interest in the invention, and would these lords and gentlemen help in the matter of finance. But none of them rose to the occasion.

The Baron was no more successful in an application to the *Illustrated London News* and a similar one to the *Graphic,* to be commissioned to proceed to Tripoli and photograph the sunken H.M.S. *Victoria.*

As I have said, it is not my intention to transcribe the whole of the attack on Rolfe. Its compiler was industrious in recording every minor misdeed of his subject, and in giving actions which would have been ordinary enough when performed by ordinary people a sinister colour when performed by Rolfe. Some of the stories set out are, it must be admitted, definitely discreditable. The Baron tendered a cheque for £5 in settlement of some purchases, the balance to be paid to him in cash; but on inquiry the cheque was found to be, 'to say the least of it, very far from satisfactory'. On the other hand, his efforts to sell his paintings 'in the mediæval style' to the inappreciative people of Aberdeen were pathetic in their futility. After beseeching the interest of all the leading Catholics in Aberdeen, he offered them to the Lord Provost with the ingenuous yet ironical recommendation, 'I venture, My Lord Provost, to suggest their appropriateness as a gift in connection with the Royal wedding, especially as they are the work of an artist who has settled in Aberdeen because of its exquisite suitability for his work'. But even that failed to draw.

There is a certain humour in even the gloomiest of Rolfe's adventures in the North. I quote again:

The Baron continued to reside with [a] family in Skene Street from October 1892 until the beginning of August 1893. The head of the family was a hardworking tradesman, and he and his wife had taken a largish house with a view to keeping a superior class of boarders. Mr. Rolfe was their chiefest venture in that direction; and when ultimately they got rid of him—in a highly dramatic way—he was due them the sum of £37 . 2 . 9½. . . . At length the Baron's landlord and landlady realised that the hope to which they had clung of receiving payment of his board and lodging in a lump sum was utterly baseless. They had taken no end of trouble with him. He was a vegetarian and a perfect epicure in the matter of his diet, making out each day from a cookery book the recipes for the day's meals. . . . But, as already said, the people resolved to get rid of him. When the Baron realised that it was literally coming to a push, he would not stir out of the house: in the end he would not get out of bed lest, peradventure, he should be thrust forth. One evening about 6 o'clock the landlord besought the aid of a fellow-workman. They entered the Baron's bedroom, and the Baron was given ten minutes to dress and clear out. He refused to move, and when the ten minutes was up he seized hold of the iron bedstead and clung for dear life. He was dragged forth, wearing only his pyjamas, out to the staircase, where he caught hold of the banisters, and another struggle ensued. Thence he was carried down the long staircase and was shot on to the pavement, as he stood, to the wonderment of the passers-by. His clothing was thrown after him, which he ultimately donned—and that was the last of Baron Corvo in that particular locality.

Poor Rolfe! His detractor calls this a 'quaint experience', but no doubt it was more miserable than 'quaint' to the man who suffered by it. On his ejectment he went to the Bishop, who enabled him to get supper and shelter for the night. Two months later, doubtless in desperation, the wretched

outcast asked the House Surgeon at the Royal Infirmary to
certify him as insane, in order that he might have free
quarters, if only in the asylum. He besought recommen-
dations so that he might try for the post of Librarian to
Aberdeen University, but failed again. Then (according to
the merciless record of his sufferings) the 'Association for
Improving the Condition of the Poor in Aberdeen' took
him up. The would-be photographer was given chemicals
with which to carry out his experiments, and even money.
From the 2nd September 1893 to the 16th November he
received as gift the total of £5 19s. od. This hardly seems
an excessive amount spread over ten weeks, more particularly if the circumstance is afterwards to be published (as in
this case) that on the 11th September one was handed
half-a-crown, and on the 26th, sixpence. Charity seems
dearly purchased on such terms. But even so Rolfe was
regarded as a 'hopeless case', and 'the Association declined
to help him further'. Was there a lower depth for him to
plumb? 'It was on a Saturday afternoon', continues the
disagreeable Recording Angel, 'when discarded by even the
Poor Association, that the Baron found his way to Mr.
Champion [at that time a well-known Labour leader] . . .
Mr. Champion and a friend were at dinner when he called—
dressed in knickerbocker suit and wearing generally a pretty
respectable appearance. He was shown into the dining
room, but drew back on seeing that Mr. Champion was
not alone, and beckoned him out. Mr. Champion followed
him, and thereupon received a tale of exceeding woe. He
did not know very well what to make of his visitor, but,
following the advice of the friend, he gave the Baron a
hearty dinner to begin with.' [The anonymous author's
comment on this reasonable action is characteristic: 'This
in itself was an inestimable treat.' Doubtless it was, to a very
hungry man.] After this unconventional introduction Rolfe
worked as secretary to Champion for some time, and was
befriended by him in London as well as in the inhospitable
city of Aberdeen until February 1894, when the Labour

leader departed for Australia. At that point, more or less, this queer newspaper account of an even queerer man comes to a stop; though its end deserves to be quoted as a pendant to its opening:

We are not concerned with his fortunes in London [after Champion's departure]. Sufficient to say that he was soon 'starving' in the old way again, with occasional lifts into more fortunate conditions—[though] it may be mentioned that on one occasion at least, in the summer of last year (1897), he revisited Aberdeen [intrepid Rolfe!] in company with a gentleman who is understood to have had in view the purchase of property. But for the present we have done with Baron Corvo. As already mentioned, there is matter at hand with regard to this personage's proceedings that would amaze the public for weeks on end. But enough has been said, one would imagine, to induce Mr. Rolfe to follow the sensible advice of his best friends [among whom the author of the article was assuredly not to be counted] to drop the use of this foreign title and betake himself to some industrious calling. And the *Wide World Magazine*, which puts forward the Baron and his story, and which declared at the outset of its career that nothing but fact would be admitted to its pages, may see in the story of the Baron a new reading which it never intended, of the motto still displayed on its front page that 'Truth is stranger than Fiction'.

THE RELUCTANT BROTHER

AFTER reading this extraordinary article (of which I have transcribed little more than half) I went for a long walk, to ponder the facts and the character that it revealed. Mr. Jackson's account of the Christchurch affair corroborated it on the one point which I could check; but I could not resist the feeling that the writer had satisfied a long-standing debt by this unfriendly account of Rolfe's doings. Still, it was useless, I felt, without further knowledge, to attempt to assess the material of the newspaper attack. At least it gave me dates and information to cover the period from 1886 to 1898. Twelve years; in that time Rolfe had changed from an eccentric and curious painter into a writer of challenging gifts and powers. How? There lay the real problem and wonder. I could not forget that the rapscallion so ruthlessly exposed had written *Hadrian the Seventh*. Save for my knowledge of that circumstance, I might have read the attack, as one reads so many similar accounts in newspapers, with nothing more than a passing smile at a quaint impostor. But the author of *Hadrian* could not have been a mere landlord-bilking impostor. It seemed undeniable that, even apart from Venice, there were sinister episodes in his life; but he had survived them; the shabby figure that stalked the Aberdeen streets had added to the laurels of English letters. I must learn more. I counted the hours till I could call on Mr. Herbert Rolfe.

Need I say that I was prompt in fulfilment of my appointment at Mr. Rolfe's chambers in the Temple? The lawyer proved to be a heavy, ponderous man; amiable, I judged, when not confronted by an unwelcome reminder (such as mine) of events which, I could plainly see, he would have preferred forgotten. As his letter foreshadowed, he was 'not unwilling', and equally not eager, to give me information. What did I want to know?

No great degree of penetration was needed to see that Mr. Rolfe was in two minds as to how much to tell me; and I soon discovered the reason for his reluctance. He was furious at the tone and 'inaccuracies' of Mr. Leslie's article, and in particular at the statement that his brother's remains were committed to a pauper's grave. He himself, he told me, went to Venice on the day that his brother's death was announced in *The Times,* and secured decent Christian burial for the remains, paying the ordinary fee. At that time the Municipality refused to grant a grave in perpetuity, and he was therefore obliged to purchase a ten years' lease. On the expiration of that, he had, after much negotiation, procured a permanent resting place for his brother's body in the cemetery of the island of San Michele.

The situation was a delicate one. I was mortally anxious not to offend the man who, above all others, could help me; but with the assertions and insinuations of the Aberdeen Press attack still in my mind, I was afraid that, by some chance remark, I might. However, I set out my questions with all the diplomacy I could contrive; and Mr. Rolfe listened with unmarred patience. I summarize his replies.

Frederick William Rolfe, the eldest of five brothers, was born at 61 Cheapside on July 22, 1860. The Rolfe family had been manufacturers of pianos since the eighteenth century; but, despite being among the pioneers of their trade, had from about 1850 onwards lost ground to their competitors. Frederick was from the first gifted and flighty. He was sent to a sound school in Camden Town (which had long since ceased to exist, Mr. Rolfe told me) and made progress when he chose. But drawing and enjoyment counted with him before Latin exercises, though he was well grounded in classical studies, and proved himself a proficient scholar. Much against his father's wish, Frederick left school in his fifteenth year; I did not discover if there was any reason, beyond 'waywardness and discontent', for thus cutting short his schooldays. He idled for a time, worked as an unattached student at Oxford, and then (as I already knew) became, first a schoolmaster, then a Catholic, and then a candidate for priesthood. Each of these steps had in turn increased the family disappointment and disapproval, and left a wider gap between the prodigal and his relatives. Mr. Rolfe, senior, a firm Dissenter, had hardly known whether to regret or rejoice at the failure of his eldest son to become a Catholic priest. Thereafter, as Fr. (which stood for Frederick, not Father) Rolfe found it more and more difficult to secure himself a livelihood, his letters home became fewer and briefer. He had never lost touch completely; but the Rolfes had necessarily watched his later career from afar, and were not, therefore, able to give me close details. With regard to the Christchurch episode, Mr. Rolfe would express no opinion, though he was surprised to hear that his brother had ever possessed any freehold houses, mortgaged or otherwise. He could give no further information regarding the Duchess. The Barony he regarded as a bad joke. But on the subject of the Aberdeen Press attack, which had been copied into other newspapers, Mr. Rolfe came very near warmth in his contempt. It had been made at a time when his brother, endeavouring to set the past behind him, had started a new career as a writer; and its effect, not only on public opinion, but also on Frederick Rolfe himself, had been disastrous. As a consequence of it, Fr. Rolfe had for years shrunk from notice, morbidly convinced that everyone with whom he was in contact had read and believed its charges. He had never fully recovered from the blow. If I wanted a reply to it, I had only to look at the Pope's interview with his Cardinals at the end of *Hadrian*.

Were there any definite misstatements in the *Aberdeen Free Press* article, I asked? Mr. Rolfe seemed to think not; but circumstances, not in themselves shameful, had been so presented as to give a very wrong impression. He thought that the best answer would be to read to me a testimonial which his brother had received from Dr. E. G. Hardy, who after being Rolfe's headmaster at Grantham School had later become Vice-Principal of Jesus College at Oxford. I listened.

Applegarth, Bardwell Rd. Oxford

22 July 1904

Mr. Frederick William Rolfe has been an intimate and valued friend of mine for more than twenty years; and, if anything which I can say, or any testimony which I can give, as to his ability and worth, should prove to be of assistance to him in his present difficult and entirely undeserved position, I shall be more than glad.

From the time when I first knew him, Mr. Rolfe has been a man of many interests and tastes, all of which he cultivated as occasion served, with energy and enthusiasm. Owing to circumstances, however, he has been gradually attracted more and more to literature, for the sake of which, indeed, he has resolutely turned his back for years upon every pleasure and recreation which might distract him from success. As to what measure of this he has already achieved, it would be unfitting for me, as his friend, to give an opinion. What I wish to dwell upon—and I speak with intimate knowledge of the whole of his career—is the unfaltering devotion with which he has given himself up to his work. He has been, as I well know, at every disadvantage throughout. He has had no influential friends to back and encourage him; and he has been almost hopelessly weighed down by want of means. But notwithstanding this, he has never lost heart. In spite of loneliness and poverty and too often, I fear, actual privation, he has year after year continued to struggle. I do not attempt, as I say, to appreciate the value of his work; but I know that it represents an amount of self-denying labour, almost wholly unrewarded, which in almost every other profession could hardly have failed to win success.

But it is not only the indefatigable industry, perseverance, and thoroughness of his work which has commanded my admiration and respect.

I should like also to record my thorough belief in Mr. Rolfe as a refined and honourable gentleman, whose moral character is without reproach, and of whose genuineness and bona fides in all relations of life I have no doubt whatever. Mr. Rolfe has been frequently a visitor in my house and college, both in past years and quite recently: indeed during each of the last five years he has spent several months or weeks with me, assisting me with portions of my work for which defective eyesight has incapacitated me; and, even if I had had no other opportunities, during the many years I have known him, of forming a judgment on his abilities, his social charm, and his moral worth, I should still be justified in bearing what I hope will be considered this emphatic testimony to his deserts.

As a matter of fact, however, I speak from a much more thorough knowledge of his whole career than probably any other of his friends.

E. G. Hardy, M.A., D.Litt.
*Vice-Principal and Tutor of Jesus Coll. Oxford
formerly Head Master of Grantham School.*

Once more Fr. Rolfe had astonished me. Who could have supposed that the adventurer who had so signally failed to impress the residents of Aberdeen could have deserved this glowing testimonial from an influential Oxford don? I was lost in surmise, when Mr. Rolfe recalled me to the active present by suggesting that, as our interview had already been a long one, I should take away and study certain letters from his brother which he had brought for my inspection, and then consult him again. He emphasized the necessity for discretion in anything that I might write. Frederick Rolfe had made many enemies during his life, not all of whom were dead; and there were incidents which, if I revived them, might bring about a renewal of attacks upon his memory, which the Rolfe family urgently wished to avoid. For that reason he would not at present aid me, even if he could, to a sight of *The Desire and Pursuit of the Whole*. Later, he would be willing to discuss the whole matter with me again; for the present, I must rest content with the material he offered.

This last decision was a disappointment; nevertheless I felt profoundly grateful to Mr. Rolfe; and after thanking him cordially, I left his chambers with the packet of letters burning under my arm.

Before reading the letters, I turned again to the refutation which he had reminded me I should find in *Hadrian*. It takes up most of Chapter XXII in that strange book. When I first read it I had missed its significance, not knowing then of the article in the *Aberdeen Free Press*. Rose, like his creator, has been grossly attacked by a newspaper; and, assembling his Cardinals, he gives his answer. He asks his audience to understand that

I tell you what I am about to tell you, not because I have been provoked, abused, calumniated, traduced, assailed with insinuation, innuendo, mispresentation, lies: not because my life has been held up to ridicule, and to most inferior contempt: not because the most preposterous stories to my detriment have been invented, hawked about, believed. No. Please understand that I am not going to speak in my own defence, even to you. I personally and of predilection can be indifferent to opinions. But officially I must correct error.

He does. He explains his retirement from Grantham as due to his conversion to the Catholic faith, not to disgrace. He gives reasons for the cessation of his Oban employment. His debts at Rome are dismissed as insignificant, and incurred on the advice of the Vice-Rector. On the subject of bilking landlords, he exclaims (in a 'rictus of rage'):

Do you suppose that a man of my description goes about bilking landlords for the sake of the fun of the thing? It's no such deliriously jolly work, I can tell you. However, I've never bilked any landlords, if that's what you want to know. Never. They saw that I worked like nineteen galley-slaves; and they offered to trust me. I voluminously explained my exact position and prospects to them. I was foolish enough to believe that you Catholics would keep your promises. . . . So I accepted credit. I wish I had died. . . . When I was defrauded of my wages, my landlords lost patience (poor things—I don't blame them), harried me, reproached me, at length turned me out, and so prevented me from paying them. I dug myself out of the gutter with these bare hands again and again; and started anew to earn enough to pay my debts. Debts! They never were off my chest for twenty years, no matter what these vile liars say. . . . They say that I gorged myself with sumptuous banquets at grand hotels. Once, after several days' absolute starvation, I got a long-earned guinea; and I went and had an omelette and a bed at a place which called itself a grand hotel. It wasn't particularly grand in the ordinary sense of the term; and my entertainment there cost me no more than it would have cost me elsewhere, and it was infinitely cheaper and tastier. They say that I ate daintily, and had elaborate dishes made from a cookery book of my own. The recipes (there may have been a score of them) were cut-out of a penny weekly current among the working classes. The dishes were lentils, carrots, anything that was cheapest, cleanest, easiest and most filling—nourishing—at the price. Each dish cost something under a penny; and I sometimes had one each day. That's the story of my luxurious living. Let me add though that I was extravagant, in proportion to my means, in one thing. Whenever I earned a little bit, I reserved some of it for apparatus conducing to personal cleanliness, soap, baths, tooth-things, and so on. I'm not a bit ashamed of that. Why did I use credit? Because it was offered; because I hoped. . . . I never was idle. I worked at one thing after another. . . . I courted semi-starvation and starvation, I scrupulously avoided drink, I hardly ever even spoke civilly to a woman; and I laboured like a driven slave. No: I never was idle. But I was a most abject fool. I used to think that this diligent ascetic life would pay me best. I made the mistake of omitting to give its due importance to the word 'own' in the adage 'Virtue is its own reward'. I had no other reward except my unwillingly cultivated but altogether undeniable virtue. . . . I repeat, I never was idle. I did work after work. I delineated saints and seraphim, and sinners, chiefly the former: a series of rather interesting and polyonomous devils in a period of desperate revolt. I slaved as a professional photographer, making (from French prints) a set of negatives for lantern-slides of the Holy Land which were advertised as being 'from original negatives' . . . I did journalism, reported inquests for eighteenpence. I wrote for magazines, I wrote books. I invented a score of things. Experts used to tell me that there was a fortune waiting for me in these inventions: that any capitalist would help me to exploit them. They were small people themselves, these experts,—small, in that they were not obliged to pay income tax: they had no capital to invest: but they recommended me, and advised me, to apply to lots of people who had:—gave me their names and addresses, dictated the letters of application which I wrote. I trusted them, for they were 'business men', and I knew that I was not of that species. I quieted my repugnance; and I laid invention after invention, scheme after scheme, work after work, before capitalist after capitalist. I was assured that it was correct to do so. I despised and detested myself for doing it. I scoured the round world for a 'patron'. These were my begging letters. . . . I knew that I had done such and such a new thing: that I had exhausted myself and my resources in doing it: that my deed was approved by specialists who thoroughly knew the subject. I was very ashamed to ask for help to make my inventions profitable: but I was quite honest—generous: I always offered a share in the profits—always. I did not ask for, and I did not expect, something for nothing. I had done so much; and I wanted so little: but I did want that little,—for my creditors, for giving ease to some slaves of my acquaintance. I was a fool, a sanguine ignorant abject fool! I never learned by experience. I still kept on. A haggard shabby shy priestly-visaged individual, such as I was, could not hope to win the confidence of men who daily were approached by splendid plausible cadgers. My requests were too diffident, too modest. I made the mistake of appealing to brains rather than to bowels, to reason rather than to sentiment. . . . By degrees I had the mortification of seeing others arrive at the discovery which I had made years before. They contrived to turn it into gold and fame. That way, one after another of my inventions became nulled to me. . . . When I think of all the violently fatuous frantic excellent things I've done in the course of my struggles for an honest living—ouf! It makes me sick! . . . Oh yes, I have been helped. God forgive me for bedaubing myself with that indelible blur. A brute once said that he supposed that I looked upon the world as mine oyster. I did not. I worked; and I wanted my wages. When they were withheld, people encouraged me to hope on; and offered me a guinea for the present. I took the filthy guinea. God forgive me for becoming so degraded. Not because I wanted to take it: but because they said that they would be so pained at my refusal. But one can't pay all one's debts, and lead a godly righteous sober life for ever after on a guinea. I was offered help: but help in teaspoonfuls: just enough to keep me alive and chained in the mire: never enough to enable me to raise myself out of it. I asked for work, and they gave me a guinea,—and a tacit request to go and agonize elsewhere. . . . Regarding my pseudonyms—my numerous pseudonyms—think of this: I was a tonsured clerk, intending to persist in my Divine Vocation, but forced for a time to engage in secular pursuits both to earn my living and to pay my debts. I had a shuddering repugnance from associating my name, the name by which I . . . should some day be known in the priesthood, with these secular pursuits. I think that was rather absurd: but I am quite sure that it was not dishonourable. However, for that reason I adopted pseudonyms. . . . In fact, I split up my personality. As Rose [Rolfe] I was a tonsured clerk: as King Clement [Baron Corvo] I wrote and painted and photographed: as Austin White I designed decorations: as Francis Engle I did journalism. There were four of me at least. . . . . And of course my pseudonymity has been misunderstood by the stupid, as well as mispresented by the invidious. Most people have only half developed their single personalities. That a man should split his into four and more, and should develop each separately and perfectly, was so abnormal that many normals failed to understand it. So when 'false pretences' and similar shibboleths were shrieked, they also took alarm and howled. But there were no false pretences.

A curious, not entirely convincing defence. What of the cheques that had not been met, the attempted purchase of Gleeson White's house, the suggestion that he might invest a thousand pounds in the photographic firm in Aberdeen? Yet 'from a much more thorough knowledge of his whole career than any other of his friends [possessed]', Dr. Hardy had spoken unhesitatingly for Rolfe. In search of further light, I turned to the letters.

They helped me very little. As I expected, they were written in that fascinating hand which I already knew; and ranged from 1894, perhaps six months after the Aberdeen ordeal ended, to eleven years later, just after *Hadrian* was published. But in the main they were concerned with the literary activities of Rolfe's later life, not with the period of the attack and the opening of his career as a writer, with which, at that moment, I was most concerned. If I were to print them here, they would confuse the reader, as they did me: I shall therefore reserve them for their chronological place. At least, however, they confirmed my feeling that there must be a Rolfe other than the rascal exposed in the *Aberdeen Free Press*.

It was not by accident, I was certain, that these letters selected for me by Mr. Herbert Rolfe threw no light on his brother's end in Venice. Evidently the same motives had dictated his choice as those which were behind the refusal of *The Desire and Pursuit of the Whole;* and, remembering the Millard letters, it was not difficult to guess what they were. But in any event it seemed useless to attempt to break down Mr. Rolfe's reluctance till I had learned what there was to be learned from my other correspondents. Mr. Shane Leslie was an obvious source: he must have made inquiries over the whole ground before writing his biographical survey. Perhaps he had notes which would set me on fresh paths. I wrote to him.

V

THE THEOLOGICAL STUDENT

IN reply I received an amiably worded invitation to lunch
a week later. I wished that the interval had been briefer;
but, as there was no way of abridging it, I occupied myself
meanwhile in reviewing the notes I had gathered. Up to
1894 my information covered most of Rolfe's movements;
he was never out of sight for long. From his birth in 1860
till the end of his schooldays in 1875 I had only his brother's
brief description, it is true; but it seemed to me sufficient:
sufficient for the moment, at least. My interest in the early
years of the eminent is far less than that which the tradition
of biographical writing painfully imposes on its devotees.
The facts of infancy may be vital when they refer to a
prodigy such as Mozart, interesting when relevant to a rebel
such as Shelley, valuable when they show the growth of a
man out of his place, as Poe; but in Rolfe's case I felt that
his childhood was by much the least interesting part of his
life. Moreover, it is possible to reason backwards as well as
forwards, to infer the child from the man; and I proposed
to do so. I knew enough to picture the bright attractive boy,
a natural Catholic in a household of Dissenters, interested in
drawing, music and the arts, not over-given to sport, and
with that love of experiment which so frequently seems
instability in youth. I could well understand his cutting
short his schooldays from a desire to be in, and to see, the
world; he was precocious, not in ability to pass examinations,
but in the general development of his personality. On the
other hand, the period between leaving school and becoming
a schoolmaster was more interesting; and I hoped that
later I should learn more of those formative years. But here

again one can to some extent reason backwards; the choice
of schoolmastership is significant, particularly in one whose
own schooldays were cut short. What sort of master, I
wondered, had he made? A good one, at least so far as
Grantham was concerned, or his headmaster Hardy would
not have spoken so highly of him in later years. No doubt
I should find traces at his other schools.

His becoming Catholic I could easily understand. The
attraction of the Catholic Faith for the artistic temperament
is a phenomenon which has been the subject of many novels,
and is one of the facts of psychology. Even among Rolfe's
immediate contemporaries, Francis Thompson, Aubrey
Beardsley, Ernest Dowson and Lionel Johnson had followed
the same path, a path which has been charted by Joris Karl
Huysmans. Rolfe had become a Catholic at twenty-six;
and, shortly afterwards, aspired to priesthood. That, undoubtedly, was more unusual than his conversion; and yet
perhaps it is not surprising that one in whom nature had not
implanted a love for women should embrace a celibate
career. And then Rolfe, as his books showed, was a mediæ-
valist, an artist, and a scholar in temperament; so that to him
the tradition of the Catholic Church, with its championship
of learning and beauty, must have been a real and living
thing. On reflection it seemed reasonable enough that he
should have desired to ally himself more intimately than as
a layman with an institution that represented the best side
of his character and his hopes. Yet somehow he had met
squalls at Oscott, which he had left hurriedly; though
squalls clearly not severe enough to deprive him of the
chance of ordination, or he would never have been sent to
Rome. His expulsion from the Scots College was plainly a
matter that I must investigate. As for his assumption of
baronial rank, it might have been a bad joke, as his brother
said, inspired by an impish sense of humour and a desire
for the picturesque; or the story he had told Mr. Kains-
Jackson might be true. At all events, his clerical career from
1887 to 1890, from twenty-seven to thirty, was dated, and

might be documented. His period in Christchurch, and his vicissitudes in Aberdeen, lasting from 1891 to 1894, were also plain enough. From that point my knowledge was more hazy. He had found his way to Wales, how or why I knew not; he had become a writer; and, four years after the end of his adventures in Aberdeen, he had endured the newspaper attack. With what consequences? Was it that which had provoked the suspicions and touchiness clouding his later years? I knew very little of his life as an author beyond what could be gleaned from the letters to his family. In 1904–5 he was busily engaged in writing; in 1913 he died.

I made a similar mental tabulation of his writings. The first was *Stories Toto Told Me,* published in 1898 after a previous appearance in *The Yellow Book.* Rolfe had been moved by their success to write more, and so form his second book, *In his Own Image.* The same year (1901) had seen his *Chronicles of the House of Borgia.* Then in 1903, 1904, 1905, his translation of Omar, *Hadrian the Seventh,* and *Don Tarquinio* had successively appeared. After that, nothing till 1912 (a gap concurrent with that in his biography), when his last-published work, *The Weird of the Wanderer,* seemed to have fallen flat. The ground on which I should question Mr. Leslie began to be clear.

It was with a certain excitement that I rang Mr. Leslie's bell: I knew him well by name, by his writings, by the commendations of friends, but we had never met. His smile of welcome was reassuring after the reserve of Mr. Rolfe; and I discovered with delight at lunch that my host (though he grieved me by leaving his excellent hock untasted) shared my own sense of verbal humour, and neither reserved all his intelligence for his writings, nor all his cordiality for those whom he knew well. Moreover, voices have always been one of my tests for new acquaintances: Mr. Leslie's intonations charmed my ear.

As to helping me, he was wholly at my service, though he thought Rolfe's life impossible to write. As before I was asked, what did I want to know? I put my questions under two heads: first: Rolfe's life at Oscott and Rome; secondly, his last years. As to the second, Mr. Leslie professed himself hardly wiser than I; he knew little more as to how Rolfe spent his time in Venice than could be derived from those letters belonging to Millard which I had read for myself. Regarding Rome and Oscott, however, he could be more helpful. He handed me a manuscript of several pages, written by a contemporary of Rolfe's at the Scots College, and numerous addresses of Catholics who had known Rolfe at one time or another in his life. In particular he recommended me to approach Fr. Martindale, S. J., biographer of Robert Hugh Benson. Concerning Benson, Mr. Leslie gave me a few details, which I reserve for their appropriate chapter. I left him with the feeling that my quest for Corvo had made me a new friend.

I will not impede this narrative with an account of my numerous letters beseeching information from those who had been, or might have been, at either of his two clerical colleges with Rolfe. Some came back marked 'Gone Away'; some to whom I wrote were dead; some refused to help me. But I did not draw all blanks, as will be seen.

Abbot's Salford
Near Evesham

Dear Sir,

I am afraid that I cannot send you much information concerning Frederick Rolfe that will be of value. I will, however, tell you what I can remember, in the hope that you may possibly be able to pick out something which may perhaps corroborate some piece of information you already possess.

I left Stonyhurst College in 1885 and came to Oscott in that year, while it was still a lay-College under the presidency of Mgr. Souter. It was about that time, before Oscott was changed into a seminary, that Rolfe arrived and joined the 'Divines'. The

'Divines' were the Church students of the College, wearing the cassock and biretta and studying for the priesthood. So far as I can remember, Rolfe was with us only a short time—a thin, somewhat emaciated, rather good-looking young man. In the course of his first week he took us by surprise one dinner-time by exclaiming aloud, in an interval of silence—'Oh! what lovely legs!' This, in those far-off days of the past, was considered a somewhat outrageous exclamation to come from the lips of a Church student, and Frederick McClement expostulated with him. But it turned out that the legs he was referring to were those of a small insect which was creeping towards his soup-plate. (Fr. McClement is still alive, I believe. He followed me from Stonyhurst to Oscott, and was ordained for a Scotch diocese: he has changed his name to McClymont.) Several of us figured in *Hadrian the Seventh*—I was Mr. Whitehead, having in those days fair golden hair; but I cannot remember further details. We also figured in some of his illustrations, which were excellent and very true portraits. The painting of John Jennings as an Angel was particularly lifelike. (Jennings, afterwards Canon of Flint, is now dead.) In fact there are so few of Rolfe's contemporaries alive to-day that I can be of very little help to you. Possibly Fr. Grafton, Blackmore Park, Hanley Swan, near Worcester, might remember something about him. Rolfe left Oscott unlamented, and at that time I never thought to hear of him again. But not long afterwards I went with my brother to visit some people at Seaton, Aberdeen, named Hay, and there I saw him once more. He was tutor to the two little boys Malcolm and Cuthbert Hay. He was leaving, however, that very day, so I had no opportunity of an interview. I regret I can give you no further first-hand information. I *heard* that he spent several months in the Poor Law Workhouse somewhere near Southport, and occupied his time writing bitterly about the Jesuits, who had refused to accept him as a student; but that may be quite incorrect.

Yours faithfully

Gerald G. Jackson

Fr. Grafton proved a disappointment, but I was luckier with Fr. McClymont:

Ardcolm, Kingussie,
Inverness-shire

Dear Sir,

I received your letter regarding a life you are writing of F. W. Rolfe. I think Fr. Jackson could have given you as much as I can about him. However I will give you my slight recollections. Rolfe was only at Oscott for a short time, as doubtless you know. He was regarded by us students as eccentric and a subject of jokes, perhaps because he was so different from everybody else. He kept much to himself, and seemed more interested in art than in theology. I remember he was engaged in painting a picture on some historical subject, and used to get one or more of the boys from the lay school which at that time formed part of Oscott to stand for his picture. My impression of the picture is that it was good to a high degree for anyone not a qualified artist. He also went in for beating out brasswork. I suppose you know that before coming to Oscott, the late Lord Bute had engaged him to take charge of the Catholic Choir in Oban? Amongst his books he had Lord Bute's translation of the Breviary, no doubt given him by Lord Bute. His outstanding eccentricity was to stamp everything available with his crest, the raven (*Corvo*). But most noticeable was a *stuffed* raven which had the place of honour on his table. He explained to me about his name that 'Rolfe' really came from 'Rollo', the common ancestor of himself and William the Conqueror. He had an overweening vanity. His usual mood was taciturnity. Amongst his lighter achievements he professed a knowledge of palmistry, and for fun we used to get our fortunes told. I believe I was to have a mental illness—I may mention that it has not come off yet. I don't think I can tell any more. The main thing is that it was and is a wonder to me why he ever became a clerical student.

Yours sincerely

F. B. McClymont, o.s.b.

The Bishop of Shrewsbury was also able to tell me something:

Bishop's House,
Shrewsbury

My dear Sir,

I fear I cannot tell you much about poor Rolfe at Oscott, although he had a room next but one to me. I am afraid we boys looked upon him as a *poseur*. Before he came to Oscott he was heralded as an 'Oxford man', and we looked forward to such a one who would take interest in cricket; and when we found he took no interest in games, and when rumour went round that he had not been at the University but had lived there for a short time in the City, his stock fell badly. He was to me personally very kind, but most of his fellow-students in 'Divinity' were afraid of his caustic tongue and his unmistakable sense of superiority.

He came out to Rome early in 1889 (I think) and lived for a short time at the Scots College. As the English College men and Scots went to the same University I saw a little of him there, but he was just the same F. W. R. The morning that I remember best was after he had had a stormy interview the night before with the Rector of the Scots College—Mgr. Campbell. I think the cause of it must have been that Rolfe had not paid for his *pension* and had been given hurried notice to quit. Rolfe said to me, 'The man is fully paid really. He has seized a meerschaum pipe that I value at forty pounds.'

That week he went to live with the Sforza-Cesarini. One of the family—Mario—was at Oscott when he was there. I don't think I ever saw him afterwards. I am afraid these are trivialities, but they are the only memories I have of him. He was at Oscott about a year only.

Yours sincerely

✠ Ambrose
Coadj: Bp: of Shrewsbury

Finally, I was delighted to receive the following:

Oscott College
Birmingham

Dear Mr. Symons,

I was a contemporary of Rolfe's at Oscott, though not in the same year. I was a senior boy: he was a junior master. This was in 1887–88, I think. Later on, I knew him rather better, when he was living in Holywell. This would be some ten years later. He certainly caused astonishment and talk at Oscott and elsewhere in this period. I am not sure that I should care to write down recollections of him. One remembers so easily the oddities of a man—and I should not care to write what may be a caricature rather than a portrait. However, if you could find it convenient to come to Oscott (where I should be delighted to entertain you) I could talk for a couple of hours about him, and you might sift what seemed needful for your purpose. We can be easily approached from Birmingham, and I really think you would get better value from a chat between supper and bedtime than if I tried to commit my impressions to writing.

Yours faithfully
J. Dey

I jumped at this chance of a visit to Oscott, which I knew well by the description of another of my idols, George Moore, who also had been an unsuccessful student at the famous Catholic College. I wrote to Mgr. Dey (present Rector of Oscott) to propose a date; and when the appointed time came, set off by car, full of hope that I might be able to discover in a lumber-room or loft some of those paintings mentioned by my correspondents. I arrived in full sunshine. Oscott College is a vast red-brick Pugin-Gothic structure, superbly placed on top of a tableland commanding a long stretch southwards. The entrance is from the back by a long drive which winds amid shrubberies and gardens to the front, so that I was quite unprepared for the sight that awaited me at my journey's end. Standing with my back to the College entrance, I looked out over the edge of the tableland past a small farm with its fields and buildings, to a full, a panoramic, an appalling view of the slate roofs of Birmingham's suburb, Erdington. Compared with the trim walk, lawn and shrubbery amid which I stood, compared with the farm below, it looked like a vast, hastily-set-up mining camp, built by men devoid of all sense of form and dignity, concerned only with a temporary covering while the ore lasts. Such sights, alas, are common enough in England now. My indignation at Erdington was still alert when Mgr. Dey came to meet me: tall, handsome, dignified, be-cassocked, with the smile of humour in his eyes and on his lips. I expressed my regret at the grim spectacle before us; and he answered with a sigh that there had not been a single house in sight when he and Rolfe first came to Oscott.

Before turning into the Rector's study to talk, I walked with him round the College. Architecturally it is not remarkable, but it houses some fine things, mainly the gift of a former Earl of Shrewsbury. The Library has some good illuminated manuscripts, and in the Museum are a number of magnificent fifteenth- and sixteenth-century vestments, heavy velvet gleaming still with gold thread, ornamented and embroidered with superb panels showing the passions and passings of the saints. They had been on show even in Rolfe's day, I learned; I could imagine how his mediæval mind must have revelled in their rich, unsubdued display. We walked through long corridors hung with pictures, to Mgr. Dey's study; there he set himself at my service, and, without prompting, told me all that he could remember of Rolfe.

They had met in 1887 at Oscott, which was then (as I knew from Fr. Jackson's letter) a secular Catholic College, and not, as now, exclusively a seminary for those preparing for the priesthood. Rolfe was a member of the limited class of 'divines' receiving instruction for ordination. His fees were paid by the (then) Bishop of Shrewsbury; Mgr. Dey could not tell me how the Bishop had come to take Rolfe up. Rolfe had certainly proved no ordinary student: he developed an inordinate passion for painting, and three sides of his bedroom wall were covered by a remarkable picture of the burial of St. William of Norwich, in which the corpse was carried by a hundred-and-forty-nine bearers dressed in varied vestments, but all alike contrived as to countenance in Rolfe's own image! Even the Saint (what could be seen of him) was marked with Rolfe's nose. This unconventional divinity student sported fanciful meerschaum pipes, and carried quite the largest tobacco pouch Mgr. Dey had ever seen. He was ruthlessly ragged by the students, though he had his friends, including Mgr. Dey himself. After the greater part of a year had passed, Rolfe left Oscott at the instance of the Bishop, who was dissatisfied with the progress of his protégé, and not prepared to pay for him to indulge his hobby of painting. So far as Mgr. Dey knew, not a single one of his canvases survived in the College.

Several years later young Fr. Dey was astonished to receive a letter claiming Oscott acquaintance, and inviting a visit, from a 'Fr. Austin' of whom he had no remembrance. Eventually, however, he discovered that this pseudonym covered the identity of his former friend Rolfe, and, mystified by the change of name, sought him out at Holywell in Wales. There he found the erstwhile student lodged in a schoolroom, engaged in painting banners for the local priest. His circumstances were miserable, his complaints numerous, chief among them being the poor pay for his work, and the shabby behaviour of his priest-employer. Cardinal Vaughan also, it appeared, had disappointed (Rolfe's word was 'defrauded') the unlucky painter, by abandoning a promised, or half-promised, contract for ecclesiastical pictures, on the ground that all his funds were needed for Westminster Cathedral. I was particularly interested in this part of Mgr. Dey's narrative: it filled in the one substantial gap in Rolfe's pre-literary career, and explained the position of George Arthur Rose at the opening of *Hadrian*, where he is shown as suffering poverty through the defalcations of his Catholic

employers. Evidently he had laboured under a deep grievance: how well-founded, my informant could not say. All
that he could add to my knowledge of the Holywell episode
was that in the end Rolfe had moved his quarters to the inn,
where, from the balcony of his first-floor bedroom, he would
(during the religious processions that passed by) point an
accusing finger at the priest by whose hand, in his view,
he was suffering.

Again Rolfe had passed out of Mgr. Dey's life for some
months, until the end of 1898, when the Aberdeen attack was
reprinted almost verbatim in the *Catholic Times*. Moved by
the manifest bias of its tone, Mgr. Dey had written in
expostulation to the editor, urging the injustice of dragging
up old history against an unfortunate man who had paid
dearly for his follies, and was trying hard to support himself
by his pen. The letter was garbled and cut down; but
Rolfe had noticed it, and written in gratitude. He expressed
his thanks in more abiding form also, for, long after, Mgr.
Dey was amused and touched to find himself promoted into
a Cardinal in *Hadrian the Seventh*, wherein, as Sterling, he
is faithfully depicted, even as to the mole on his nose and his
manner of speech. The two friends never met again. In 1913
Mgr. Dey heard (in South Africa) of Rolfe's death in Venice.

Unfortunately he had preserved no letters; and I learned
with regret that there were no records surviving of Oscott
in its pre-seminary days. We looked in vain through albums
of old photographs. But, even more to my purpose, Mgr.
Dey was able to put in my hands a printed testimonial,
possibly the means by which Rolfe had brought his clerical
aspirations to the notice of his superiors, which gave me
exact information of his pedagogic career:

TESTIMONIALS IN FAVOUR OF MR. FREDERICK ROLFE

I

F. W. Rolfe conducted himself to my satisfaction while a pupil
in this School, and left with an excellent character. He is steady,

industrious and persevering, and I think will do his best to give satisfaction.

CHAS. WM. WILLIAMS, D.D.

(Trin. Coll. Camb.)

Head Master, North London Collegiate School.

II

I have much pleasure in recommending Mr. Frederick Rolfe, who was my Assistant-Master for a year and a half. Mr. Rolfe's work consisted entirely in teaching the youngest boys in the School; but that work he has done thoroughly well. His questions are always simple but searching, and he never shrinks from the laborious repetition which is requisite for driving home ideas in very young minds. Mr. Rolfe likes his work, and is thoroughly methodical and conscientious in the discharge of his duties, while his powers of maintaining discipline are quite sufficient for the successful management of a fairly large class of junior boys. He rendered valuable aid in training a young Choir, and undertook successfully a class of beginners in Drawing. I may add that Mr. Rolfe came to me strongly recommended by Mr. Isbister, Head Master of the Stationers' School, under whom he had previously worked, whose good opinion of him appears to me to be fully justified.

R. M. LUCKOCK, M.A.

(Corp. Christi Coll. Camb.)

Head Master, King Edward VI Grammar School, Saffron Walden, Essex.

III

Mr. Frederick Rolfe has taught in this school for two terms. I received his resignation with regret, as I have found him constant and methodical in work, and believe him to be actuated by the best motives. During his stay here he has taught History throughout the School, and to Junior classes Latin, French, English, Arithmetic and Divinity. He has assisted us considerably with choir work, conducting the boys' practice and playing the harmonium in chapel. He will exercise a good influence over boys, both by the conscientiousness displayed in work and by the cheerful interest he takes in their games and occupations out of school.

JOHN M. OGLE, M.A.

(Clare Coll. Camb.)

Head Master, Winchester Modern School.

IV

Mr. Frederick Rolfe has been a non-resident assistant master with me since Easter, 1882. His engagement was a temporary one. He had charge of the second form. I have had ample opportunities of observing his powers of teaching and maintaining discipline, and I can confidently say that he excels both as a teacher and disciplinarian. He is neat and methodical in his work, and regular and punctual in his attendance.

J. ATKINS, M.A., LL.B.

(Trin. Coll. Dublin)

Head Master, S. Bartholomew's Grammar
School, Newbury.

V

I have known Mr. Frederick Rolfe for more than three years, during the latter portion of which he has assisted me with my pupils. He has always attended assiduously to his duties, and has won a good reputation as a teacher. He excels as a disciplinarian, while gaining the goodwill of boys by the great interest he takes in them out of school.

GEORGE HOWES, M.A.

(Pem. Coll. Camb.)

Balsham Manor, Cambridge.

My visit to Oscott had been a very fruitful one. As I was taking my leave, one more remembrance came to Mgr. Dey: that the poet Vincent O'Sullivan, later the friend of Oscar Wilde and most of the writers of the 'nineties, had also been Rolfe's contemporary at Oscott, and might have kept some memories of a minor feud with him. By a lucky chance, O'Sullivan had been a more or less regular correspondent of mine for many years, and I was able to get details without difficulty:

                                        Hotel Bristol,
                                        Biarritz, France

Dear Symons,

I am glad that Dey remembers me so kindly. It is always a pleasure for me to think of him, and I have a great respect for him.

You ask me about Rolfe (pronounced Rofe). Any 'feud' I had with him I forget, and it could only have been very slight, on account of our relative position, which was that of school-master and school-boy. I never saw him after I left Oscott. My brother was much more his friend than I was, but my brother, who returned home to the United States after leaving the school, and never came again to Europe, never saw Rolfe again either. I believe he corresponded with Rolfe for some years and kept him in funds for a while, which the financial situation of our family at that time enabled him to do.

I suppose he was about twenty-six or twenty-eight when I knew him. He had a handsome sensitive face. Although he was never a member of the University, he had passed somehow or other a good deal of time at Oxford, and he had what used to be known as the 'Oxford accent' to the extreme. A low musical voice. Very charming manners once his timidity was broken down. One Christmas holidays, as my brother and myself were alone in the College, our home being too far off to go there, we were sent under the charge of Rolfe to make a tour of the Cathedral cities—Worcester, Lichfield, Lincoln etc. and he was very good company. He had a way of giving boys a very good opinion of themselves which made them unable to measure accurately their strength and value afterwards when they were face to face with disagreeable events in life.

His reading was not wide and it was very peculiar. One of his favourite books was Reade's *Cloister and the Hearth*. He also liked the books of Mrs. Ewing, and had one or two of them in his room, and would read aloud from them sometimes. The people in vogue at that time—Stevenson, Meredith, Hardy, Henley etc. he didn't know at all. I had them in my room, but Rolfe could never have asked for them, for I certainly never lent them to him. He adored the Gilbert and Sullivan operettes and would sing the ditties and play the accompaniments on the piano. He had many small accomplishments of the kind that make a man or woman welcome in dull country houses where everybody is boring one another. He wrote verse, atrociously bad most of it. I got some of his poems by heart, and I remember bits of them still. They were about boys and saints, generally both together— altogether objective, by-the-bye.

He was a man, as I think of him now, who had only the vaguest sense of realities. I never knew anything about his people or what class of the population he came from. In those days I took no interest in such matters. He was surely English, but it is not impossible that he had a Jewish strain. I have since known Jews not unlike him. I don't even know what he was doing or how he existed before he came to Oscott, nor what diocese it was that sent him there. He would talk by the hour about people we had never seen or heard of before, and make them interesting too—at least to boys. Thinking of him with my present experience of life, I imagine he must have lived for long spells together with more or less wealthy friends until the inevitable quarrel came.

He was born for the Church: that was his main interest, and if the Catholics had kept him as a priest he would have done them credit and might have been useful. He was not fitted of course for a big dirty parish, but he could have done many things well. The Jesuits, I think, would have had more insight. So far as I know, his chief offence in the eyes of the Oscott people was his propensity to run up bills which he had no chance of paying. His books, breviaries etc. he had bound in the most expensive way. Ugly things really hurt him. It is quite possible that he was of very modest origin. I have known some rather like him, booksellers' clerks, etc. In happy circumstances he would have led a life like Pater's. But he had not Pater's curiosity. If he had had a fortune he would have been defrauded by trustees.

I suppose you have fathomed the 'Baron Corvo' business? If you have not, I can't help you much. In one of the few letters I wrote him after I left Oscott, I began as usual 'Dear Mr. Rolfe'. He replied 'Baron Corvo, if you please—a designation I picked up in Italy'. My explanation is this:—the Duc Sforza de Santafiore was at school at Oscott at the same time as I was. He was a friend of my brother, and through my brother came to know Rolfe. I was told that Rolfe went to Italy with Sforza as a tutor or something, and that he was quartered for a time in one of the Duke's palaces, where he was free to do as he liked. I believe the Italian nobles have a right to bestow one of their minor titles on whom it suits them, and Corvo may have been one of Sforza's minor titles.

You know, of course, that Rolfe was not originally a Roman Catholic? Whether he had been Church or Dissent I cannot say. He was very pious. He knew nothing about religion scientifically and he had none of the mental reservations found in many of the clergy. His life was blameless. There was no guile in him. He was as innocent as a three years' child of the ways of the world. He had enemies among the ecclesiastics: such a man outraged all their Irish peasant and little English shopkeeper notions. One of their charges against him was that he carried an arm-chair about with him whenever he changed his abode.

When I came to know Andrew Lang, his voice and something in his manner reminded me of Rolfe. Another point of resemblance was Rolfe's devotion to the Royal Stuarts. When he had a class in history, I gave one day an uncomplimentary account of Charles I, inspired by Carlyle. Rolfe was more distressed than angry, but he *was* distressed.

'I bathe in a row', he would say. But as a matter of fact I think he was probably a bad hand at a row. He was far more shy and timid than self-assertive and bullying. As certain contacts offended him, he preferred to shun them. This was taken for disdain by some of the theological students—'divines' as they were called—

among whom he was. I believe he was given some kind of sacerdotal orders. I know he shaved the crown of his head—a large round spot such as I sometimes see on the heads of the Spanish seminarists about here. 'Whenever they come to the horrors I stop listening and draw pictures' was all I ever heard him say of his lectures in moral theology. By 'horrors' he meant sex-questions. But he was really devout. I was told that he used to go down to the chapel late at night and stay there an hour sometimes when he could have had no notion that he was observed.

I remember reading some years ago an article by D. H. Lawrence praising *Hadrian the Seventh*. Another who praised the book to me was Charles Whibley. What he liked was what he called the description of a 'rotten' life in London. Yet Whibley had no good to say of George Gissing, who has done that kind of thing supremely well, I think.

I hope that these random notes will be of some use. It has given me some pleasure to recall Rolfe, and made me forget for an hour or two my wretched condition in all ways and my smashed up frame.

With all good wishes

Vincent O'Sullivan

VI

THE REJECTED PRIEST

IT was less necessary for me to rely upon correspondence in regard to Rolfe's second bid for the priesthood than for his first; for that manuscript of several pages already mentioned as handed to me by Mr. Leslie was an eye-witness account of the career of 'The Rev. F. W. Rolfe' at Rome. It was written by Canon Carmont of Dalbeattie, and contradicts the impressions of Vincent O'Sullivan. I did not find the inconsistence of the two accounts surprising, however: evidently the reactions to Rolfe of those who met him depended less on what he did and was than on the temperament of the observer. O'Sullivan, himself a writer of distinction in later years, already interested in literature and art, sympathized with the queer student's feeling for form and surface; whereas Canon Carmont, a priest concerned with other things, is impatient at what he considers trivialities, and a personality preoccupied by interests he did not share.

My acquaintance with F. W. Rolfe dates from about October 1889, and lasted for rather over six months—the period during which he was at the Scots College, Rome. I know little of his after career, beyond what might be derived from a casual reading of an attack made on him in the *Catholic Times,* an article by 'Baron Corvo' in the *Wide World,* and one or two of his books, especially *Hadrian the Seventh*, in which he was good enough to make me a Cardinal. Previous to his coming to the Scots College he had been for a time at Oscott; before that a sort of an assistant master at a school for boys at Oban, established by the late Lord Bute. He had been accepted as a candidate for the priesthood by the late Abp. W. Smith, then Metropolitan at Edinburgh, and was sent to Rome to study. At that time he must have been about thirty years of age. As he insisted on having entire liberty to make 'afternoon calls' on his friends in Rome, the Rector, Dr. Campbell, rather unwisely allowed him to 'wear the black soutane', which made him exempt from all but the fundamental rules of the College. (The students' costume, as you are possibly aware, is a purple soutane, black 'soprano', etc.) Thus privileged, he might have lived in the College with next to no intercourse with the ordinary students. On the contrary, he tried to mix with them a great deal. The first impression he made on us was his tendency to 'swank'—a detestable word that I must use, it is so apt. He talked in a vague way of the importance and status of his family, who apparently had severed connection with him when he became a Catholic. Some weeks after his arrival he developed an attack of what he was pleased to call gout, and I recollect his anathematizing his ancestry. 'Oh, that beast of a grandfather', he would exclaim during a twinge of his malady. We fancied he was a vegetarian, as he invariably refused meat at meals. Afterwards we understood that he had no dislike for flesh meat, but imagined the meat served in the College to be horseflesh. In the restaurants of Rome he often made up for his abstinence, the friend who paid on these occasions being a man called Thirstanes—tutor in an English or American family then in Rome.

He possessed a large fund of stories and anecdotes—of the anti-Anglican type—a few also of a slightly Rabelaisian cast. I have heard some funny 'Anglican Confession' stories in my time, but none so ingenious and ornamental as his. Some of his stories were really good: a certain 'cheese' story almost challenged Mark Twain. He was wont to condemn the alleged laxity of the Roman Communion in the matter of truthfulness, and its sub-distinguishing the lie. He himself, brought up as a strict Anglican, had all the Anglican horror of lying and equivocation of every description. He seemed to be quite serious about it, which surprised us, as he was universally regarded as about the biggest liar we had ever met.

Everything about him suggested one who dabbles. His room was a miniature museum. A fine stand-camera betokened the photograph enthusiast, though I don't remember his doing any photography. He had a number of pictures said to be painted by himself. I was and am no judge, and I don't know what their artistic worth might be. There was something distinctive about them, a sort of affectation which repelled me. He sang, nicely enough, being endowed with a pleasant but not very strong tenor voice, and could play the piano. Musically I could diagnose him. He had a 'good ear', and could read music a little, but there was a bizarre something about his improvised accompaniments that made it evident to me that his technical knowledge of harmony was practically nil, and his understanding of the art very superficial. He used to toy with triolets and fidgetty trifles of that sort. He wrote articles weekly to the long-defunct *Whitehall Review*. His parade of Greek in *Hadrian the Seventh* I regard as swank pure and simple. I don't believe he knew any. I presume he had enough Latin to follow the drift of the theological lectures. But I had my doubts at the time. Once he came to me, Gury in hand, demanding to know the meaning of 'eccur'. I expounded. 'Then why can't he say "et cur"?' But I don't think he interested himself much in the course of studies he was supposed to be pursuing, and his attendance at lectures left something to be desired. In innumerable ways he said and did odd things, both in and outside the College, and for a time, no doubt, it was very interesting. But we were a set of young cubs, ignorant and opinionated, with none of the tolerance and understanding that age brings, and mixing in the world. And so a certain savage annoyance and scorn towards Rolfe slowly grew up among the students. When we began to hear stories from outside the College, which indicated that his presence among us was making us a subject for gossip and comment, the annoyance became rage, and the end was in sight.

Rolfe was no student. He gave no indication of any real piety beneath the surface—if there was any 'beneath'. No earnestness and fineness of purpose, no discernible interest in the souls of others—so we judged. His general laxity and carelessness lowered the tone of the college. And then the inevitable 'What is this man doing here?' We put our ideas regarding him before the

Rector, and the Rector expelled him. He got a fortnight to look about him, a week was added to that, three days, one day more, then his departure. I quite assented to the action the students took, though I took no leading part, and looking back I do not regret, and would not alter that attitude. If Rolfe had any vocation for the priesthood at all—I don't think he had—he certainly had none for the missionary work of the Scottish province, and he would only have proved an encumbrance and a nuisance, at the best. At the worst he might have been a positive menace, and a danger. After his expulsion Fr. Mackie O.P. gave him three days' hospitality. Later he got in tow with an Oscott contemporary—an Italian principe, whose name I forget—though it may have been Sforza-Cesarini.

A word or two of my personal views concerning Rolfe. He seemed to me to have a keen sense of externalities of all kinds, little or no apprehension of the inward spirit that is in most things. He painted and photoed and wrote about the outsides of things. He tinkered with triolets, because they are a manner, a form—nothing else. Nobody with anything to say would say it in triolets. I am convinced that a critical reading of his various books would serve to show that he had a very clear and discerning eye for outside values and superficialities—and little else. My rather dim recollection of *Don Tarquinio*, for example, is a sort of movie—a cinema picture. The moral and intellectual and spiritual status of the Don and the young Cardinal is a blank in my mind, and, I suspect, in the book also. Forms, manners, colours, sounds, shapes, and, beyond, a region of vague uninteresting shadows—a sort of spiritual and intellectual myopia—there, I hold, you have the key to all Rolfe. Everything he said or did or wrote should be considered in the light of that. In his tenacious desire for the priesthood was nothing sinister, nothing elevated or fine,—he saw himself doing picturesque things in a picturesque way. He did me the honour of making me a Cardinal, not because we were intimate or friendly—we were not—not because of anything unusual in my character or abilities—there is not—but I imagine because he saw something in me that satisfied his artistic sense, though what that could be I myself am utterly unable to divine. This limitation of his imagination to the external may have increased his power of dealing with what he could apprehend, for there seems no doubt that he was a man of ability.

There was in him little pride, in the better sense of the term. He did not disdain to beg. In fact he seemed to consider that he had a right to expect assistance and favours from those in a position to grant them—I have heard him say so. As to gratitude —less said the better.

There was a sort of ruthless selfishness in him which led him to exploit others, quite regardless of their interest or feelings or advantage. This trait, in small matters, I saw many instances of. He was dressy and particular about his appearance. Church matters were mostly a matter of millinery to him.

There was little or no warmth or affectionateness in him. Probably this was why he was so selfish and self-centred. No geniality. His humour, such as it was, was of a thin and rather sardonic kind. I don't know if he could be called revengeful— perhaps not. The short descriptions of the students in *Hadrian* are certainly not friendly in tone, and might perhaps be regarded as a payment of old scores. I doubt it. I fancy he loathed most of them for the same reason that he apparently liked me—artistic sense.

Take him all in all, he was not very human: he was a sort of sub-species. He must have been very tough and elastic, or he would have been utterly crushed and destroyed by the opposition and enmity he met with, and did so much to excite. Was there an element of greatness in him to account for this? Or was it perhaps something more analogous to that appalling saying of Parolles: 'If my heart were great 'twould burst at this. . . . Simply the thing I am shall make me live'?

This is rather a hasty and scrappy account—written at one sitting—midnight oil. If there is any point you think I can elucidate further, don't hesitate to say so. I shall willingly do what I can.

This article of Canon Carmont's is evidence of an exceptional memory, and of the strong impression that Rolfe made on those who met him. And, despite the Canon's evident lack of sympathy with his eccentric fellow-student, he gives a true picture of a remarkable man. I could imagine very clearly this unusual divine, with his passion for fine clothes, his distinctive paintings, bizarre musical accompaniments, verses, articles, photography, fabulous stories and artistic sense. Out of place, no doubt, in the Scots College at Rome: not fitted, as Vincent O'Sullivan said, for the dirty work of a large parish; but a man of character and accomplishments nevertheless, not to be matched in a day's march; a man who would have adorned the court of a mediæval prince or pope, or won esteem in one of the less rigorous monasteries in the days when a fine manuscript was regarded as a worthy occupation for a lifetime. He was conscious, obviously, of his manifold abilities, and regarded the rewards that he exacted from the world (on credit!) as no more than his due: 'he seemed to consider that he had a right to expect assistance and favours from those in a position to grant them'. I found myself in disagreement with many of the views expressed by Canon Carmont in his diagnosis. He seems to me too hard on the fancy which embodies itself in the triolet; too censorious of Rolfe's acute sense of surfaces; singularly modest in his failure to understand Rolfe's unreturned liking for himself; too incredulous of Rolfe's Latin (he had taught it in Winchester Modern School, and, at Oscott, written at least one Latin poem); wrong in thinking that there was 'no warmth or affectionateness' in the tantalized author of *Hadrian the Seventh;* and wrong again in his view that there was 'nothing elevated or fine behind Rolfe's tenacious desire for priesthood'. I wrote to something like that effect, and in the course of his letter giving me permission to publish his account, Canon Carmont observes with great fairness:

As the years roll by I find I have better insight. At the time when I knew Rolfe I was hardly fit to form any reliable judgment on him. I had no experience of mankind, and was swayed by impulsive and immature prejudices. I came to the conclusion that he was merely a clerical adventurer, and I could see no good and nothing remarkable in him. About eighteen years ago, when Fr. Martindale S.J. was writing his Life of R. H. Benson, I wrote for him a similar account of Rolfe, and Fr. Martindale rather took exception to the uncharitableness of its tone.

In later letters Canon Carmont amplified one or two points for my benefit:

There was a *universal* prejudice against Rolfe in the College. His eccentricities of conduct made the institution a subject of unfavourable comment in other colleges . . . I may mention one item. Rolfe ordered £20 of clothes from a tailor called Giomini— I acting as interpreter. When Giomini realized that he wasn't going to be paid, he came and annexed £20 worth of Rolfe's effects. The students bitterly resented this transaction as a humiliation of the College. . . . As to further reminiscences, the only one that occurs to me is [that] Rolfe had in his room a large sheet of cardboard, marked with ink into irregular compartments each of which contained a motto, epigram or atrocity culled from Catholic or Anglican hymnology. . . . One day Cary-Elwes (deceased Bishop of Northampton) and I paid a surreptitious visit to Rolfe's room while he was out for the purpose of studying these curiosities. I read them out while Cary-Elwes scribbled them down. Some time later Cary-Elwes gave me his copy, which I probably still have, though I tremble at the task of unearthing it. . . . In person Rolfe was about 5 ft. 7 in. in height—perhaps slightly less. He was pale, rather demure and ascetic in expression, wore eye-glasses, smoked rather heavily.

From Dr. Clapperton at the Scots College I obtained a list of Rolfe's surviving contemporaries (to all of whom I wrote) and also a note of two of those mottoes mentioned by Canon Carmont; the first a reference to the College fare, 'And he ate nothing in those days', the second a reference to his companions, 'And he lived with beasts'. It is also remembered that he was reported for saying that he was like Newman in that he had nothing to learn when he entered the Catholic Church.

From Fr. Stuart, of Fauldhouse, I received an interesting note:

St. John's, Fauldhouse,
West Lothian

Dear Mr. Symons,

I do not think that I can add anything to what Canon Carmont has told you about Mr. Rolfe. He has doubtless told you of many of his eccentricities—his musical ability and his gift of song, his weird sermons in the refectory, with their stinging hits at our somewhat uncultivated Scottish manners, and his own rather scant treatment of respect; his saying his office in his bath; and so on. I really think it was genius on the very border. I'm sorry I cannot give more details, as it's such a long time since we were together in Rome.

With best wishes for success in your undertaking

Yours very sincerely

John L. Stuart

Perhaps the truest summing up of all was sent me by the Rev. Provost Rooney, of Peebles, who was Vice-Rector of the Scots College when Rolfe was expelled:

He was most amiable despite all his little eccentricities—with ever and always an element of mystery in and around his elusive character.

*   *   *

Before his rejection from the Scots College, Rolfe adopted, by anticipation, the titular dignity of orders, and joined the Royal Historical Society, and the Royal Society of Literature, as 'The Rev. F. W. Rolfe'. And early in 1890 Mr. Elkin Mathews announced among his 'New Books':

Will be published shortly, medium 8vo, finely printed on hand-made paper, in a limited edition, with Etchings

THE STORY OF S. WILLIAM: THE BOY MARTYR
OF NORWICH.

From forty contemporary and subsequent Chronicles, all of which are given in full, with copious Notes and Translations, etc. etc.

by THE REV. FREDERICK WILLIAM ROLFE,

Late Professor of English Literature and History at S. Marie's College of Oscott.

This historical study never appeared, and was probably never written.

Rolfe left a record of his stay at the Scots College in Chapter XV of *Hadrian the Seventh*, wherein George Arthur Rose revisits, as Pope, 'St. Andrew's College', scene of his second discomfiture.

The hateful memory of every nook and corner, in which, as a student, he had been so fearfully unhappy, surged in his mind: the gaudy chapel where he had received this snub, the ugly refectory where he received that, the corridor where the Rector had made coarse jests about his mundity to obsequious grinners, the library where he had found impossible dust-begrimed books, the stairs up which he had staggered in lonely weakness, the dreadful gaunt room which had been his homeless home, the altogether pestilent pretentious bestial insanity of the place.

And Rolfe drew his own portrait in that chapter of *Hadrian* also, as Jameson, the fastidious and reserved student, mocked by his fellows for excessive personal clean-liness, who lives on bread and water and boiled eggs because he has been in the College kitchen and seen—things; who, like his creator, is very much alone.

Wall painting, situation unrecorded, by Fr. Rolfe

VII

THE NOWT OF HOLYWELL

No exact information has ever come to light regarding Rolfe's movements in the months immediately following his dismissal in mid 1890 from the Scots College. It is clear that he found a refuge with the Sforza-Cesarini family, but what the length of his stay was, and what his position in the household, remain obscure. It may be that during this uncertain interval he began to write a book—there is evidence in one of his later letters to justify the inference. Was he Keeper of the Archives, as he sometimes boasted afterwards? What is certain is that at most this Roman vacation lasted less than a year, though during it he gained a lasting insight into Italian history and character. Then, armed with the Duchess's allowance and the title of Baron Corvo, the rejected priest reappears at Christchurch in 1891. The reader is already acquainted, by Mr. Jackson's narrative, with the passage of his stay there, and with its sequel in the following year, when, desperate, much in the mood in which young men join the Foreign Legion, the Baron went to Aberdeen. The prolonged futility of that tragic farce described by the *Free Press* kept him in the North till 1894. Then (it may be remembered) he was left stranded in London after Champion's departure for Australia. Time was passing; he was thirty-four.

For the next few months the only authority is *Hadrian the Seventh*:

I began life again with no more than the clothes on my back, a Book of Hours, and eight shillings in my pocket. I obtained from a certain prelate, whose name I need not mention, a commission for a series of pictures to illustrate a scheme which he had

conceived for the confounding of Anglicans. He saw specimens
of my handicraft, was satisfied with my ability, provided me with
materials for a beginning and a disused skittle-alley for a studio;
and a few weeks later altered his mind and determined to put
his money in the building of a cathedral.

From Mgr. Dey's information I could place the nameless
prelate as Cardinal Vaughan, the Cathedral as Westminster.
The abandonment of that contract must have been a sore
blow to the penniless painter; he refers to it several times
in *Hadrian*, always with bitterness.

I don't know how I kept alive until I got my next commission.
I only know that I endured that frightful winter of 1894–5 in
light summer clothes unchanged.

Moved by his straits his brothers tried to help him; but he
refused their proposals.

Then a hare-brained and degenerate priest asked me to undertake
another series of pictures. I worked two years for him: and he
valued my productions at fifteen hundred pounds: in fact he
sold them at that rate. Well, he never paid me.

By a series of chances, I was to learn the inner story of this
incident.

*   *   *

The scene was set in Holywell, near Flint. What impulse,
or indeed what conveyance, took Baron Corvo to North
Wales I do not know; midway through 1895 a shabby,
pious, itinerant artist, calling himself 'Fr. Austin', sought
aid and work from the Franciscan brothers of Pantasaph.
He was admitted to make a retreat, and engaged to clean
the great bronze crucifix. Both plans were aborted; the
second when the monks learned with alarm that their
property was to be cleaned by an untested secret preparation made up from a mediæval recipe, the first when the

wanderer, after three days of retirement, was found reading a Kingsley novel instead of the edifying book provided by his spiritual director. From Pantasaph 'Fr. Austin' progressed to the neighbouring town of Holywell, where he laid his needs before the Rev. Fr. Sidney de Vere Beauclerk, S.J., who was in charge of the miraculous well of St. Winefride. Fr. Austin was destitute, hungry, and full of invective against 'those spurious Franciscans' who had turned him away. The charity of the Church was not invoked in vain: the stranger was engaged to paint a set of banners for the Shrine (it was his own proposal), and in return was assured of the necessities of life. Lodging was found for him in a boarding house kept by a kind Lancashire lady, and a studio set apart for him in an unused schoolroom. Oil and pigments were provided, and, after his brushes had been formally blessed, the new arrival set to work.

Rolfe has left his own record, in a short story, of the impression that he considered he created in Holywell, which, in allusion to the fact that it had then no drainage system, he calls 'Sewer's End'.

The Nowt was a Mystery. No one knew from whence he came, nor what, nor who he was. He dropped down upon Sewer's End from 'the back of beyond', settled there, worked like a slave, spoke to few, and made no friends. His dress was not only shabby, but fearfully and wonderfully common and stained. He had no luggage, no change of clothes, and no effects. He was proud and reserved in manner, though he could hold a roomful attentive when he chose to speak. And the meticulous delicacy of his habits, together with his voice and accent, stamped him as a person of culture and consideration. Sewer's End invented romances about him, said he was a 'gentleman who had come down'; and, though he told some few the truth about himself, he was not believed. The bumpkins could not bother their beery heads simultaneously with a truth and their own patent romances; and, consequently, the Nowt practised the gentle art of answering fools according to their folly, and became a holy terror by reason of the reticent mysterious modesty of his demeanour, combined with a fashion of speech so plain, that it was undeniably ugly.

But there was an eye-witness who saw him in a somewhat different light. A few weeks after Fr. Beauclerk made his benevolent bargain, John Holden, the young nephew of the Lancashire lady who was looking after the tattered traveller, came to North Wales to recover from a serious illness, and found himself a fellow-boarder with the 'Nowt' of Holywell.

Fr. Austin appeared to be about thirty-five years old. (I never learnt his real age.) He was a little below the average height, with fairly broad shoulders and decidedly bandy legs. His face reminded me of that of a monk. (Later I saw him in the garb of a Franciscan and he suited it to perfection.) He had a smooth high forehead, a rather pointed nose, and a somewhat aggressive chin; his hair was of a faded light-brown, and he was bald over the temples and the crown; he was clean-shaven, and I think that if he had let his beard grow it would have been reddish brown; his mouth was small, and his lips, particularly the upper lip, were thin; he was very short-sighted and wore a pair of extraordinarily powerful glasses. He was very shabbily dressed. I was most struck by the mouth, it looked so hard and cruel. I found him what he would have called 'antipatico'.

His manner was impressive. He walked and spoke with great deliberation, and seemed to be unaware of the existence of those about him. (Later I told him he reminded me of a priest returning to the sacristy after he had celebrated mass.) The immobile mouth and the extremely powerful glasses, the glint of which hid his eyes, made his face almost inscrutable. Most people went in awe of him. My aunt's servants were terrified.

Despite this formidable appearance, Fr. Austin proved a pleasant companion at the dinner-table, and even invited his young new acquaintance to smoke a pipe with him in the studio. Such was the beginning of one of the queerest of Rolfe's many queer friendships.

Mr. Holden continues:

I went up to the studio. We passed a really pleasant evening, and I began to find him less repellent. When we parted, he asked me to come up any evening when I had nothing better to do. Not finding the company of the pious old ladies downstairs much to my taste, I got into the habit of spending every evening with him, and I often dropped in on him during the day if the weather was bad.

His eyes were very weak, and without his glasses he was quite helpless. When he painted at night by the aid of a powerful paraffin lamp, he wore a big eyeshade. When we went to bathe in the swimming basin below the Well, he would enter the water first, and I would stand on the side of the bath, shouting to direct him and tell him when to turn.

He was a great smoker. Every two days I bought a four-ounce tin of Capstan Navy Cut, Strong, of which he smoked more than two-thirds. He put the dottles into a stone jar, and when the jar was full he spread them out on a newspaper and dried them in the sun or over the stove.

His hair was falling fast. He bought a tin of some ointment that was advertised to 'touch the spot' and smelt like furniture cream, and after washing his skull with almost boiling water, he smeared it with the preparation. After several applications he asked me to see whether there were any signs of new hair. I examined his scalp and said that red spots were appearing but that I could not say whether it was new hair pushing itself through the skin, or incipient erysipelas.

Though he seemed to be oblivious to all about him, I have never known a man or woman who had so insatiable an appetite for gossip as he. He knew everything that took place in the town. Anything scandalous was a tit-bit. One day I happened to mention some little thing, and he badgered me so much with his questions that I became impatient and said I could not understand how an intelligent man could be interested in such trifles. 'It's useful to me for literature', he replied. 'And besides, knowledge is power.' I learned later what he meant.

I well remember his snort. It was characteristic of him. It expressed surprise, impatience, contempt, and a host of other things. He could express more by that one inarticulate sound than another could express in a volume.

What was perhaps most extraordinary about Austin was that he would never speak a word if he could write it. We lived in the same house, a very little one, yet he would always communicate with me by note if I was not in the same room with him. He had dozens of letter-books. He seized upon every opportunity for writing a letter, and every letter, whether to a publisher or to a cobbler, was written with the same care. When closing a letter to some insignificant person about the veriest trifle, he would say 'And that's literature, Giovanni, that's literature'. I have never seen him happier than when he had to answer an unpleasant letter. Before he sat down, I would hear him bubbling and chortling for quite a time. 'Now for it', he would say at last; 'I'm going to flick that gentleman with my satire.' 'I cultivate the gentle art of making enemies', he would say. 'A friend is necessary, one friend — but an enemy is more necessary. An enemy keeps one alert.' I do believe he made enemies, or fancied he made them, for the sole pleasure of being able to 'flick them with his satire'.

All this was strange enough, but stranger still was the picture of himself and his past history that 'Fr. Austin' drew for the benefit of his young friend. First he inferred and then admitted that 'Austin' was not his name, and that he was not the humble painter that he seemed; on the contrary, he was the Baron Corvo, partly Italian by birth, and related to several of the most noble Italian families. Nor was this all; his reasons for his retirement and disguise were numerous and mysterious. In the first place, he was hiding from very powerful and persistent enemies, who had already wrecked his life by preventing him from the priesthood for which he had been trained; what further they might do when they found him could only be guessed, though prominent among his fears was incarceration. Certain Catholic dignitaries had pursued him relentlessly; even his family and most of his friends had cast him off when he was converted to the Roman faith. Yet despite the machinations of his opponents and the indifference of his relatives he was resolved to win fame as author, painter, sculptor, or inventor; indeed, of the outcome of his unequal fight he had no doubt whatever: it was Corvo against the world, with the odds on Corvo. Though his discovery of colour photography lay fallow, already his paintings were favourably known, and he contributed regularly to important reviews, and certain manuscripts were under consideration by wealthy publishers.

So much was definite; but there were vague hints that went further. He several times alluded to his 'godfather', slightly emphasizing the word. One day Holden related to him something he had read in a newspaper concerning the German Kaiser, whereupon 'Baron Corvo' observed: 'So my godfather has been at it again, has he?'

I continue Mr. Holden's narrative:

Sometimes before telling me something about himself he would hesitate a short time and then say: 'This is strictly between ourselves, you will understand.' At other times he would ask me to give my word that what he was about to say should never be divulged to anyone in any circumstances. I would give my word and keep it, only to learn that others had not been so honourable and discreet as I. Corvo was already a man of mystery when I arrived in Holywell.

I told him my simple history: I, too, had been in a seminary for some years, until I discovered that I had no vocation for the priesthood. I took good care not to say more about myself than he probably already knew. I mistrusted him.

I had known Austin-Corvo about a month when he said he had a proposal to make to me. I asked him what it was. After reflecting for a few minutes he answered, 'You are the man I have been waiting for. We are flint and steel to each other. I need you and you need me. My proposal is that you and I go into partnership.' I was much too astonished to speak. I looked at him steadily for a minute or two. He was evidently in earnest. 'The man's quite mad', I said to myself; then, aloud: 'What's the object of the partnership?' 'We work together and share all we earn.' 'Very well,' I said; 'let's draw up the articles of association.' (I knew that I should have to spend some time in Holywell, the winter was approaching, and the society of the prim, pious old ladies would not be congenial to me, a scatterbrained youngster of twenty-two. This partnership offered me a pastime, and there ought to be some fun to be got out of it.) 'Of course you will have to choose a *nom-de-guerre*,' Corvo went on. 'How would John Blount do?' I asked. (I had made a few attempts at writing short stories for the popular magazines in this name, but modesty forbade my telling him that.) 'I like it,' he said. He produced a letter from Henry Harland, the editor of the *Yellow Book*, to say that he had accepted the first *Toto* story. 'That's our beginning,' said he. 'We shall have much to do.'

I told my aunt of what had taken place, and we had a hearty laugh.

The next day I transferred a number of my books and papers to the studio.

Corvo was engaged on some banners. I did the borders and the lettering on them.

At the end of our first day's work Corvo said to me in a casual tone: 'Now you will wash the brushes and make up the fire.' 'Is that included in the articles?' I inquired. 'Of course,' answered he; 'everything has to be shared.' 'Good,' said I. 'While I am washing the brushes you will see to the fire.' I thought it prudent to make a good start.

Our other department, literature, was not neglected. We pinned to the studio walls sheets of foolscap, and jotted down on them ideas as they occurred to us. If we were dissatisfied with a word or a phrase, we ringed it in red, and then from time to time scribbled against it another which we thought more fitting. Saturday night was revision night, and we went over the week's work. If we disagreed as to a word or an expression, Corvo was umpire. To anything nearly ready we gave the final touch. The better things were signed 'Corvo': those more or less predestined to rejection were signed 'Blount'.

It was also very amusing to compose sestinas, triolets, etc. This we did only for our own pleasure.

We also produced a number of Limericks. These were not for publication either. In the writing of Limericks I excelled Corvo. He even acknowledged that.

I asked Corvo why he did nothing more for the *Pall Mall Gazette*. He said that Sir Douglas Straight (I think that was the editor's name) and he had quarrelled, and that Sir Douglas was no gentleman.

This collaboration, which Mr. Holden laughed at with his aunt, was regarded in a very different way by Corvo. It was a feature in Rolfe's friendships which recurred time after time during his troubled life; though I was unaware of its significance when I first read Mr. Holden's account.

After our day's work we would often read together till midnight. We read Marlowe, a selection of verses made by Gleeson White, the plays of W. S. Gilbert, some extracts from Chaucer, the Bible (particularly the Book of Proverbs, Ecclesiastes, and the Song of Songs), the *Memoirs* of Benvenuto Cellini, *The Cloister and the Hearth*, and Pepys's *Diary*. In the end we knew the Book of Proverbs, the *Mikado* and *Patience* almost by heart. We both revelled in Cellini's *Memoirs*. Corvo soaked himself in them.

I believe his favourite character in fiction was Denys of Burgundy.

All the books named above belonged to me.

These evenings we spent in reading and discussing books were some of the pleasantest in my life.

All our evenings, however, were not so peaceful and pleasant. Before long we began to quarrel. Corvo was not an easy man to get on with. His sarcastic tongue and, above all, his impassive ways used to drive me mad. I was young and hot-headed, accustomed to speak and act first and do my thinking after. I was pert, too, and cheeked him awfully. We often quarrelled over trifles. I think we quarrelled at times just to keep our hand in.

After our first squabble I did not go to the studio for nearly a week. Corvo met me as we were coming out of church and said in a very indifferent tone: 'Pax?' 'Pax, if you wish it,' said I. 'Very well, then. You have only to ask my pardon.' 'Then it's war, bloody war,' I cried. My aunt reconciled us, but I didn't beg his pardon.

When we had a row, it was as a rule Corvo who made the first advances towards a reconciliation. Sometimes it was I. Life in Holywell is dull, especially in winter, but one was never dull with Corvo.

I will copy one letter he sent me after we had had a quarrel:

'June 17th, 1896. I have your letter of the 8th. Let us begin again on the original compact. Come back here as soon as you like, and let us have a clear understanding with your aunt that you must have the days fairly free in which to write. Make up your mind to take me for better or worse. It's the worse now, and if you are steadfast the better will come. I shan't do anything alone. I am not in the mood to. But I have a Kampf's Safety Razor now which you can share and which will give you no end of joy. Corvo.'

Corvo's self-control when he was in a rage was my despair. He turned white and his tongue became more venomous, but he never raised his voice and he was even more deliberate in his speech. I once broke a maulstick over his head. Not a muscle of his face moved and not a word did he utter. I wished the maulstick had been a scaffold pole.

One Sunday afternoon after a little skirmish we both sat reading. The door and windows were closed, and the stove was burning full blast. I opened the door and he shut it. I opened a window and he shut it. I shut the door of the stove to diminish the draught and he opened it. (Neither of us had spoken.) I felt that I was losing, and I was fast losing my self-control. What could I do next? My eye fell upon a jar of water in which the brushes were soaked. I picked it up, and, lifting up the lid of the stove, poured the contents over the red-hot cinders. There was an explosion and I was half-blinded by the steam and ashes. When I recovered my sight, I looked at Corvo. He hadn't budged. He only interrupted his reading from time to time to blow the ashes off his book. I had lost again. To keep up appearances I read on for another half-hour, but I went home with murder in my heart.

I know he took pleasure in provoking me.

We had been speaking of the resemblance we saw in some of our acquaintances to certain animals, quadruped and biped. 'What am I?' he asked. 'A porcupine,' I answered promptly; 'you are so beastly prickly! And I?' 'A badly broken-in young colt.' I think we were both right.

One reconciliation was brought about in a most extraordinary manner. He had written me half a dozen letters in his most virulent style. The last had goaded me to fury. 'Now it's your turn, Corvo, and you're going to have it,' I said to myself. I didn't spare him. I called him a consummate humbug and many other things. When I had finished I thought 'This is an end to you and I'm jolly glad.' I gave my letter to the girl when she went to do Corvo's room. In a quarter of an hour a boy came with an answer. It ran: 'Gorgeous! Drop whatever you are doing and come round at once. I've a bottle of nectar awaiting you. Corvo.' I was mystified. I had said things calculated to bring him round with a tomahawk, and here he was asking me to pass a convivial evening. I went round. He was prancing about the room, my letter in his hand. His welcome was most cordial. He filled my pipe and poured out a glass of Chartreuse for me. (Fr. Beauclerk occasionally made him a present of a bottle of liqueur.) He read my letter aloud, chortling over my most malignant passages. Was he making game of me I wondered? Ought I to crack him over the head with the bottle? When he came to the end of the letter, he said 'It's splendid, Giovannino. I couldn't have done much better myself.' The man really was delighted. We had a jolly evening.

In his attitude to women he was peculiar. Here are a few of his sayings regarding them:

'Women are a necessity at times, but as a rule they are super-fluous.'

'A friend is necessary; influential acquaintances are useful; but never encumber yourself with a woman.'

'The worst of a woman is that she expects you to make love to her, or to pretend to make love to her, first.'

'What you can see to admire in the female form I don't know. All those curves and protuberances that seem to fascinate you only go to show what nature intended her for—all that she's fit for—breeding.'

'There's no more loathsome sight in nature than a pregnant woman.'

But despite these hard sayings, and others from early Christian writers which he sometimes repeated at table, he was so far interested in women that at intervals he would pay a visit to Rhyl or Manchester to seek what your namesake Arthur Symons calls 'the chance romances of the street'. On his return he would tell me of these experiences at some length. They did not seem to give him a great deal of satisfaction; on one occasion he asked me if I thought he was impotent. In such matters he was an enigma, and I could not understand him. He would go to mass every Sunday and to confession and communion every month, but quite as regularly he would make his pleasure trip.

When Corvo had to begin another banner, he would go to Rhyl for 'inspiration'. After a Turkish bath and luncheon, he would have himself wheeled in a bath chair up and down the front for two or three hours and then go in search of a 'chance romance'. I more than once suggested, rather maliciously, that he would have done better to make a retreat.

His linguistic capacity, where I could test it, was far from marked. He asserted a knowledge of Latin, Greek, French, German and Italian, but I soon found out that he had little or no Greek or German; and I soon came to suspect that his other claims were no better founded. At all events he gave me no encouragement whatsoever when (languages being a hobby of mine) I took up Italian. Though I frequently tried to draw him by asking the gender of a noun or tense of some irregular verb, he would never answer me. 'I know Italian,' he said; 'you should learn languages I don't know, and so increase our common fund of knowledge.' In the same way he declined to converse in French with a visitor who was more accustomed to that tongue than to English, and sat at our table. But he may have been able to read more Italian and French than he could speak; vocally at least he was no linguist. He knew enough Latin to read the Missal and the Breviary fairly well.

On one occasion I brutally told him that he had a wonderful knack of making people believe he knew thoroughly a subject of which he had only the most superficial knowledge. He took that for a compliment and said: 'That is the art of arts.'

Corvo professed to have a horror of reptiles. He told me that he had once fallen into a trance after stumbling over a lizard, and had very nearly been buried alive. (This he worked up into a story and published in the *Wide World Magazine* under the title *How I was Buried Alive*. Corvo claimed that the first paragraph was autobiographical, and he alludes to his Imperial godfather in it.) I thought this was another of his 'tall' stories, but later I was persuaded there was some truth in it. One Sunday afternoon we had taken a walk down to the river, and when we got back we found the house empty, it being church time. I climbed over the yard door and got through the kitchen window, then I opened the house door for Corvo and went upstairs. Suddenly I heard a blood-curdling shriek, and on rushing downstairs I found him in the kitchen, his face as white as chalk, his mouth twitching. He was staring fixedly at something I did not at first see. I followed his gaze, and under the table I saw a little toad. I spoke to him, shouted to him, but he did not answer.

I got a chair and pushed him into it, and he sat there for more than an hour quite motionless except for the working of his mouth. When he had recovered enough to stand and walk, I accompanied him to the studio and laid him on his bed. He fell at once into a deep sleep, and when I went round early the next morning to see how he was, I found him still asleep. I didn't wake him, and he slept on till eleven without stirring once. When I questioned him later, he told me he remembered nothing after first seeing the toad.

Mr. Holden's vivid account, though written from such close quarters, is that of a man who was young, perhaps younger than his years, at the time of the incidents which he describes with such fidelity; and, naturally, he was more concerned with his own problems than with those of the strange man whom chance had thrown into his company. Nevertheless he had brought Rolfe to life for me more completely, perhaps because he knew him more closely, than any other of my correspondents. And he had answered the most urgent of my questions. Rolfe is revealed for the first time as a writer in fact and intention; for his conscious habit of letter-writing must have been the whetstone of his literary power, just as his tall stories were the restless signs of stirred imagination—though there were obviously other reasons for them also.

For nearly two years this fantastic friendship continued to develop; and during that time 'Fr. Austin', despite his vagaries of conversation, patiently continued to paint his banners, which are still the pride of the church in which they hang. Did he begin to tire of his six-winged serafini, his four archangels, 'St. Peter in scarlet', 'St. Gregory in purple', and (favourite subject) Chaucer's 'Swete Seynt Hew'? It would seem so; for now the Holywell adventure takes a darker turn.

Early in 1897 (Mr. Holden continues) I noticed that the relations between Corvo and Fr. Beauclerk were less cordial. My aunt told me that Fr. Beauclerk always spoke of Corvo as 'My Old Man of the Seas', and was most anxious to get rid of him.

Fr. Beauclerk dropped in upon us one day and after wishing me good morning asked me to take a walk for half-an-hour. When I returned I could see that something was amiss. As soon as Corvo and I were alone he said: 'You and I will soon be off now.' 'On tramp?' I asked. 'No, in a first-class railway carriage,' he answered. There was a long silence. Corvo was thinking hard. At last he looked at me in a very strange manner and said slowly: 'You have often been here when Fr. Beauclerk has called, and you have heard him say that I was to have £— (I have forgotten the amount) for each banner I painted?' I replied: 'I have very often been here when Fr. Beauclerk has dropped in, but never once have I heard him speak of paying a penny for one of your banners. I have always understood that he was finding you work until you got on your feet again. And this is the first time', I continued, 'that you have ever told me you expected to be paid.' 'So you have gone over to the enemy, have you?' he asked. This time I spoke calmly. 'Look here, Corvo,' I said, 'you know that ever since I first met you I have never asked you one question about yourself or your affairs. I tell you plainly that I don't know anything of any arrangement you may have come to with Fr. Beauclerk. If you have a quarrel with him, I am neutral.' He gave me a look I remember well. 'There are a few things that belong to you here,' he said; 'I will thank you to take them and yourself away. You shall hear from me again.' That was my final break with Corvo.

*   *   *

Before transcribing Fr. Beauclerk's account of these occurrences, I quote again from the story in which 'Fr. Austin' set out the affair as he saw it, or tried to see it. The main villain of the story is, of course, the Priest, Fr. Beauclerk, who is thus described:

His religion consisted of eternal principles modified to suit temporal requirements. But he had a good heart, and he meant well. Ladies said he was the most graceful man they had ever seen, and so he was till this story's middle, after which he jerked like an electrified marionette. . . . [He] craved notoriety . . . [and] was unhappy unless he was thumping a tub or punching a pillow before the public. . . . So he organized pious prances, or crawls, according to his mood, which were neither Salvationist nor Ecclesiastical, nor fish, nor fowl, nor good red herring; but whose fashion was so deliberately frantic, and of so purposeful a violence, that his end was gained and immediate conspicuousness assured.

He commissioned the Nowt to paint a set of banners, promising that, if he would be content to work hard, on the bare necessities of life, for a time, he would deal very generously with him later. The Nowt put his back into this business, and laboured early and late, leading the life of a pig at his patron's direction and expense, hoping for better things bye and bye; and, after nearly a couple of years, he had produced a series of ecclesiastical paintings of a kind which everyone admitted to be something above the ordinary.

Then, the Vicar of Sewers End refused to pay for the work that had been done; actually saying that, as no legal contract existed (the Nowt always trusted to the honour of clerical patrons), he acknowledged no obligation to pay an honorarium, but was willing to give a few pounds in charity. This the Nowt emphatically scorned, and sent a statement to the Vicar's diocesan, who summoned that cleric to explain. What kind of apologia his reverence made is not exactly known . . . but he subsequently instructed the Nowt to set down his actual claim in writing, for the Episcopal consideration. Accordingly the Nowt wrote that the Vicar had had, from him, compositions including one hundred and five figures; that he (the Vicar) had taken ten guineas from a private donor for one of those hundred and five figures: and that, on this scale, the Vicar's valuation of the series amounted to one thousand and fifty guineas. But, he added, for his incessant and painful labours of twenty-one months, he was willing to accept an honorarium of seven hundred guineas; and from that sum he would make an offering to the Vicar's charities of two hundred guineas. Further, to show that he was only fighting for the principle that he deserved honestly earned wages, and not the insult of proffered charitable relief, he said he would accept *any sum* as honorarium, even a single six-shillings-and-eightpence.

The Vicar replied that he would pay nothing, except as charity or friendship; whereupon the Nowt promptly skipped in next door and instructed a solicitor to issue a writ for the full value of the work in question.

After a month [the Vicar] climbed down very suddenly indeed; and, pleading poverty, offered a sum of fifty pounds as honorarium. The Nowt took it, in accordance with his promise; and paid it straightway to an institution of the diocese; for, having gained his point (honorarium *not* charity) he wished to act disinterestedly; and then, without more ado, he joined the staff of the local paper, intending to get a living by journalism till the dawn of brighter days.

But here he reckoned without the Vicar . . . [who] assiduously set himself to carry out his threats of ruin and revenge, first by counsel, and secondly by example. His counsel took the form of 'insinuendo' derogatory to the Nowt's employer and his paper, and the successful corruption of his printer; and his example consisted of the severest form of boycott, with the refusal of the rites of the Church. Fired by this . . . spark the Vicar's parishioners withdrew their advertisements; his officials openly robbed the Nowt and his employer, and conducted machinations against their business, all with the Vicar's cognisance and tacit consent; the tradespeople refused to supply their household . . . the Vicar had the Nowt county-courted for a debt incurred by the Vicar's authority.

And the Nowt preserved an equal mind and demeanour; and took neither notice of nor action against . . . the Vicar, or any of his gang, beyond nailing up in black and white a record of each villainy as it occurred, and driving [them] to fury by contemptuously refusing to correspond, and by a sort of heartless immutable adherence to his usual habits, careless of or indifferent to each manifestation of the malignant spite of his foes.

'The malignant spite of his foes!' Even without the letters
that Fr. Beauclerk had sent me I should have realized, I think,
how completely Rolfe was his own enemy. Vincent
O'Sullivan's words recurred to me: 'A man with only the
very vaguest sense of realities.' It was true. When the film
came over the eyes of his mind, Rolfe saw himself as a
permanently picturesque figure oppressed by a circle of
enemies jealous of his talents or exhibiting their own mean-
ness. It was his compensation for the maddening sense of
failure, for his poverty, for his inability to dominate circumstances as he desired. Not, however, always. For those who
stop on the hither side of insanity, there must be moments
of self-realization, moments when an interior mentor
whispers 'I am wrong; they are right.' And, as I saw by his
letters of that period, despite his constantly-expressed
conviction of his utter rightness, Rolfe had spasms when
he saw things as they were. But they passed; the shutters
came down again; and then he was once more 'the Nowt'
ringed round by foes. His letters tell an interior story which
is very different from the surface meaning that he meant
them to wear.

Loyola House
March 15, 1896

Dear Fr. Beauclerk,

Many thanks for your welcome letter and Postal Orders.

Also for the damper which was certainly needed. If I have
been unduly elated, forgive me. I will try not to do it again. But
I could not help feeling pleased with what I have done because
I felt that I had contended successfully with many difficulties. At
the same time I by no means infer that I have anything like
reached my goal.

I NEVER SHALL, for the goal goes higher always. I only mean
that I have gone up *one* little step. Nor do *I* claim the smallest
credit for that. It is the saints who have deigned to impart some
modicum of their radiance. As I correspond more closely with
the graces they impart so much the more beautiful will my work

become. The difficulty is for a worldly wretch like me to detach myself entirely. There was a hypnotizer once who could not hypnotize me and from whom I rose from the cataleptic trance solely on account of my strong selfishness.

Nor is it for want of diligence that I fail if continuous work is diligence. But I do not concentrate all the time and so I fail. Faces? Yes. They are only the shadow of what I have seen. And I fail to reach the reality for the reasons of hurry and human respect and worry. And really dear Father Beauclerk my worldly worries are very bad indeed and lately I have felt that I must shriek or burst. Also I have developed a violent and raging temper, blazing out at what I suppose are small annoyances, and overwhelming people with a torrent of scathing and multi-lingual fury. I make amends for it afterwards but it leaves me weak in mind and body. It's the Mr. Hyde surging up.

But I will take care not to show you ugly or horrid faces again. I will stick at them and pray at them till they are right.

I think if I had a clear mind I could do better. Well I *know* that. But perhaps it would be more creditable to do better for all my obstacles! I will try. There's a Retreat at Manresa in Holy Week. I made my first and last one there in 1886.

Your faithful son in Xt,

F. A.

P.S. I see that I have failed again to put down what I really want to say. It is this chained impotence, this powerlessness to reach the point I am after that makes me chafe, and I boil inwardly the more because outwardly I insist upon keeping a demeanour most marble and which I find people call proud and cynical!!! (or as one of your fathers cuttingly said, 'I'm *afraid* he's a genius'! *Afraid!!!!*) Enclosed is a Litany I have written. It's badly put down *causa incapacitate meo* (can't write Latin now!) but you should hear me play it. It's a duet for a high bass and counter-tenor with chorus, and is meant to be accompanied on the strings. There's a magnificent instrument yclept citherna or theorbo on which it would make you faint for joy. But it would be lovely played on six small harps in a procession. If you can get someone good to play it to you you may get some idea of it, and if you like it perhaps you will let me offer it to you. I would be glad. I did better things which are now illuminated on vellum at Oscott, but I was young and had not had ten years of hell then.

*   *   *

Fr. Beauclerk gives the facts behind this contradictory disturbance:

The Presbytery,

Accrington

Corvo came to me soliciting work, attracted by the fact that the Shrine was prospering through my action in initiating public daily services at the Well. I made an agreement with him that I would give him the opportunity of supporting himself by finding him in lodging and board, and supplying all materials, if he would paint banners for the Shrine. He lodged quite comfortably with a good Lancashire lady, who treated him with uniform kindness.

He must have painted some ten banners for me, when one day he asked me for the sum of £100. On my assuring him that I could not give it, seeing that I was under orders from my religious superior, he retaliated that the Society (Jesuit) had plenty of money. He then sent me in a bill for £1000, and I put the case into the hands of a Liverpool lawyer. This man offered Rolfe £50 for himself and £10 for his counsel; and to my surprise Rolfe accepted it.

He then declared open war. A local magazine, the *Holywell Record,* had been started by a speculator, named Hochheimer, and Rolfe attached himself to the concern, his writing ability gaining him ready acceptance. He let loose in this publication all his views and grievances. He built up a wildly illusioned tale of my supposed hostility, which indeed only began and ended in my refusal to go beyond our first agreement, viz. that I would find him in everything essential.

His statements of my 'excommunicating' him and persecuting him and threatening to 'hound him out of the town' are absolutely baseless and ridiculous. In fact it was he who boasted that he worked for and secured my own dismissal from Holywell. My superior removed me in November 1898, after Rolfe had written letters against me to the Bishop of the Diocese, to my Superior General in Rome even. In *Hadrian* you may find me acting two parts. First I figure as that 'detestable and deceitful Blackcote, who came fawning upon me, and then robbed me of months and years of labour.' See page 15.

Page 273 *et seq.* shows me in my second personality as General of the Jesuits, the Black Pope, Father St. Albans. (We Beauclerks belong to the Duke of St. Alban's family.) The interview described, wherein Hadrian tirades against Jesuits is characteristically venomous and funny, especially the final words 'Fr. St. Albans looked like a flat female with chlorosis'!

On page 30 you read how he was commissioned by Cardinal Vaughan who, like myself, was struck by his apparent artistic talent, to execute a series of pictures. Vaughan found reason to discharge him, and hence Rolfe couples him with me 'and other scoundrels' whom he charges with defrauding him.

Lower down on the same page you can read his accusation against me. 'A hare-brained and degenerate priest asked me to undertake another series of pictures. I worked for him for two years: and he valued my productions at fifteen hundred pounds: in fact he sold them at that rate. Well, he never paid me. Again I lost all my apparatus, all my work: and was reduced to the last extreme of penury'!

And what was the real truth? That Rolfe had been provided with a comfortable home for two years, had been able to display his powers to the many visitors and priests who frequented the Shrine, and further, as I told him, had enjoyed ample leisure to employ his talent for writing, and so earn money for himself.

And note the madness of the man! When I asked him how he calculated up the £1000 he charged me with, he replied 'I have counted the figures on the banners I have painted, and find they number one hundred. I charge them at £10 a head.' Now the facts are these. There were some ten banners painted, each a single figure: but he had executed a larger banner in which was portrayed a crowd of people in the background, their heads the size of a thimble! When I asked how he was justified in assessing the figures at £10 a head, he reminded me that I had told him of a visitor having given me £10 for a banner of St. David!

On page 324 he vents his full resentment on my poor efforts to befriend him, when he speaks of me as 'the very detestable scoundrel', etc. Then follows this interesting bit of history misread. 'What became of him? The bad priest, I mean? He ruined himself as we predicted. He persisted in his career of crime till his Bishop found him out. Then he was broken and disappeared.—Maison de Santé or something of that sort, for a time. He is in one of the Colonies now.' Yes, I was sent to Malta for two years and acted as Chaplain for the troops. Thank God I am turned seventy-six and anything but broken; in fact I have more to attend to now than at dear old Holywell.

I had heard that Rolfe committed suicide? He used the name 'Austin' till he fell out with me.

What a wasted genius the man was.

> Yours very sincerely
> Charles S. de Vere Beauclerk, S.J.

*   *   *

Mr. Holden gave me details of the vindictiveness with which, once the final breach had been made, Rolfe pursued his ends.

Corvo joined the *Holywell Record*, and through its columns attacked all whom he was pleased to call his enemies. He lashed out right and left. Now I knew what he meant when he said 'Knowledge is Power'. Everything he had been told in confidence was blared out by the *Holywell Record,* of which Corvo was now master, and which he used for his own purposes. He caused much trouble in Holywell and in the surroundings of the town.

I heard from him again as he had promised.

Among the few things about myself which I had told him was an escapade known only to my aunt. (I had once toured the provinces for two months as an actor. I was not so much enamoured of the dramatic art as of one of the feminine exponents of it.) Through Corvo, news of this reached the ears of my mother.

My aunt had related to us an event that had taken place some ten years before. I worked this up into a humorous tale, laying the scene in Spain, but Corvo took a fancy to it and made a *Toto* story out of it. I refer to *How Some Christians Love one Another*. My aunt was the one who went to the aid of 'the respectable woman in her hour of need'. Some of the persons concerned were living at this time, and Corvo let them know that he was in possession of their secret.

I was enraged by these treacherous attacks. Our previous quarrels had had their humorous side, and I had got a considerable amount of fun out of them. This time we were both in deadly earnest.

On the 12th June 1897 Corvo wrote to my aunt: 'Dear Mrs. Richardson. By all means continue to direct your nephew to write me threatening letters. . . . I am delighted to have your written confession that you are boycotting 3 Bank Place, the *Record,* its owner and his wife, because I lodge and am employed at the *Record* office. No doubt you think your crime will ruin the *Record* and force my employer and me to the Workhouse. . . . If that is your idea, I wish it may do you much good. But remember, each act of you Irish against me or my friends is regarded as instigated by the counsel and example of Fr. Beauclerk, and each act will be met with a fresh disclosure of his villainies. We do not war with women and children, but with the knave who makes tools of you. But you are very useful to me for literature. Meanwhile you have not yet sent me my clothes. Faithfully yours, F. Austin.'

I at once got one of the girls to make a bundle of Rolfe's washing; then, taking the bundle to his solicitor's office, I threw it down at the feet of an astonished clerk and said: 'Tell your master I have brought some more of his client's dirty linen for him to attend to.'

I met Corvo in Well Street and stopped him. 'Corvo, this must stop,' I said; 'If it doesn't, I shall do you a mischief.' The same day I had a letter from him to say he had instructed his solicitor to take out a summons for threatening language. To this I answered: 'Tell your solicitor to wait for another twenty-four hours and then take out a summons for assault and battery. You will only have to produce yourself in evidence to have me convicted.' In the evening I went to Bank Place. The door was opened by Mrs. Hochheimer, who told me that Corvo and her husband were away. I told her what I had come for. She burst into tears and said she and her husband had had no peace since Corvo came to them, and he had ruined the *Record*. I prowled about the town all the next day looking for Corvo but I didn't come across him. A few days later I left Holywell for good.

I never saw Corvo again.

* * *

It must have been about this time that, from the first floor of the Greyhound Inn, Rolfe, a gaunt and gloomy figure, pointed his accusing finger at Fr. Beauclerk as the latter passed in procession to pray at the Shrine. An unpublished story, which must be contemporaneous, opens: 'I write this in the fervent hope that I may wound one Jesuit. I desire that some of his candid friends shall read to him what I have written; and give him pain.'

Among the dozens of recriminatory letters which Fr. Beauclerk sent me, many were signed and purported to be written by the *Record's* proprietor, F. W. Hochheimer, though the handwriting remained undisguisedly Rolfe's. Some are comic, pathetic, and childish at once; for, far from refusing to correspond (as he claims in his 'Nowt' story), Rolfe wrote almost daily; it was he, and not Fr. Beauclerk, who was infuriated by his opponent's silence. At the risk of overcrowding my narrative, I quote one more letter, written though not signed by Rolfe.

The Record Publishing Co.
Record Office, Holywell, N. Wales.
June 18th, 1898

Dear Fr. Beauclerk,

I fear Mr. Austin's troubles have been quite too much for him, and I have been compelled to resume the Editorship of the *Holywell Record* as I do not consider him competent any longer to reply to letters addressed to him in such a capacity.

He has chosen to go without food since Wednesday morning, solely for the purpose, I believe, of dropping down and creating a scene and a scandal, a mode of proceeding which I strongly disfavour.

We are not without food in the house, at present, as we have several times been during the thirteen months you have boycotted us, and therefore I, finding no excuse for such conduct, dissent from it and wish to dissociate myself from any evil effects which may be caused by it.

I would ask you to make a pastoral visit to him, but could not guarantee you ordinary decent treatment.

Yours faithfully in Xt.

Frank W. Hochheimer

Under the spur of the virulence Rolfe imparted to the *Record's* pages, its circulation waned; and midway through 1898 the whole edifice of this strange provincial feud crumbled into nothingness. When the paper died, Rolfe ostentatiously took up quarters in the workhouse, whence he continued to disseminate, to the best of his ability, the story of his 'wrongs', now immovably fixed in his distorted mind. It must have been almost a relief to Fr. Beauclerk when his superiors, disturbed by the scandal and animosity darkening the well of the Saint, removed him to another sphere of usefulness. Rolfe had won a discreditable victory; and he paid for it later in the year when his *Wide World* fiction gave his enemies their opening. With Fr. Beauclerk's disappearance there was nothing more to keep Fr. Austin in Wales, and so, with all his possessions tied in a bundle on the end of a stick, the 'unhappy Catholic vagabond' set out to walk from Flint to Oxford, to find Dr. Hardy at Jesus College—almost the only friend with whom, during his stormy life, he never quarrelled.

In after years Rolfe often spoke of this Holywell episode as the close of his second career. His first was the Church, and he had been driven from that; his second was painter, and he had been cheated of his due. Now he turned from cassock and brush to the pen.

VIII

THE STRANGE HISTORIAN

NOTE

Among the privileges of the biographer is an assumption of omniscience in respect of his subject. And, when sufficient material is available, something very near full knowledge is possible. The evidence of a man's letters, of his contemporaries, his work, and the indisputable facts of his life, do sometimes make it possible, when the material has been collated and sifted, to write with certainty. In the present study a different method has been employed. So far, I have set before the reader (not an analysed summary of my researches but) an account of the search itself; and I believe that in regard to a man so exceptional as Rolfe this exceptional method is justified. Truth takes many forms; and the dramatic alternation of light and dark in which my inquiries discovered Baron Corvo has, I am convinced, more value as verity than any one man's account. I have tried, accordingly, to be the advocate for neither side, but rather the judge impartially bringing out all aspects of the case for the benefit of the jury. At the point in Rolfe's life which my narrative has now reached, however, that method ceases, for the moment, to be advisable. The evidence concerning his career immediately after the Holywell episode came into my possession in fragments, over a long period of time. To present it as I obtained it would set so great a task to the reader's attention that the resulting knowledge would almost certainly seem insufficient reward. In the chapters following I have, therefore, combined numerous testimonies and information obtained from various sources into a coherent and chronological account without detailing the course of my investigation, though (as will be seen) without, on the other hand, abandoning the framework of my Quest.

FEW onslaughts on London and literary fame can ever have seemed more hopeless than that of the baffled, exposed, threadbare Baron, with his dismal record of unsuccessful painting, priesthood and photography, his kinks of quarrelsomeness and sexual feeling. Penniless, friendless, out of favour with the authorities of his Church, smarting from exposure by newspaper, he had not even youth, which can outweigh many odds, to balance the scale. He was nearly forty, the age at which most men who are to make a mark in the world have struck the first impressions. But Rolfe had made no mark: the world had stamped him, not he the world: no rolling stone ever gathered less moss. Nevertheless there were three things on his side. First was the habit of hardship, which enabled him to accept poverty in the spirit which has dignified so many artists' garrets. It is easier to tolerate the accustomed, than deprivation. And if the outcast had no cash, he was at least immune from the quotidian responsibilities that chain the lives of the free. Second, his excellent, still unimpaired constitution and sense of the physical, which, when he was not hungry, brought him a ready, thrilling appreciation of the world around him. And thirdly, he possessed a genuine talent, so far hidden behind the bushels of his other aspirations, but now to be revealed. Still, when all this has been allowed, it must be admitted that he wore thin armour against fate.

His only literary acquaintance in London (if the term may be used of one he had never met) was John Lane. Lane, too, was in his way a remarkable man, a self-taught railway clearing-clerk who had graduated by way of bookselling into the ranks of established publishers. He set new standards for his trade, and sponsored many good books. By a flair, perhaps less for literature than for men, by luck, by hospitality, and by natural business sense, he had reached prosperity and the opportunity of power. Among his many enterprises, *The Yellow Book,* a quarterly miscellany of literature and art which represented (and misrepresented) the noisy, gifted younger generation of that time, is perhaps now best remembered. The eighteen-nineties was a decade in which many new ideas and mental attitudes were born, many old ones died, many new talents first flowered. It was marked by an unusual expectancy of fresh things, and readiness to consider unknown men. Perhaps for that last reason Henry Harland, the literary editor of *The Yellow Book*, accepted and published six short stories which 'Frederick Baron Corvo' sent from Wales.

But the stories deserved acceptance, and the applause they provoked, on their own merits. Though they were Rolfe's first serious effort at writing, his ability suddenly appears in them full-fledged. There is a vivid and arresting novelty of style, pose and theme in these *Stories Toto Told Me* which charmed sceptics equally with the devout. Baldly described, they are retellings of folk-lore legends of the Catholic saints as presented by one Toto, a handsome, ingenuous, vivacious Italian peasant-lad. His quaint attributions of human characteristics and motives to the saints in their heavenly functions remind the reader irresistibly, though without irreverence, of the Gods of Olympus. Toto's audience is his English patron, the Baron; and his manner of speech is represented by an effervescent mixture of archaisms and broken English. No summary can do justice to these modern fables, which Rolfe, as he told his brother, 'rewrote nine times in honour of the Nine Quires of Angels'. They did not pass unobserved in the pages of the *Yellow Book*: such was their reception that Lane was encouraged to reprint them in a booklet uniform with Max Beerbohm's *The Happy Hypocrite*, which had also aroused a wide admiration on its first appearance in the famous quarterly. He did more: he invited the unknown author to submit a second series of *Toto* stories; and it was with the fate of this further batch that Rolfe first concerned himself in London.

In the February of 1899, then, on a Monday morning, Baron Corvo presented himself for the first time to the astonished eyes of his publisher. John Lane (whom Rolfe describes as a 'tubby little pot-bellied bantam, scrupulously attired and looking as though he had been suckled on bad beer') was confronted by a gaunt figure shrouded in a tattered mackintosh which might hide anything or nothing, who spoke with 'an arctic highness which strangely contrasted with his frightfully shabby garb', an un-Baronial and yet impressive scarecrow. Rolfe's account of this meeting survives: 'The publisher had a curiosity to see the writer whose first book he had published. . . . The writer, on the other hand, took no more interest in the publisher than one takes in the chopper which one seizes at random for hewing-out steps to fortune: he had no fear at the back of his mind; and he had something quite definite to say.' The 'something' concerned that second series of *Toto* stories, commissioned the year before, and delivered nine months previous to this visit. Nothing had been heard of them since, and their author now requested that 'terms for publication should be settled out of hand'. Behind this 'definite' request a good deal remained unspoken, as Lane was shrewd enough to see.

Lane was impulsive as well as shrewd. He could be hard; but he could also be humane. It is no injustice to his memory to say that he often kept his authors waiting unduly for their due; yet he frequently backed books which he knew would involve him in loss, or supported men whose work could never pay. On meeting the haggard yet haughty Baron, who was frank that he had no friends or funds in the world, he was moved to pity, praised his work, gave him the names of other publishers for whom he might read manuscripts, pressed a sovereign in his hand, advised him to call on Henry Harland, and promised to arrange matters in respect of the book next day. Baron Corvo left the Albany office almost in elation.

Next morning, alas, his day-dream was swiftly shattered. Lane's impulses had reversed themselves overnight, and he now offered only £20 as the purchase price for the new *Toto* stories on which Rolfe had built his hopes. The unlucky Baron could, and should, have refused. But it had taken

nearly a year to extract even this offer; if he opened negotiations with someone else an equal period might pass
before he benefited at all by his labours. And the prospect
of an immediate cheque was irresistible. So, hiding his
disappointment behind a blank mask, Rolfe assented, and
left the publisher's office richer by £10. The balance he was
to receive when the book came out. It was a bad bargain;
and he never forgave the man who made it.

Where and how did Corvo live, then? (One is almost
tempted to add, why?) There is no clue to the quarter of
London in which he hid his poverty and rage; but at least
he did not despair. The autobiographical romance in which
he consoled himself by setting down an acid recital of his
wrongs narrates that 'on the way back' he bought a lamp
and an oil-can, a ream each of standard linen bank- and
green blotting-paper, a large bottle of Draper's Dichroic
ink, a Japanese letter copybook, and a fountain pen which
held a quarter of a pint of ink. With these slight weapons
he renewed his fight against his penury and the indifference
of the world.

He had hopes of Harland. The editor of the *Yellow Book*
and his friends were fascinated by the equivocal Baron, an
impressively shabby figure at the Saturday tea-parties in
the Cromwell Road. The slight, eagle-nosed, reticent,
unsmiling worn wanderer, in corduroy trousers and jacket,
with his appalling cap and withered cloak, his Vandyke
beard grown during the walk from Wales, his strange rings
and stranger words, was indisputably a man of parts. It was
apparent when he talked. On those occasions he kept his
eyes cast down, raising them abruptly to disconcert inter-
rupters. His topics were very various and yet akin. In a
lucky moment you might have heard a surprising panegyric
of the Borgias or a vivid description of modern Rome, a
profession of Catholic faith or a bitter denunciation of contemporary Catholics. He was manifestly a mine of liturgical
knowledge. On occasion he would relate his past life for
hours, and tell of his privations, his paintings, and his

oppressors. He explained that he was a tonsured clerk as well as a Papal Baron. By his own account he was a singularly friendless individual, who for a variety of reasons had been treated with shameless treachery by those in whom he had trusted. Once started on this topic he was difficult to stop, and a modern observer would have found the label of 'persecution mania' ready to his hand. Nevertheless there was evident, abundant ability in the man; and, partly on account of it, partly because of the mystery of his circumstances, Baron Corvo was treated with respect by Harland and his circle.

But though this audience and their attentions doubtless gratified his vanity, the hungry author was still without the means to live. He besought editors with unsolicited articles, he entreated publishers for work as a 'reader' (or, as he put it, 'asked for a chance of showing his skill as a judge of commonplace literature'). Few listened; fewer still employed him; he lived on oranges and oatmeal. 'The Baron' was almost destitute and desperate when he met Mr. Grant Richards, a young newcomer among publishers, on the look-out for talent.

Here, in a way, he was in luck. Grant Richards had read and admired the *Toto* stories, and was eager to consider further work by the same hand. The first meeting between the publishing novice and the pseudo-Baron is unrecorded; but out of it, after an interval, a book was born. 'Frederick Baron Corvo' was engaged to produce a history of the rise and fall of the Borgia family which should be at once a gallimaufry of living pictures and a studious chronicle. How Rolfe had managed, in the course of his worried and wandering life, to acquire sufficient knowledge of Italy and Italian history to equip him for the task is an interesting problem. Was this the legacy of those unrecorded Roman months? At all events he was able to satisfy Mr. Richards of his competence to write the book; for he had studied under the best of all masters—his own desires, his own curiosity, and with such masters one learns quickly.

For payment he was to receive a sovereign a week (for not more than seven months), ten pounds on publication, and twenty-five pounds on the issue of a second edition. In return he sold, irrevocably, all rights. Not very generous terms; but they were his own suggestion, and the best he was to get during the whole of his life. At least the arrangement promised a roof overhead for half a year. Accustomed as Rolfe was to hardship, he believed that he could live within the means proposed, which he hoped to supplement by extra work. So the contract was signed, and the weird scholar departed to his task.

How he progressed can be shown in his own words:

Dear Mr. Richards,   *Hogarth Club, Bond St., W.*

I have got through the first week on 18s. 10d., which I think is a bit of a triumph! It was achieved by the simple expedient of cutting dinner: and it has left me furious for work. Now I find the evenings intolerable after the B.M. closes; and think you might let me have something to read by way of change. Mss. for choice, *for which I shall not expect you to pay unless you like.* It's *reading* I want *hic et nunc.*

V ty

Corvo

For weeks the quaint, shabby Baron haunted the British Museum, reading and making notes all day. But, as he wrote subsequently, 'a man cannot work eighteen hours a day during seven days a week on insufficient food and with total absence of recreation without feeling the strain'. The bargain as to payment was made in November 1899. Three months later (it will be seen) the strain began to tell:

Jesus College, Oxon.
xxvij Feb. 1900

Dear Sir:

The Borgia book is progressing. I should very much like to have photographs of the various portraits etc., which I selected some weeks ago; for, with these before me to assist the human air, I shall be able to work without let or hindrance, as long as my health endures the strain.

I may say that I find living on a pound a week, while working as intensely as I do, to be a very difficult task. May I suggest the desirability of increasing that amount to thirty shillings—a sum which would save me many petty worries? Of course, I do not for a moment propose any interference with the agreement which I have made with you; but that the extra ten shillings should come out of the sum which you are to pay me on publication.

I should be much obliged if you would give this proposal early consideration; for the work on the book is far greater than I, or any one, anticipated; and, very naturally, I wish to put into it a great deal more than that of which I am deemed capable.

I am staying a few days in college with Mr. E. G. Hardy, who is V. P. of Jesus, and an old friend of mine; and to whose care a letter may be addressed to me till Thursday.

Yours faithfully

Baron Corvo

This pathetic, modest request went unanswered. Perhaps the young publisher with a business to establish would or could not go beyond his contract. Shortage of money was not, however, Corvo's only trouble. His artistic conscience was alarmed by reductions proposed in the number of illustrations planned for his book; he fought for portraits and medallions like a wildcat for its young, in long and earnest letters in which he bewailed the poverty which prevented him from supplementing them from his own pocket. On a pound a week he could not afford to pay for process blocks.

For the moment, actually, he had found a home. Among the few figures from his past life with whom he remained on speaking terms was a young Catholic solicitor, Edward Slaughter, to whom he had acted as tutor thirteen years

before. One afternoon about this time the two met unexpectedly in Bond Street, and the Baron was invited to dine
next day with his former pupil in his Hampstead lodging.
The meeting was repeated, and then repeated again. The
landlady had a tiny room to spare; why should not the
Baron use it till the publication of his book brought him
fame and funds to take a proper apartment? The suggestion
was welcomed, and the move was made. Certainly Rolfe
worked hard. When not investigating by day in the British
Museum, the indefatigable chronicler spent his nights in
constructing a vast pedigree of the Borgia family from its
origin in Aragon to the present day. It was made on some
forty squares of squared paper each two feet long, engrossed
in inks of many colours and blazoned with the Borgia bull.
When finished and assembled, this labour of love measured
nine feet by five, and nearly covered the floor of its compiler's room. Slaughter, returning from his day's work,
marvelled to find that his ex-tutor had written a whole new
chapter, or added a fresh line of descent to the giant family
tree. But still that extra ten shillings eluded the strange
historian:

> 69 Broadhurst Gardens, South Hampstead
> xvi May 1900

Dear Mr. Grant Richards:

In reply to yours of today:—

I suggested that you should pay me £1–10–0 per week instead
of £1, upon which last I could die but not live; and that the
extra 10/– could come from the £10, which you were to pay
me on completion of my task; if that is what you mean. If not,
I have a copy of my letter somewhere. Also, I beg you to be
reassured that *La Borgiada* will be in your hands at the time
stipulated in our agreement. I suppose 'July' will bear without
straining the interpretation 'July 31st'. I am taking that for
granted: because, as you will readily imagine, with all the delays

I have endured, as long as possible a time will not be a day too much. . . .

Yours faithfully

Corvo

Luckily, he did not have to live entirely on a pound a week. In addition to the timely aid of Slaughter, who made a small but regular contribution to his friend's revenue, Rolfe benefited by the good nature of Grant Richards's manager, Temple Scott, described with the Baron's usual asperity as a 'broad-nosed dough-faced dwarf with thin woolly hair scattered over his big head'. 'I visited him every Saturday', writes Temple Scott, who shared his employer's admiration for the unconventional and harassed writer, 'and found him as a rule happy and engrossed in his monster genealogical tree of the Borgia family. I used to bring him twelve packages of different tobacco, named by him, which he would blend for his cigarettes. He liked, he said, to have twelve emotions of taste in smoking. He would come nearly every evening to my apartments in Welbeck Mansions for meals and the opportunity to read to my wife and myself what he had written. I found him a most pleasant companion with a store of archaic lore that was at times weird in the form in which he imparted it. He was childishly superstitious and childishly romantic. You may translate this as you wish, but the children in my home listened to him with wide-eyed faith.'

Weeks sped by and became months; August arrived; and at last the Borgia book was finished. Even with the help of his two friends Baron Corvo saw that he would be unable to make ends meet without the much-discussed pound, and so he sought more work. He implored Grant Richards for a new commission, in letters which are a mixture of dignity and tragedy. The publisher temporized; he felt that he had experimented sufficiently with this unusual author. Corvo wrote again: 'The week or two of which you spoke expired more than a month ago; and it becomes an urgent necessity that I should complete my plans for the winter.' Who can say what would have happened had a fresh commission been vouchsafed? Though at that moment Rolfe would have welcomed any labour, for almost any pittance, ultimately, probably, he would have rebelled in some dramatic unreasonable form (as at Holywell) against the rigid poverty of his life. But his patience was tested in a quite different way; the historian of the Borgias was not fated to write a second book for Mr. Grant Richards.

* * *

The completed manuscript of Rolfe's 'gallimaufry' was submitted to an expert 'reader'; and, unexpectedly, the report contained criticisms and suggestions for alteration to the text. Passages were rebuked as showing 'acrostics and effeminacies of intellect and strange clumsiness of thought and style'. The reader's remarks and requests were communicated to Corvo, who exploded like a bomb. 'Dear Mr. Grant Richards' became at once 'Dear Sir', and Rolfe's letters took on an instantaneous tone of sullen dignity:

Dear Sir: *xxvj Sept.* 1900

I have your letter dated 25th, the Second Report, and the Borgia MSS.

I have taken the trouble to think out a method, and a style of writing. I believe that you know this. I believe that it was because you liked my previous work that you gave me this commission. It appears to me, therefore, perfectly amazing that you should now agree with your Reader's opinion, i.e. that the style is 'loose', 'clumsy', the spelling 'incorrect';—the method, in short, unsatisfactory. As though all these things were not relative, and only relative.

In reference to the Reports (while sternly denying that 'Il Cardinale del Gonalla' [your reader persists in the small g] is a sentence [v. Report II, 3] seeing that it lacks a predicate), I must be allowed to regret the impatience, perhaps animus, which appears, particularly in Report II; and to say that I incontinently and utterly abjure 'the incurable mania for self-justification' (a phrase which I should not have expected to find in a Reader's Report) now that I am aware of the futility of the same. And concerning these Reports, and your decision, I have no more to say. The work shall be recopied, revised, and gelded, in accordance with your instructions. I estimate that it will take two months from the date of commencement. That date depends on *a*, my recovery of strength, which circumstances make uncertain, *b*, my obtaining a commission which will enable me to pay debts incurred for living while waiting for your delayed decision, and which will provide me with means of living on.

You are perfectly aware that I have nothing except my literary earnings.

Of course, I need hardly say that on no account will I allow myself publickly to be connected with this New Borgia book, written in a style which is not mine. I can only accept responsibility for works of which my own judgment approves—things quaint or curious, and distinguishable from the works of the million. So, kindly invent a man of straw, John Brown, or James Black or St. George Gerry, and put him, in those lists of which you wrote in July, as the author of the *House of Borgia*.

'An Ideal Content'—term in Logick—shall be omitted.

Understand that you shall have exactly what you want, as soon as I am in a position to do it; and without any reference to my natural rights or sentiments, or future commissions: and that I will communicate with you directly I have regained health (if I ever do) and have concluded arrangements which will enable me to give my spare time to your work.

Faithfully yours

Frederick Baron Corvo

After taking up this position, the outraged author dug his toes in, and it was only with the greatest difficulty that he could be persuaded even to discuss the matter.

He had said that he would revise the book; he had said that he disapproved of the revisions; he had withdrawn his name from a book which did not fulfil his wishes; what could there be to discuss?

xviiij Oct. 1900

Dear Sir,

In compliance with your request, I will come on Monday; although, as my health is declining and not improving, this week would have suited me quite as well: but, in view of the mysterious reticence which you observe regarding the object of this interview,—a reticence which prevents me, in my dejected condition of health, from being prepared to give adequate attention to matters over which I have had no opportunity of pondering,— I think it as well to try to define more clearly than before, the position which I have taken up in reference to the *Chronicles of the House of Borgia*.

I am sure that I very gladly should have welcomed an intelligent criticism of, and an intelligent correction of minor pen-slips and clerical errors which may have crept into, a work that cost me such infinite and ceaseless pains; but you do not seem to be aware of the sad injustice which you have done both to the book and to its writer, in subjecting it, not to your own promised consideration, but to the judgment of one so manifestly incompetent as your Reader. I mean that I resent the opinion of a person who could not read the Varchi passage without ultimate blunders; who denounces as 'strange clumsiness' a sentence which I did not write; who displays a defective knowledge of spelling; who calls a name devoid of predicate a 'sentence'; who has not a word to say on the Greek and Latin extracts (where my rusty classical knowledge may have led me into error); who alleges, in mitigation of his intemperate remarks, that his report is the report of a printer's devil—but I will not fill the page.

Having thus (in his own view) 'reduced his publisher to a fitting state of mind', the appointed meeting took place, with no particular result. The ensuing deadlock was unexpectedly broken when Rolfe received a letter from Count

Cesare Borgia, existing head of the family, who offered Rolfe assistance and information to make his *Chronicle* and pedigree more complete if he would come to Italy to examine the Borgian archives. This proposal transported Rolfe to the seventh heaven. Italy remained the haven of his hopes; the thought of being the guest of a Borgia enhanced the romantic dreams provoked by the letter. So an enthusiastic proposal was made to Mr. Grant Richards, that the Borgia book should be delayed pending the investigation of the new material in Italy, and (of course) that a new bargain should be made with the author whereby he should be provided with funds to pursue his investigations. How much will it cost? was the publisher's natural reply. Rolfe's answer, written as usual in beautiful script, with a new, affected, and effective punctuation, offered to make 'your book so complete that there will be nothing left for future historians to say about the Borgia / until two little boys / aged fourteen / aged three / have grown to manlihood / and either relieved the necessities of another English King / or mounted on the Throne of Peter / in the approved Borgian mode /', in return for an 'adequate honorarium' of two hundred and sixty guineas, payable as to two hundred guineas in cash on the signing of the contract, with ten guineas per week for six weeks thereafter. 'I should then be willing to allow my name to be appended to [the book]', wrote the optimistic author!

Poor Rolfe. This was the foolish bluff of Holywell all over again; and naturally enough it was ineffective. A publisher who had paid him £48 10s. to write the book was not likely to pay him £273 to revise it. The offer was refused. But the thoroughly roused Rolfe found another plan. He suggested that he should seek a publisher willing to take the book over and repay the amount so far advanced. 'I imagine', he urged, 'that you would welcome the opportunity of ridding yourself of a ms. which I am determined to alter or to refute, and which can bring you nothing but irritation with failure.' The stalemate was renewed, this time by Mr.

Richards, who was not at all willing to allow Rolfe to place his book elsewhere. The deadlock was a second time broken in unexpected fashion:

69 Broadhurst Gardens, South Hampstead

vj Mar. 1901

*Dear Sir:

Will you kindly note that I disapprove of, and entirely dissociate myself from Mr. Edward Joseph Slaughter's perridiculous mismanagement of my affairs; and that I have cancelled the authorisation to act for me, which I formerly gave him at his own request, he being my creditor to a small amount.

I find that my confidence once more has been abused by a stupid and dishonourable Roman Catholick: though I have no doubt but that Mr. E. J. Slaughter's aboriginal instincts and casuistick breeding will enable him to pitch some such elaborated, and delicately distinguished, yarn into his hebdomadal confessor, as will justify his treachery to me, or at least reduce it from the category of mortal, to that of venial sin; and so maintain the integrity of his idiotick self-conceit.

If these, of his, be 'business methods', and for more than a year I have had it rammed into my head that they are, I can only say that I thank the Goodness and the Grace which made me not a 'business' man.

I have no idea that you yourself will be feeling very genial: but, had it not been for your evident desire to negociate through Mr. Slaughter, and that pious deceiver's perfervid protestations that he regarded me as a promising speculation in which he was

*Note: In justice to Mr. Slaughter, I desire to emphasise to the reader that Rolfe's strictures in this letter are unfounded, as also is his statement that Mr. Slaughter was 'managing' his affairs. In fact, Mr. Slaughter did no more than call two or three times on Mr. Grant Richards (as a friend without charge, not as a solicitor for a fee) in the hope of persuading the publisher to allow Rolfe to place his book elsewhere. When it became clear that Mr. Richards would not relinquish his rights, Baron Corvo reopened negotiations by 'dropping' his 'agent', as he ungratefully chose to call his friend.

concupiscent to engage, I never should have submitted, against my own judgment, to his direction, or to have my affairs so involved and embroiled by this precious 'commercial capability' of which he so dogmatically has boasted. I imagine you to be extremely sick; and I well know that I am—*usque ad nauseam*. . . .

And now, will you please note that I am managing my own affairs; and having communications addressed to me *directly* from this date. And will you consider this as an intimation of my final rupture from the Slaughter gang, and from Roman Catholics generally. I find the Faith comfortable and eximious; but its professors utterly intolerable. In seventeen years I never have met one R. C., except the Bishop of Menevia, who was not a sedulous ape, a treacherous snob, a slanderer, an oppressor, or a liar; and I am going to try to do without them.

Yours faithfully

Frederick Baron Corvo

The answer to this revelatory letter, which touched Mr. Richards's sense of humour, was an invitation to lunch, accepted in terms which it is given to few to command:

Dear Sir: *xviiij Mar.* 1901

I do not want to appear ungracious, nor do I ever eat lunch, and you know that to interrupt my work even for a couple of hours is a grave inconvenience; indeed, I actually have not been outside this house since the exsequies of the Divine Victoria: but I feel that something is due to you on account of the exasperation which you have endured from the idiomata of Slaughter; and therefore, if you can meet me on friendly terms, remembering all the while that my mind is concentrated on the xvi not the xx century, and if you agree to consider our conversation as privileged and in no wise binding, I will be at Romano's between 1 and 2 p.m. on Tuesday or Wednesday next. . . .

Faithfully yours

Frederick Baron Corvo

It is to be hoped that the lunch was enjoyable to both parties. But, enjoyable or not, it did not pacify the thoroughly suspicious Rolfe for long. Some fresh problem again required his presence in the publisher's office: an invitation he declined in terms appropriate to the fly countering the spider:

Dear Sir: *viij April* 1901

I cannot leave my work on Tuesday because it is a long way from here to Henrietta Street; and as I have no draft of your proposals there is nothing to occupy our time.

> Yours faithfully
> Frederick Baron Corvo

IX

THE CHRONICLES

ROLFE had told Vincent O'Sullivan that he 'bathed in a row'; he might now fairly claim to be up to his neck in a series of them. He was embroiled with Grant Richards, at arms length with Slaughter, not on speaking terms with Harland, distrustful of John Lane, and amiable to Temple Scott only because the 'dough-faced dwarf', having left the service of Grant Richards to act as Lane's American Manager, had accepted a private mission to push the Baron's interests in the United States. Why was Corvo so unreasonably asperous to those who had befriended and helped him? 'I have never been able to account for his strange conduct', Temple Scott writes, 'except to put it down to a nature tortured by disappointment and a megalomania that could not be satisfied with what the world had to offer it by way of value, either in money or praise. It was dangerous to praise his work, for the more you praised it the more he demanded. His intellectual vanity was colossal.' This diagnosis is, I think, in essence true. Rolfe's megalomania and mental conceit cannot be doubted; but they were in part his compensation against the feeling that others, far less gifted than he, were enjoying the pleasant fruits of a world in which he had no share. His own observations on the subject reveal the man: 'To all these people who came professing friendship, he grimly said: "Actions before words. If you wish me well, employ me: or help me to get a proper price for my work, and to become your social equal; and we will begin to ponder the matter of friendship." For he failed to understand how anyone could be friendly, who did not act wholeheartedly on his behalf.' Rolfe never wrote anything more true than that last sentence.

*　　　　*　　　　*

The imbroglio with Grant Richards grew more entangled. After lengthy vicissitudes of correspondence, he offered to do what was needed to his book for a further £50, plus 'the typescribe's fee which I saved you last October-November in copying the m.s.', at the same time reminding the publisher (in an axiom which he would have done well to have borne in mind himself) that 'this is commerce in which I am engaged, not euchre'. But that proposal was of no avail, and he was soon as tart as ever:

Dear Sir: *xxiiij Apr.* 1901

I cannot regard your letter as being in any way a straight reply to mine; and you leave me no option but to take professional advice.

Yours faithfully

Frederick Baron Corvo

Even 'professional advice' could not help, and the book appeared without further correction from its author, with all its imperfections on its head. Doubtless its publication (in October 1901) must have secretly rejoiced Rolfe's heart (he wrote by postcard, 'The writer of *Chronicles of the House of Borgia* notes that the usual Author's copies are withheld from him, after publication'); at least it gave him new ground for his hobby of correspondence:

69 Broadhurst Gardens, Hampstead

Dear Sirs: *xiij Oct.* MCMI

I am surprised to see, in the *Athenæum*, that you are advertising your Borgia Book by my name.

I beg leave to remind you that, more than a year ago, I withdrew my name from your Borgia Book, on account of your demand for the reformation of the style in accordance with your two extraordinary 'Reader's Reports' of Sept. 1900.

Since that date, I several times have informed you that your book is a tissue of historical inaccuracies, owing to your refusal to provide me with opportunities for original research, and owing to your refusal to avail yourself of the new material obtained by me from Conte Cesare Borgia after the expiration of my agreement with you.

I now have to intimate to you that I formally prohibit you from using my name in connection with your *Chronicles of the House of Borgia;* not only on the grounds before-mentioned: but, also, on the additional grounds, that I decline to accept responsibility for your mutilation of, and excision from, my MS.; and, that there is no stipulation in our contract obliging me to lend my name to a work which I consider subturpiculous, and which, frequently during the last twelve months, I categorically have disapproved.

This is without prejudice; and I reserve all rights in this letter.

Yours faithfully

Frederick Baron Corvo

Indeed, the ground of his grievances continued to widen:

69 *Broadhurst Gardens, Hampstead*

xvij Dec. 1901

Sirs:

I do not know by what law, either of business or of common courtesy, you justify your disregard of my request, dated xviiij Oct. 1901, that you should refuse all letters sent to your care for me—a rule which I asked you to construe as absolute, to which no exception can be made under any circumstances.

The thing which I ask of you is a very small thing and not, I believe, an unheard-of thing: and your repeated disregard of my wishes impels me to remind you that, in view of your mutilation of my work, and the libellous liberties which you have taken with my name, you should avoid converting my present attitude of forbearance into one of reprisal.

Your obedient servant

Frederick William Rolfe

Nevertheless one other letter was sent on to him, doubtless by clerical inadvertence; and in consequence the correspondence was closed by a final letter, too libellous for transcription, which, after mentioning that Mr. Richards had few friends and many enemies, concluded:

but I doubt whether you ever have made a more ruthless and persequent enemy than

Your obedient servant

Frederick William Rolfe ★

★   ★   ★

The fruit of Baron Corvo's harassed labours was presented to the world late in October 1901. Though a financial failure at that time, *Chronicles of the House of Borgia* attracted wide notice, and has since influenced other writers and become a rare book. In form it is a substantial and handsome octavo of nearly four hundred pages; in content it abounds in passages of epigrammatic excellence and insolence, and in Rolfe's individual eccentricities of spelling, language and treatment. He tells a fascinating if diffuse story of the rise and fall of the great, sinister, perverse family which, sprung from a King, gave Christendom two Popes, and a Saint and General of the Jesuits. The Preface defines the author's attitude, without admitting that it is that of counsel for the defence. He explains that 'The writer does not write with the object of whitewashing the House of Borgia: his present opinion being that all men are too vile for words to tell. Further, he does not write in the Roman Catholic interest;

★ Note: I quote these letters by the courtesy of Mr. Grant Richards, who bears no resentment to the memory of the strange being who promised him undying enmity because letters sent to him 'care of' the publisher were forwarded instead of refused. As will be seen subsequently, so far from being 'undying', Rolfe's sense of grievance did not last long enough to prevent him from proposing a fresh alliance and more publications to Mr. Grant Richards a few years later.

nor in the Jesuit interest; nor in the interest of any creed, or corporation, or even human being; but solely as one who has scratched together some sherds of knowledge, which he perforce must sell, to live.' But, although he professed not to wish to whitewash the Borgia, Rolfe was unwilling that they should be condemned. 'No man, save One, since Adam, has been wholly good. Not one has been wholly bad', he wrote (again in the Preface). 'The truth about the Borgia, no doubt, lies between the two extremes. They are accused of loose morals, and of having been addicted to improper practices and amusements. Well; what then? Does anybody want to judge them? Popes and Kings, and lovers, and men of intellect, and men of war, cannot be judged by the narrow code, the stunted standard, of the journalist and the lodging-house keeper, or the plumber and the haberdasher. . . . Why should good hours of sunlight be wasted on the judgment seat, by those who, presently, will have to take their turn in the dock? Why not leave the affairs of Borgia to the Recording Angel?' This attitude, in its widest sense, might be taken to preclude even his own book; which, however, he justified by adding, 'All about the Borgia quite truly will be known some day; and in the interim, more profitable entertainment may be gained by frankly and openly studying that swift vivid violent age when . . . "there was no check to the growth of personality, no grinding of men down to match the average".'

There is no doubt that Fr. Rolfe wrote himself into his Borgia book as he did into *Hadrian*. He worked from a boarding house in Hampstead, but he dreamed himself in Rome, the Rome of the Middle Ages. He turned from the twentieth century in which he was born, and in which he had failed, from its 'jaded physique and sophisticated brain', to what he called 'the physically strong and intellectually simple fifteenth, when the world—the dust which makes man's flesh—was five centuries younger and fresher; when colour was vivid; light, a blaze; virtue and vice, extreme; passion, primitive and ardent; life, violent; youth, intense,

...ne; and sententious pettifogging respectable medio-
..., senile and debile, of no importance whatever'. Reading
th.. book (with its denunciation of 'that curse to real
civilisation, the printed book', denounced because it ended
the amenities of manuscript), with its joy in the 'raw reality
and glittering light' of Italy, its cult of magnificence in
manners and habiliments, its strenuous love of action and
insistence on hardihood of nerve, it is easy to see that Rolfe
had accepted himself as a contemporary of Cellini, and
suffered from that nostalgia of the past which, of all tempta-
tions of the mind, is the most destructive of contentment.
So constituted, his attitude to the Borgia can be imagined.
He admired them. To him the infamous Alexander, with
his simony, bastards and murders, was 'A very strong man,
guilty of hiding none of his human weaknesses', who made
'malefactors feel the flail which, like Osiris, he wielded
equally with the crook'; Cesare Borgia was a governor
whose power, justice and ever-present indefatigable energy
seemed superhuman. 'He was hated: hated by the great
Baronial houses which he had ruined, whose heirs he had
slain; but he was not even disliked by the people whom
he ruled. It was not extraordinary; for the mob always
adores the strong bowelless man, the rigid fearless despot,
the conquering autocrat who brings peace with security.'
As for Lucrezia, she was a 'pearl among women', a second
Lucrece, who 'won fresh fame by her goodness to young
girls, whom she provided with dowries, to tempt them to
keep continency by marrying well'.

This patchwork book is not history as it should be
written; but it is history that can be read. Corvo's sentences
sing: 'sumptuous brocades, fairest linen of flax, furs from
the East and delicate enduring leather, adorned these men
and women who had not learned to change their garments
as often as they changed their minds; and who went to bed
at night simply as nature made them'. Sometimes he em-
ploys the emphasis of brevity: 'This year died the twelve-
toed, chin-tufted excommunicated little Christian King

Charles VIII of France, and was succeeded by his cousin Louis XII, a thin man with a fat neck and lip, and an Ethiopic nose, and exquisite attire.' Sometimes he reaches his effects by expressive images, as when relating how the news spread of the disbanding of Cesare's army: 'Colonna and Orsini heard, in their ugly exile, in their battered fortresses. Like the chained wolves on the Capitol who know when rust makes thin their fetters, they lifted up their horrid heads and waited till the ultimate link should part.'

Or he gives dramatic pictures of such incidents as the punishment of Ramiro d'Orca: 'On the twenty-second of December, when the setting sun cast blood-red lights across the snow, without warning Duke Cesare galloped into Cesena with an armed escort of lancers. The cowed Cesenisi, turning out of doors to do him reverence, caught bare glimpses of flashing mail and the bull-bannerols of Borgia passing over the drawbridge of the citadel. Presently, from that citadel came Messer Cipriano di Numai, the Duke's secretary, to the house of Messer Domenico d'Ugolini, the treasurer, seeking the Governor of the city. Messer Ramiro d'Orca was arrested, and conducted to the presence of his chief. Surmise that night was rife as to the import of these acts. New vengeance? New taxes? New horror? None could say.'

There are touches of Rolfe's ironic humour in his summary of the scientific learning of that time. 'Messer Giambattista della Porta appears to have used his science and magical art to invent "Some Sports against Women"; which will show what the Borgian Era regarded as permissible practical jokes. He says that, if you wish to discover paint on a face, you must chew saffron before breathing on her, and incontinently she yellows: or you may burn brimstone near her, which will blacken mercury sublimate and cerusa (white lead): or you may chew cummin or garlic and breathe on her, and her cerusa or quicksilver will decay. But if that you yearn to dye a woman green, you must decoct a chameleon in her bath.'

A final quotation will show Rolfe's sympathy for the classic learning of the Renaissance:

During many years, since the first signs of Muslim activity, fugitives from Byzantium descended upon Italian shores. The glory of Greece had gone to Imperial Rome. The grandeur of Imperial Rome had returned to Byzantium. And now the glory and grandeur of Byzantium was going to Christian Rome. When danger menaced, when the day of stress began to dawn, scholars and cunning artificers, experts skilful in all knowledge, fled westward to the open arms of Italy with their treasures of work. Italy welcomed all who could enlarge, illuminate her transcendent genius: learning and culture and skill found with her not exile but a home, and a market for wares. Scholarship became the fashion. 'Literary taste was the regulative principle.' It was the Age of Acquisition. 'Tuscan is hardly known to all Italians, but Latin is spread far and wide throughout all the world', says Filelfo. But to know Greek was the real test of a gentleman of that day; and Greek scholars were Italy's most honoured guests. Not content with the codices and classics of antiquity that these brought with them, Italian princes and patricians sent embassies to falling Byzantium, to search for manuscripts, inscriptions, or carven gems, and bronze, and marble. Greek intaglii and camei graced the finger-rings, the ouches, collars, caps, of Venetian senators, of the lords of Florence, of the sovereigns of the Regno, of the barons and cardinals and popes of Rome.

Baron Corvo seems after all to have had his way, very largely, in the matter of punctuation and spelling. At least, 'Sistine' is 'Xystine' throughout; all the characters are referred to by their ceremonial titles (Caesar Borgia, for instance, is not so called, but 'Duke Cesare de Valentinois'); and all the Popes are accorded capitalized pronouns. Another whim which may be noticed is his avoidance, in the chapter entitled 'The Legend of the Borgia Venom', of the word 'poison', which only defiles his pages in a quotation. He revived an old form, and for 'poison' wrote 'venom', for 'poisoned' 'envenomed', for 'poisonous' 'veneficous', and 'venenation' for 'poisoning'. This chapter on the Borgian poisons, in which Rolfe refused to believe, is the most interesting in the book, and as ingenious as the lock of a Milner safe. By a pharmaceutical examination of the ingredients and recipes asserted to have been used, Corvo came to the conclusion that the stories of assassination by spiked ring, and the rest of the romantic Borgian murders in similar modes, were merely fabulous; in short, that 'These Borgia could no more poison artistically, than they could send telegrams.'

He is equally dexterous in manipulating the theory that Cesare was not the son of Alexander, but of his rival and successor Cardinal della Rovere (defined as a 'psychic epileptic'), and uses this alternative of paternity to explain Cesare's strange inactivity after Alexander's death. Indeed, the whole book is full of ingenious surmises.

The critics were variously impressed by Rolfe's queer pages. To one, the 'breathlessness of his exaggerations, and the freedom of his criticisms', seemed like 'an icy shower-bath after the tepid ablutions of average historical research'. Another condemned his 'mixture of asterisks and hysterics'. Harland, magnanimously sinking his resentment at the ingratitude with which he had been treated, wrote: 'Your Borgia book is GREAT. To say nothing of the labour and the learning of it—the historic imagination, the big vision, the humour, the irony, the wit, the perverseness, the daring, the tremendously felicitous and effective *manner* of it. It is like a magnifical series of tapestry pictures of the xv century. Of course I think you are *advocatus diaboli*, but *what* an advocate. In any land save England such a book would make its author at once famous and rich. It is GREAT.'

Equal uncertainty existed as to the identity of the author. Some critics accepted him as Baron Corvo; others, more cautious, as Mr. Frederick Baron Corvo, or Mr. Corvo simply; while *The Bookman,* having questioned if the author was Italian, referred to him as 'the Signor Corvo'.

All alike praised his learning and research; and most, the powerful audacity of his style. Even the most unfriendly of his critics conceded that 'when the mighty family of Borgia is dealt with in future this volume will be a standard work of reference'. Perhaps the best word was spoken by a reviewer who, after noticing the author's obvious close acquaintance with Catholic ritual, inferred that the *Chronicles* were written by a man 'not old in years, but worn with experience and unafraid', and concluded: 'Baron Corvo must pardon the many readers he will have interested if they consider him almost as great a problem as the strange family whose fortunes he has traced.' He was.

X

THE DIVINE FRIEND

WHILE the feud with Grant Richards was developing to its climax, Rolfe had sunk his resentment and sought fresh work from John Lane, who was persuaded to buy a few more stories concerning Toto for £10. The whole collection was published shortly before the Borgia book under the title *In His Own Image*, which covers twenty-six new fables in addition to the original half-dozen from the *Yellow Book*. It cannot be claimed that the later tales are as good as the first; nevertheless most of them are very good. The subjects are not all taken from hagiology in this second selection, though all are more or less religious in theme; but the stories retain Baron Corvo's peculiar mixture of paradoxical piety, fantastic humour, and sensuous appreciation of the lights, sounds, forms and changes of the world. Even the titles possess that artificial yet naive humour which was one of his best effects, and is sufficiently personal to deserve the epithet 'Corvine'. Two examples will serve: 'Why Dogs and Cats always Litigate'; 'About Doing Little, Lavishly'.

Taken together, moreover, these *Toto* stories afford the reader many vivid glimpses of the author's character, which, though not that of Hadrian, has proved hardly less fascinating to certain temperaments. Robert Hugh Benson, for example, delighted to read them aloud to his visitors, and jokingly referred to them as 'the fifth gospel'. Rolfe had a gift for gradually disclosing or implying personality; and as through spring and summer Toto narrates his legends and folk-tales, the Baron, who is his audience, comes to life. Perhaps to those who have never felt any admiration, even reluctant, for the Mother of Churches, and her record, and what she stands for, most of these stories will have little appeal; but to those who possess faith, or envy its possessors, they have an airy and amusing charm. Corvo's central characteristic is, of course, a religious belief and fervour which is tender, profound, childish and childlike in turn, but he reveals far more than that. Indeed, it is surprising how complete a picture of himself he draws.

What 'the Baron's' exact purpose in Italy was at the time the stories were told does not appear, though we learn that he was a painter, photographer, writer and observer. He is attended by a bodyguard of youths who are both models and servants; and it is their leader, Toto ('a splendid, wild (*discolo*) creature from the Abruzzi') who tells the tales which make the book. To these unlearned peasant lads their master seems a marvel of knowledge, wealth and power; the Baron's manner to them is that of a benevolent despot to his slaves. He reveals himself in countless ways. He is a priest (he speaks of 'the clergy (of whom I am, in private life, the least)', and also an epicure ('Breakfast was ready, under the magnolia tree. I like these late-spring breakfasts in the sun. Guido and Ercole had executed a masterpiece in their simplicity, with three great bowls of beaten brass, one in the middle to support my book, one each at the opposite ends of the table, all filled with damask roses of the darkest purple, fresh, and breathing liquid odours as of cloves celestial. I gave the creatures compliments, and sat down to breakfast. Cocomeri ripieni, Port Salut, olives, perfumed oranges, pitch-flavoured wine,—delicious.') He is a Royalist; all his emotions are roused by the sight of a college founded by Henry IX, that Cardinal-Bishop, brother of the Young Pretender, who might have been a Stuart King of England. Mary Queen of Scots is another of his idols. He hates the 'minotaur-manufacturers' of Lancashire, with ('until a few years ago') their tradition of child-labour. He is alarmed by storms and lizards. There is a fine description of 'the end of an awe-full afternoon' at Vasto d' Aimone, when 'the hot air throbbed in paralysis and apprehension' before a frightening thunderstorm in which 'the waves of the sea rode high, and dashed themselves to death against the towered rocks'. Watching the lightning flashes, the sleet and hail, fascinated, from an upper window, the Baron urgently, fervently, and nervously counts over and over the beads hidden in his trouser pocket. He is superstitious to a degree, yet with a sense of his quaint folly; easily moved by beauty, very generous. Perhaps the most reve-latory of all the stories is that entitled 'About Doing Little, Lavishly'. This tells how 'in early summer, at the very begin-ning of my explorations along the eastern coast, something happened to rouse me from the lethargy into which tem-peramental indolence had let me slip, after my life's great disappointment.' That 'something' was the circumstance that the annual procession on the Festival of Corpus Domini was about to be held in the 'wonderful little walled-city' in which the traveller found himself. The Baron entered heart and soul into the preparations; he was given his head. So he chose 'beautiful children from the schools, youths and maidens, men and women, from trade-guilds and confraternities', and gave to each 'the character of some god, some angel'. He redrew ancient designs, chose material, and cut garments for their costumes. Then, after rehearsal, himself unseen, he indulged his seeing eye in the splendour of the pageant as it made its way through the flower-decked streets. Later 'in the starlight, young eyes glittered, and white teeth gleamed on peaches. Never was complex crescentine beauty so discreetly manifested, as in this dim garden, where black cypress soars into the eternal star-sown blue, furnishing grey-green lawns with outlines, indefinite, mysterious, with infinite imperscrutable distances. Against the retirement of this background, the long contours of limbs, of old ivory, or having the transparent nacreous pallor of the flesh of turbot, and the modelling of supple forms, accented by clinging of silk, or revealed by a kithon's falling folds, undulated in inconstant curves'. All which pleased the Baron mightily.

There is another reference to 'my life's great disappointment' in a later story which tells of 'a single summer night' when 'a fire burned for no cause in my brain'. 'Lying there, as still as death, clutching crucifix and rosary, and the miniature of my dead, my closed eyes saw myself as I was, driven from my road, my life's career wrecked, blocked, checked—whichever you will—thrown out of my stride, thwarted in my sole ambition, utterly useless. Other men envied the freedom which was mine; they would have welcomed the happiness, and health, and power, which were offered to me in mocking substitution for the bonds I craved'. Whether or not 'elevated' or 'fine', in Canon Carmont's phrase, Rolfe's desire for the priesthood was certainly 'tenacious'.

He reveals another side of himself in the tale *About some Friends,* in which he deplores his loneliness: 'No one ever loved me well enough to take trouble to find out that which would give me pleasure. No stranger in the street ever said to me, "O, sir, why are you so unutterably sad?" Friends do not to me, as they would that I should do to them. There is some impenetrable mail of ice about me, which only one dead heart ever has been warm enough to melt.'

It had been agreed that *In His Own Image* should be dedicated to Henry Harland; but the quarrel put Harland out of court as a dedicatee; and when the volume appeared, it carried instead the inscription:

Divo Amico

Desideratissimo

D. D. D.

Fridericus

This dedication, 'To the Divine Friend, much desired', did not pass unnoticed.

*　　　*　　　*

By what side-wind did I hear the name of Trevor Haddon as that of one who could tell me much concerning Rolfe if he chose? I started down so many blind alleys at that time that I cannot remember who gave me the hint to write to Haddon at the Savage Club. His answer came from Cambridge:

11 *Little St. Mary's Lane,*
Cambridge

Dear Mr. Symons,

I have come to live here, where I am busy at work as a portrait painter, and fear there is no prospect of our meeting unless you are in these parts.

I have a lot to say about Corvo, and in fact I wrote a good deal of it some time ago, as the result of a suggestion from a bookseller-friend of mine, for a pamphlet to be sent to America. But I went abroad for four years, and all my things are in store. I don't know where my MS. is, but of course I could replace it.

These two points may amuse you. Rolfe lent me the manuscript of a book, the diary of a priest, Dom——(I shall remember the name). It was never published, but it was a most remarkable production. He was going to dedicate it to me, but we quarreled first.

I had a large collection of his letters, of the deepest interest from a psychological point of view, but my wife so detested the man that she said she would not stay under the same roof as those letters, and I must destroy them. Like a bloody fool I did not make a package of them and hand them in to my bank, but burnt them. How I have kicked myself since!

I am quite willing to spin my yarn; this is only a hasty reply to your enquiry. There is this about it, however. I want to treat my recollections in my own way, not to have them kneaded up and confected by another mind. What I write would have to be an intermission by T. H. and to be acknowledged suitably. I might want a little help with names, dates etc.

Yours sincerely
Trevor Haddon

Mr. Haddon's condition accorded very comfortably with the plan that I had already half-formed for this book, and after several meetings he sent me the following 'intermission':

It is a curious experience in these later days to drop one's line into the almost forgotten waters of thirty years ago and see what one can land. The 'Nineties then were dead though not quite buried; the row of 'Yellow Books' was completed on the shelf, Wilde had died in Paris, Henry James was about to desert whiskerdom, Aubrey Beardsley had burned out his marvellous flame; yet even after all those prodigies it was still possible to find new books which proved remarkable as experiences: at least, so I found *In His Own Image*. A review in the *Star* newspaper indicated in colourful words that these *Toto* stories were something quite out of the common, and hinted at an unusual personality behind the tales. I bought the book, and fell at once under the charm of its style and its spirit. Perhaps I was susceptible from personal causes. My Catholicism was then Roman in its orientation, I was newly returned from six months in Italy, and I had a hunger for friendship which responded immediately to a book dedicated to 'the Divine Friend much desired'. The chapter 'About some Friends' contains some of Rolfe's most beautiful writing; and here again its opening seemed to me almost a personal appeal. I was attracted, also, by the picture which the book gives of a free, artistic, and apparently opulent life led in ideal surroundings in the Roman Italy I loved so much. More than that, however, was the hint that this interesting personality suffered under a secret sorrow, and almost openly desired a friend who could 'understand'.

What is it that attracts us to the personality of an unknown writer, particularly to that of a writer of fiction? He may amuse us, thrill us, or impress us by his penetration into the psychology of his characters, but it is perhaps most of all by his understanding of and sympathy with those frustrations of emotion and buffetings of fortune which are our common lot. Thus it happens that a writer may arouse in us a set of vibrations so personal that we feel that he has shared our suffering, and is releasing in us a sorrow long buried, unvoiced, and unshared, in our own heart. So it was with me, at least; and in this case the author concerned, Corvo, went further: he seemed to *invite* someone to grasp the hand he held out in his own hope for friendship.

Knowing, as I did, a similar need, I felt that I could offer such a friendship; so, though it was rather like taking a leap in the dark, I wrote to Baron Corvo, care of John Lane.

I only half-expected an answer, but I got one. This was what Rolfe wrote:

'I do not know whether to thank you for your letter: or to exsecrate you. I do not know whether to thank you for Hope: or to exsecrate you for another illusion dispelled, for additional matter for Despair. I rejoice that my book has delighted you. But you terrify me when you mention your connections. Then what have you to do with me? Do you not already know me? If you do not, I beg of you to ask all or any of my thirteen worst enemies, whose names and addresses I have written here, to tell you about me. Till you have done this, I have no more to say. In secret I am fled away; and I will live alone, until——. I dedicated my book to the Divine Friend, Much-Desired. I do not know whether you are he—or another.'

Naturally I refused to inquire of the thirteen enemies, and answered that I should probably find them hateful, egotistical, wishful to chain divine things down to petty personal limitations. I denied that I was under the influence of any of the Catholic 'connections' which I had mentioned in my letter. I said that I wished to take Corvo as I found him, in spite of enemies. I even said, I remember, that the mystery of personal magnetism was all-wonderful, and that if it was propitious, I was the Divine Friend—I claimed the title—to the death. (I was much younger then!) I begged Rolfe to confide in my honour.

At this Rolfe melted, and soon after came to see me in my studio at Westminster. When he arrived, I realized that he was not the kind of being my imagination had painted. In person he was somewhat short and spare; he wore glasses which accentuated a myopic expression; moreover there was a cold shyness in his manner, due, as I found out later, to the fear and mistrust which were part of his general make-up. He told me fragments of his story, mostly his experiences at the Scots College in Rome. I was amazed to hear of his penurious circumstances. It was somewhat of a shock to learn that the erstwhile patron of an interesting band of followers, living in a noble house and touring the Italian coast for pleasure, was now so straitened that he had lately been writing *Chronicles of the House of Borgia* 'in conditions resembling serfdom'. From what he said I gathered that Rolfe was not in a position to stand out for respectable payment, so I suggested that he should employ an agent to look after his interests. It happened that I had seen in a literary column an announcement that Mr. Stanhope Sprigge had left a publishing firm to set up on his own account as an author's agent. I offered to see Mr. Sprigge on Rolfe's behalf. He agreed, and in the end I succeeded in interesting Mr. Sprigge. When I next saw Rolfe he appeared greatly perturbed by his discovery that Sprigge was a Roman Catholic and member of a sodality at Brompton. There was evidently an uneasy suspicion in his mind that there was some backstairs reason for my suggestion and introduction. I assured him emphatically that I had no Jesuitical connections or leanings of any kind, and for the time being he was pacified. In later walks and talks he maintained that most of the offers of help and assistance he received could be traced back to a sinister intention to intern him and keep him 'safely locked up', and that even those Jesuits who were not bent on thwarting him in subtle unseen ways would not hesitate to 'kick a stone in his path'.

Indeed, he had very hard things to say of his fellow-Catholics. According to him, they did not behave in daily life as though they believed in the life to come, and he had a bitter but pleasurable anticipation of seeing them 'fry in hell'. When things went wrong with him, his retort to Fate took the form of 'SOMEBODY WILL HAVE TO PAY FOR THIS'. His own life ambition was to be a priest, and he could not understand the opposition that had barred his way. Priests in general he had a poor opinion of, and he spoke with scorn of the kind of conversation common to their gatherings—particularly of 'priests' stories' of a certain shade of blue. His descriptions of his fellow students at the Scots College, and the Rector, Mgr. Campbell (who deprived him of a dressing case with luxurious fittings on the score of worldly vanity), were devastating.

In due course Rolfe came to my house at Elms Road, Clapham Common. During dinner, bearing in mind various references in *In His Own Image* (which it seems I misunderstood), I asked him whether I was right in thinking that he had been married. His answer was evasive.

At the piano Rolfe proved himself a true and sensitive musician. He had a cult for the boy-saint William of Norwich, and had composed a lovely little hymn in his honour; I meant to get the music of it from him, but never did. He had genuine skill in transposing.

Speaking of Elms Road is a reminder that in *Hadrian the Seventh* Rolfe evidently intended a lampoon of my humble self as Alfred Elms the painter—though his description of Elms's work as a portraitist indicated a meretricious success that has evaded me. My wife instinctively disliked him, and unhesitatingly qualified him as a liar, a sponger, and sexually abnormal. He filled her with what she called 'creepy loathing'.

Rolfe always rolled his own cigarettes, and when in funds had his own 'Corvo mixture' made up at a little tobacco shop in Oxford. It had a heavy full flavour, evidently due to Latakia.

He liked the romantic richness of the Italian tongue. I was amused at his praising the Italian version of *Ben Hur*. He spoke very little of literature in general. He enveloped himself in his own atmosphere, though he would occasionally quote with glee and admiration some happy phrase or purple patch.

He lent me the manuscript of a draft version of his charming story of *Don Tarquinio*, a day in the life of a Roman nobleman.

Later on he sent me the manuscript of another book, the diary (it pretended to be) of an Italian priest, Dom Gheraldo, in the service of one of the great Renaissance nobles. He had often

spoken of it, and quoted from it. Indeed, he announced his intention of dedicating this interesting and extraordinary work to me.
The facts about that flower of Rolfe's patient genius must be
narrated by others, but it seemed to me such a marvellous mosaic
of apparently authentic detail that it could only have been
secreted from intense and persistent observation, and that under
very favourable circumstances. Wherever did he get it all? In
my letters I cautiously sounded him as to his creative methods.

The rationale of creative art is one of the most fascinating
human problems, and Rolfe's bizarre and elaborate artistry
aroused my curiosity. Where did he get his material? He undoubtedly loved, with an almost passionate understanding, that period
of life in Italy which formed the setting of *Dom Gheraldo*, and
I could not help wondering how much was invention, how much
divination, how much a systematic 'culture' of such fragments
and unconsidered trifles as his reading and research enabled him
to pick up. That much he shrewdly kept to himself, but in
answer to a letter in which I formulated as nearly as I deemed
justifiable the idea of mediumship, I practically got an admission
that the divination had to wait on favourable conjunctions.

It is possible that the inception of the *Dom Gheraldo* book was
an incident that Rolfe related to me as occurring in Rome when
he was in the town palace of the Duchess Sforza-Cesarini, who
was employing workmen to take up the pavement of the
ground-floor in connection with the installation of a new calori-
fer. In the course of the work a deep oubliette was discovered.
The household was in a great state of excitement when the
workmen who had descended reported the discovery of a skeleton, which was intensified on his remains being brought to light,
when the skull was seen to be pierced. 'That proved him to have
been a priest,' said Rolfe, and explained to me that this form of
assassination was reserved for the priesthood. The hero in the
unpublished book I have mentioned perished by that means.

More than twenty-five years later I read Mr. Shane Leslie's
essay in which he describes a visit paid by Rolfe to W. T. Stead,
'who, before testing Rolfe's literary talents, handed a penny held
by the Baron to his medium Julia, who from another room

furnished the oracular reply, "He is a blackguard! He has a hole in his head." Mr. Stead thereupon chased and seized Rolfe until he could feel his cranium, when behold there was a perceptible hole to be found in the skull! He was accordingly dismissed as a blackguard, and for once Rolfe was baffled by powers more sinister than his own.'

Julia's verdict, 'He has a hole in his head', amazes me. Surely there was more than coincidence in this? Was Rolfe a modern projection of Dom Gheraldo, or had he built up a dream-entity of such psychic stability that it coincided with himself—or what?

What a pity, by the way, that *Dom Gheraldo* (I am not quite sure if that was the name—it was also called *An Ideal Content*, I fancy) is lost. Perhaps you will be able to trace that queer freak of Rolfe's fancy, which is unlike any other of his books in the number and variety of its fanciful words. I never knew whether the proposed dedication took any definite form, for the simple reason that Rolfe chose to break with me, and this must be the conclusion of my random recollections

MALEDICTORY.

I wish I could have spelt it with a V! It came about thus. I never heard much of Rolfe's dealings with Stanhope Sprigge, but I understood he had a manuscript to 'place' which got mislaid. In the course of time Rolfe asked me to send him a statement of the various small sums of money I had advanced him, or expended on his behalf. After I had done this, I received a post-card from him written in green ink which concluded thus: '*When the manuscript which was purloined by your accomplice Sprigge has been returned to me, it will be time enough for me to consider the settling of your bill.*'!!!

SIC TRANSIVIT

Because the day was very fair & the sun warm for the time of year, after my dinner I went to take the air, at ten of the glass, on the roof of the new watergate called Saint Thomas Beket his tower. There is a parcel of silly people, who believe the superstitious nonsense written by Mr Matthew (formerly of Paris,) averring that this tower is unsafe because it fell twice during its building; & they avoid it. But I sit here in the sun, day by day, for the confusion of such fatwits as well as for other reasons. The place is quiet, & apt for meditation, being high above the ant-heap of fortress & city. Here, an old man's eyes may follow the silvery river, as far as London Bridge, on the one hand; &, on the other, lose themselves far away over Lamehythe Marsh among the clean white pinnacles of the abbey & hall & palace of Westminster.

I had many matters for my meditation. There was a great crown-wearing this day in King William Redhair his hall at Westminster. And my lord the king was to do more awful & more difficult justice than ever before during his whole long reign. I had wished to stand in my place by his throne, where I always have stood in all his grave affairs. But his sweet grace, mindful of a very old earl's infirmities, bade me to take care of my health, for his sake & the kingdom's, sitting at home at my ease. Nevertheless, I thought of naught but the king's affairs throughout this sunny day. And, in the middle of the afternoon, Fulk the Flame, vert, a heart between eight lyonceux or, came to me, hot from the crown-wearing. His fiery face was ashen-grey, & his manner quiet as cold cinders. "Hubert, the king is dead:" says he.

Fr. Rolfe's handwriting (from an unpublished manuscript
in the possession of Lord Esher)

XI

THE QUEER COLLABORATOR

ALL through my Quest for Corvo chance helped astonish-
ingly; it came to my aid now. Grant Richards, into the
well of whose memory I plunged frequent buckets,
recollected as an unimportant detail the name of Sholto
Douglas as that of a friend of Rolfe's. The name Sholto is,
I knew, a very usual one in the Douglas family; I had met
three. One of them I had encountered once only: at a
dinner given to the two of us by my friend Vincent Marrot,
a dinner made memorable by Madeira of the year 1803.
The Sholto Douglas then encountered was, I felt
unreasonably certain, the one known to Mr. Grant
Richards. Confident in my assumption, I wrote to him,
and was delighted to find that I was right.

> *27 Brunswick Place,*
>
> *Hove, Sussex*

Dear Mr. Symons,

Of course I remember well the happy evening when I had the
pleasure of meeting you. I have often hoped that we might meet
again. But I am out of Town for the present. I have a curious
job. I am in charge of a lad of seventeen. He learned to read and
write at the age of seven. He was then given a ten-year holiday.
Now I am called in. The depths of his ignorance are abysmal. At
first I thought that I could not endure. But I have come to be
interested immensely. . . . I hope to travel far with him.

But I forget to answer your questions.

I know very little of Corvo. I read his *In His Own Image* long
ago—1902 perhaps. Then I wrote to him through his publisher
to ask if he could put me in the way of the legend of Fioravanti
and Guerino. He replied in Italian that he could not do so.

I responded in French. He then tried Latin. Of course I could counter with a long answer in Greek. After that linguistic display we continued in English. I did not meet him for some time. We agreed to collaborate. Actually looking back I cannot but say that he took a series of *Reviews of Unwritten Books* which I had concocted and failed to sell. He damaged them in my estimation, but I admit he sold them—to the *Monthly Review*—when I had failed to sell them at all. And he took no money for them: I got it all. We then set to work on a satiric history of certain naughty emperors, in which I wrote everything and he made changes which annoyed me. He even took a translation I had made of Meleager of Gadara. Neither of these were ever published. But over that last we came to a final squabble. He made alterations to which I could not agree. I demanded the return of my MS and he refused because of the work he had put into it. Eventually I got it back together with most of my letters to him in exchange for all his letters to me. Well, we were both at fault. I did not make due allowance for his wayward and fantastic genius. I see now that I failed in sense of charity. He was not as other men and I was wrong in treating him as an ordinary man and judging him by ordinary standards.

I had only once the privilege of seeing him in his poor little lodging in Hampstead. It was not a pretty setting for such a man as he—a commonplace little room with a few shelves and photographs about, mostly his own handiwork. I think he had exaggerated ideas about his own power of drawing: he told me that he drew the not very attractive things which decorate the outsides of *Don Tarquinio* and *Hadrian the Seventh*.

He was not a first-rate classical scholar. His Latinity was not quite faultless: and his Greek was, shall we say, on a par with Shakespeare's. Even in Italian I remember his making one elementary slip to me. But he knew his Italian history well: even there he had a perverse way of rejecting other people's conclusions—sometimes, it would seem, differing from others simply for the sake of differing, as in his estimate of the characters of Alexander VI and Julius II.

I feel that these desultory remarks are going to be of no use to

you. It is indeed the case that I know very little of the man.
Indeed, I believe that he did not want me to know much. He
learnt much more of me than he ever told me of himself. I think
he never quite got over the fact that I was not Catholic in his
opinion.

I ought to be in Blackheath for the first fortnight in January.
It would give me much pleasure to see you then—if fate is kind.
Perhaps you will dine with me. . . .

Sincerely yours

Sholto Douglas

I could not help reflecting, after reading this valuable
letter, on the insistent eccentricity with which Rolfe
marked his way. Who but he would have lightly entered
upon a collaboration (by correspondence) with a stranger!
—a collaboration, moreover, which had as its object translation from a language which he hardly knew? What
sort of version of the immortal Meleager had been
produced by this strange conjunction? I wondered, and
wrote to ask for the loan of the manuscript. But alas;
after a vain search Sholto Douglas was forced to conclude
that it was lost or destroyed. To console me, however, for
a disappointment perhaps too bluntly expressed, he
placed in my hands those letters to Rolfe returned after
their disagreement. Knowing the story of the correspondence, it was a queer experience to read it through, and
mark the ripening of a romantic friendship between two
kindred spirits who had yet to meet. These letters must have
meant much to the lonely Rolfe: Sholto Douglas's brief
summary does less than justice to their interest. Where, I
wondered, was the rest of the correspondence? Lost with
the manuscripts, I feared; and indeed it is one of the regrets
of my quest that though in the end I found most of what I
sought, those letters to Sholto Douglas still elude me.

The modest first demand for information, just such an
inquiry as any diffident reader might send to an author
whose book he liked, told very little; nor did the French

and Greek expostulations; but I was interested to see, from a slightly later letter, that, as at Oscott and Holywell, Rolfe claimed Oxford as part of his background, and regretted that he had been sent down. 'My dear Sir' soon became 'Dear Man'. 'You ask me many questions', Douglas wrote, 'the most comprehensive is "Who are you?" I am a man no doubt somewhat older than you [in fact he was 28, Rolfe 40]. I say that because you aged so quickly between the first stories Toto told you and the coming of *In His Own Image*. I am a private tutor, doing sufficient work to reduce my poverty to the tolerable minimum. I compel the elements of accuracy into the dull unwitting brains of successive pupils'; 'My first tutorship was an easy one and a great success; my second was difficult and a failure: from it I learned many things and I have acted consistently upon them ever since. I remember that I am a male governess. I suppress myself and speak when I am spoken to. I am studiously polite. I echo the religious opinions of my employer. I eat what I am expected to eat. I smoke only when and where I am expected to smoke. I adore little girls. I have no eccentricities. I am violently interested in mechanical toys and county cricket—I am particularly good at county cricket. Therefore I am a successful tutor.'

As a counter-confidence Baron Corvo sent the friend he did not know a copy of the Aberdeen attack. The reply was reassuring. 'The cutting from the paper is interesting as a study in calumny, but I should like to be able to read it in a looking glass.' Encouraged, Rolfe suggested a meeting. Douglas was doubtful. 'Shall we get on? I am certainly at my best in my letters. And you?' They did meet. 'Dear Man, I had formed a strangely incorrect notion of you. I had absolutely failed to expect that very human kindliness which twinkles so charmingly behind your spectacles.' So far, good.

Though Sholto Douglas did not realise it, that letter written in fluent Greek had deeply impressed Rolfe.

Fresh from his Borgian studies, imbued with the spirit of the Renaissance when it was the test of a gentleman to understand Greek, Baron Corvo had plunged into the study of the classics with all the ardour of the amateur. He not only desired to know, but also to conceal the newness (and thinness) of his knowledge. So he rejoiced in this contact with the greater learning of Sholto Douglas, though without betraying the limitations of his own. The task was not unduly difficult; he was by now sufficiently well acquainted with Latin authors to give an air of erudition to his comments on the books he was reading or admired. Nor was Greek beyond him. Personal adaptations from the Greek (lexicon) star the pages of *Toto*. If this was sciolism, it was sciolism in the spirit of Edgar Allan Poe, who delighted in reviewing and correcting translations from the German, though his knowledge of that language was less than Rolfe's of Greek. Both possessed that true feeling for literature beside which mere learning is an unlit lamp.

When Rolfe learned that Sholto Douglas treasured in a drawer a number of unfinished manuscripts, and an unpublished translation of Meleager, he was delighted, and asked at once to see them. But it was one thing, in this quaint correspondence, to ask; quite another to receive. Douglas possessed a mind of tantalising nimbleness, and a sense of fun and humour that was perhaps more tantalising still to his sombre senior. In reply to a discourse on Ausonius, for example, Douglas returned, not the reasoned comment that Rolfe invited, but a denunciation of Southsea and its ways: 'It is all flat and made of plaster with esplanades and promenades and cheap coloured females and pavilions and Lipton's tea. Think of slob at low tide and boggle it up with an estuary, dry it and scratch bricks out of it and build anathematic villas, stick an esplanade and shrubs all round, decorate with barrel organs and piers and make electric trams squirt all over it—then fall on your knees and sympathise with me.'

Rolfe was not in the least amused, and asked again for
Meleager and the manuscripts.

After a delay, he got them, though with the warning,
'They are enough to make a cow scoff. My soul must
have been made of shoe leather when I wrote this stuff'.
The eventful parcel contained all the miscellaneous
writings mentioned in Sholto Douglas's letter. There
were some rough *Reviews of Unwritten Books* of which
the titles give the character: Machiavelli's *Despatches
from the South African Campaign;* Johnson's *Life of Carlyle;*
Tacitus's *De Moribus et Populis Americæ;* Herodotus's
History of England; Cardinal Newman's *Grammar of
Dissent.* There were beginnings for a book to consist of
studies of thirty Roman emperors—Carinus, Elagabalus,
Commodus, Pertinax and others (written in a breathless style
which seems a mixture of Carlyle and Edgar Saltus)—
which had been given such titles as 'A Colossus of the Bed
Chamber' and 'A Goat in Priest's Clothing'. Douglas,
sceptical of their value, described their composition
humorously: 'I have invented a new method of breeding
literature—it is a complete failure. Take three epithets, of
which one, at least, must be meaningless, and the others
such as are not used in polite society: build around them
a sentence, in the second person singular if possible (this
enables you to commence with the object and arrange
the other words so that they scan): finish every third
sentence with an exclamation mark, and there you are!'
Finally there was the version of Meleager.

Solitary in his dingy Hampstead lodging, Rolfe set
himself to revise and improve these immature works.
And, as Sholto Douglas had told me, he so far succeeded
that a number of the *Reviews of Unwritten Books* found a
place in the *Monthly Review.* Rolfe even invented some
new subjects: 'Lord Chesterfield's Letters to Mr. Pierpont
Morgan', 'Cicero's Oration for Joan of Arc', 'Marlowe's
Epic of the Borgias'. 'You have transformed my rubbish
into literature with your wondrous Attick talent', the

original author wrote enthusiastically. He had not: the *Reviews* remain unworthy of revival, though there are interesting phrases in them, as in everything Rolfe touched. For a time the Roman histories seemed more promising; and obscure sources were ransacked by both collaborators for facts and phrases. But when the amusement of research wore off, Douglas lost confidence in his work. 'I have been writing with laborious diligence for four days. I have proved to my own satisfaction that I cannot write.' 'Oh, it is damnable', he adds later, 'I knew it would happen: I have gone Carlyle. While I was writing *Commodus* the soul-sobering thought came to me. I did not dare to whisper it to myself. I did not breathe it to you. It is six months since I looked at the *French Revolution*. I ought to have been disinfected in that time. I shall have to read a lot of antidotes. I shall take a course of Whitman, Aeschylus, Cyril Tourneur, and Tacitus. Or perhaps I ought to take an emetic like Gibbon?' Finally, 'Oh man', he implored, 'do you really want me to continue with grief extracting these pilfered trivialities? Even you can never make anything out of them. It is such an utter waste of time. I do it only to please you. I wish you would give me leave to stop.' Rolfe did: he had come at last to admit the rightness of Douglas's doubts; and the *Thirty Emperors* subsided again into the limbo of unfinished books.

Meleager remained; and of the three projects this most interested Rolfe. He was flattered at the thought of being even part translator from the Greek, and earnestly scrutinised Meleager's text word by word, lexicon in hand, in the hope of imparting a personal flavour to Sholto Douglas's draft. He succeeded only too well. At first his collaborator's criticisms were temperate: 'Your sapphics don't bring conviction to the ear. I think you would be safer in iambics. You find the self-chosen metre elaborate and it hampers you so that in reading I find more Rolfe than Meleager: this is a fault.' As Rolfe warmed to his work, however, relations grew strained. Personal modes of spelling and transliterating were among his more annoying foibles. He used the obsolete final k for such words as 'public' without encountering any objection; but his conscience prompted him first to Kypris for the usually accepted Cypris, then to Kupris. Equally he resolved on Meleagros for the familiar anglicism Meleager. Sholto Douglas at first demurred and then grew indignant at Rolfe's 'blatant pedantry' and proposals. 'No. No. No. We are proposing to translate Meleager. I refuse to accept Rolfian plagiarisms and call them Meleager. You may euphuize if you can, but you must not give a false version of the whole song.' Rolfe was accused of displaying the learning of *Notes and Queries*. Later, 'a detailed study of your version only confirms my first impression, that you have failed to find the soul of Meleager, that your ear frequently plays you false, leading you into complexity where a failure for the sake of simplicity would be excusable, that my version as a whole is much better than your version as a whole'. More reproaches followed as the much amended manuscript went backwards and forwards by post. 'I have no objection to your new line, but my dear, dear man, one is Meleager and one is not: you are at liberty to say that Meleager was æsthetically wrong in ending the song as he did: but that cannot justify your desire to change his meaning.' Finally Douglas, who, though well aware that he had no gift for original writing, possessed a scholar's conscience far more active than Rolfe's, exploded: 'I have looked hastily through parts of your new version, and it angers me so that I can hardly speak. I want to take a great earth-born blue pencil and score and rage. I am simply weeping over it. Oh, why are we to disagree like this? What a fatal mistake it was of mine ever to send you my manuscript. I would give much to go back to that day and refrain from having sent it. Am I to send you every trifling change I think fit? or do you trust yourself so firmly that I am to send it back to you untouched and leave everything in your hands?'

That was the end. Rolfe had borne criticism with far more patience than I had credited him with possessing, doubtless from deference to a knowledge which he recognised as superior to his own; but at such flat correction his pride took umbrage, and the friendship and correspondence ended, though apparently without vindictiveness on either side.

Behind the literary controversy the letters showed a few darker touches. In one Douglas rejoices that bailiffs no longer perturbed Rolfe's peace; in others, evidently conscious of his friend's acute poverty, he enclosed small sums of money, ostensibly to pay for postage, paper, and other expenses incurred by Rolfe on their joint account. Evidently even while the unlucky translator hunted up alternative epithets in his dictionary, the shadow of penury loured darkly overhead.

*　　　　*　　　　*

At the time that this association with Sholto Douglas was making its flow and ebb, while Rolfe was mastering the mysteries of Greek and Meleager, he was engaged upon another and hardly less surprising literary task, and severing himself from another friend. The friend was Temple Scott, who, it may be remembered, had left England to act as John Lane's manager in America, bearing with him Baron Corvo's blessing, and also an injunction to familiarise American readers with his works and merits. This task Temple Scott was very willing to perform, so far as lay within his power.

The instruments by which the American public was to be made conscious of Corvo as a writer were the *Toto* volume (*In His Own Image*) and a new translation of Omar Khayyam. The second subject owed itself to the recommendation of Harland and of Kenneth Grahame, and to the vast popularity which FitzGerald's version enjoyed. The early neglect of the Persian masterpiece had been replaced by widespread favour; edition after edition was issued by publisher after publisher. The *Rubaiyat* suited the temperament of a generation in revolt against religious assumptions; Omar's pagan assertions expressed with poetic completeness the new materialism which had followed Darwin's doctrines. And so 'comparative' versions, 'illustrated' versions and new versions, made by those who thought they could better FitzGerald's classic, or merely wished to make money from the public demand, flooded the market. Not many of the 'new' translators knew any Persian; but that simple circumstance seems not to have troubled them. It did not trouble Rolfe.

The mine which these hardy intruders for the most part worked was the virtually complete translation into French of all Omar's quatrains made by J. B. Nicolas, a French civil servant who spent many years in the East. FitzGerald, in his first version, purposely gives no more than a hundred and one verses; and most of the other English adapters followed his example in rendering only a selection of stanzas connected by sentiment and idea. Rolfe's project, in itself a good one, was to make the first translation into English prose of the more than four hundred tetrastichs given by Nicolas. If challenged, it is possible that he would have essayed, by his own peculiar methods, to extract a meaning from the Persian original; by comparison, the task that he set himself was an easy one.

On the advice of Temple Scott, who was to write a Preface for Rolfe's new version, John Lane agreed to publish the book when completed, and to purchase the copyright for £25. In due course Corvo did complete his task. It cannot have been an easy one; and the finished product, issued to the world in 1903, bears many marks of its eccentric author. Mr. Nathan Haskell Dole, an American Omarian who contributed an Introduction, remarks that

Frederick Baron Corvo shows that he is a masterly translator. He often penetrates through the decorative filigree of the French style to something approaching Omar's own marvellous concentration, condensation. Where, for instance, M. Nicolas, with a humorous lack of humour, declares that the nightingale speaks 'dans un language approprié a la circonstance', the English reads elegantly 'whispers me with fitting tongue'. The translator often uses a Greek word with cleverness; as in the phrase beginning 'Initiate in every mystery, now for what new orgies dost thou yearn', which is Greek from beginning to end, exquisitely veiling the obscenity of the Persian. The phrase 'un verset plein de lumière' is luminous as 'diaphotick verse'; and how elegantly he introduces the Moon as 'Astrarche', the Queen of Stars. He speaks of fair Parthenian tresses, and the Greek word agapema, which means 'The object of love', and is neuter, he, by a turn of genius, transforms into a proper name, and a beautiful name at that—'the throat of Agapema'.

These praises may be deserved, but it is only by the enthusiastic that Rolfe's text can be read for pleasure. Apart from the peculiarities of his transliterations, which this time Sholto Douglas did not restrain, there is a heavy formality about his prose version which not even occasional happy turns of phrase can make more than tolerable. 'If a Stranger be faithful to thee, take him for a Kinsman, if a Kinsman bewray thee, take him for a Stranger', is a favourable specimen. 'God, moulding my Body's Clay, knew what I would do. Not without His Connivance am I culpable. Then, at the Ultimate Day, will He let me burn in Hell?' is another. However, for a time, Rolfe was very pleased with his translation, and expected it to make his fortune. 'The Philistine likes a little obvious recondity', he wrote to Temple Scott; 'Don't you misjudge by glancing. I have invented a new set of English words expressing the Persian idea *via* the Greek language, strictly following philological rule, so that, though these words hit you in the eye, they strike a spark of intelligence in the brain *instanter*. Anyone can see the meaning of Hybristick, and reference to the glossary will show it as the epithet applied by Homer to the suitors of Penelope—rude and tipsy and libidinous and gay and young—wanton, but a much more pregnant word.' Unfortunately, 'anyone' (if he was the average reader) could not. Lane would not go to the expense of printing the glossary, and so Rolfe's 'archellenisms', as a later critic called them, were unappreciated by the Philistines, though they amused students of eccentric words. This new and elaborate version of Omar fell flat in England, and was stillborn in the United States. For this failure the author blamed (not himself but) Lane and Temple Scott. 'In London I had found him deserving of pity and charity', writes the latter; 'in his letters to me in New York I found him ungrateful and bitterly misunderstanding of kindness and friendly help. Indeed, I found that it was irritating to help him. He curdled the milk of human feeling by an acidity of nature he was unable to sweeten, however he might desire to sweeten it. And I am sure he did so desire. I ceased corresponding with him when I found that he became insultingly suspicious, and that it was impossible to satisfy his demands.'

Before the final break, however, Rolfe sent his friend in America a number of letters which contain illuminating phrases. 'Do not trouble to tell me anything about your journey', he wrote following Temple Scott's departure; 'that is the most annoying convention of the traveller. I, when formerly I moved, and had friends (passez moi le mot) who expected news of my movements, used to find myself after the first few letters inditing the most enormous lies. The tale of little travels, after two repetitions, is perfectly uninteresting to the traveller; indeed, he becomes bound to create'. 'I imitate nothing. I cultivate my prominences. Hence my singularity', he wrote in another moment of self-expansion. Again, 'Collect and send me as many . . . literary papers, magazines, as you can, anything to keep me from losing my senses. All things considered it takes very little to amuse me;

and I am never amused at all; and a man without amusement cannot be serious'. These letters are for the most part friendly in tone, but at the least transgression beyond the expected the claws show:

Last night [I received] your unsatisfactory letter dated VII June.
Unsatisfactory, by reason of divers damnable heresies therein contained.

Item: that you know me now.
> You don't. No one does. I don't myself. Except that I am what I am at the moment, utterly concentrated on that, and as utterly concentrated on this at the next. You know me? *Anathema sint!*

Item: that you have nothing to do with Imagination.
> You have. Your own letter gives you the lie. It's all imagination. *Anathema sint!*

Item: that I'm satisfied with my Borgia book.
> I'm not. It's about a third as good as it might be. It wants seventy-eight more medals, a voyage to Rome, Milan, Ferrara, and two years. It's only a poor starved pretentious thing. *Anathema sint!*

Item: that I'm a luxurious sybarite.
> That is perfectly infernal. That shows how abominably the insidious calumnies of the *Aberdeen Free Press* have influenced even you. People, accustomed to classify, only can classify. It is such a common thing to say that one uncommon is luxurious. Kindly note that I am not. Strawberries I loathe, and asparagus I merely use. I do pride myself on being dainty, but my daintiness is for the little and the simple. Food doth not worry me, nor clothes. I prefer omelettes, green things, and a gown, to unnatural and splendid opulence. I crave of the unhearing gods a climate, books, precious stones, baths, five slaves, and my naked soul. But strawberries and asparagus forced—*Anathema sint!*

The most interesting of the letters sent to me by Mr. Temple Scott defines Rolfe's attitude to love and passion:

I am struck aghast every now and then by the strange thing people call Love. One would be silly to deny it—because every now and then an example crops up of a sensible man or woman having their life tangled up with the life of another in blind mystery. They actually support each the continual presence of the other. Oh, there must be something in it.

But it seems so excessively funny to me. Carnal pleasure I thoroughly appreciate, but I like a change sometimes. Even partridges get tiresome after many days. Only besotted ignorance or hypocrisy demurs to carnal lust, but I meet people who call that holy which is purely natural, and I am stupefied. I suppose we all deceive ourselves. To blow one's nose (I never learned to do it) is a natural relief. So is coition. Yet the last is called holy, and the first passes without epithets. Why should one attach more importance to one than to the other? I don't think that I want to know.

Some talk of wickedness, and vulgarly confound the general with the particular. Of course you're wicked, every instant that you spend uncontemplative of, uncorresponding to, the Grace and Glory of your Maker. That may be forgiven, for that Real Love forgives.

So that, except carnally, I fail to understand the love of man for maid. But carnally—well, of course. Extra-carnally, there is a perfectly possible relation of taste, of admiration of soul, of body.

As for me, I am rotting in my chains, and Nature only looks in at my prison window, and passes by. Mail of icy indifference encloses me, no one touches me where I can feel. I am aloof—alone.

*   *   *

The peculiar neurosis under which Baron Corvo suffered had cut him off from almost every friend he had ever made, and every source of income, but he still retained a roof over his head—that Hampstead roof to which he had first been introduced four years earlier as a guest of the friendly Slaughter. Slaughter, however, had left 69 Broadhurst Gardens to serve in the South African War, and did not return. His place as Rolfe's main benefactor was taken by another boarder, Harry Bainbridge, a young chemist, who for over two years helped Corvo with money and friendship. But now Bainbridge also left the Hampstead haven, and Rolfe became desperate.* He must have earned and borrowed small sums in one way or another, though how, it is difficult to guess. About this time he enlisted the support of J. B. Pinker, the well-known literary agent; and fortified by a recommendation, sought, but sought in vain, a publisher for the Dom Gheraldo book, now called *Don Renato,* and for the translation of Meleager, and the *Reviews of Unwritten Books,* made in collaboration with Sholto Douglas. He disavowed any desire for fame. 'I do not burn for literary success, but for commercial success', he explained to one reader who considered his unpublished books; 'I am only waiting to find a publisher with whom I actually can cooperate. It is open to the publisher of my works to invent a personality and to attach that personality's name to those works. I myself will give you a name for them, if there really is any value in a name.' It seemed clear that there was not much in 'Baron Corvo'.

What he longed for above all was some dramatic turn that would make him independent. 'I am having a frightful time with money worries', he wrote to a correspondent in America:

The booming in my ears is incessant and the top right of my skull feels like lead. My tongue is furred, mouth foul, and I am always dry. I never touch alcohol: I have not for years. Only once in my life was I drunk and that was an accident when I was six years old. But I think more and more slowly every day. I am

* Mr. Bainbridge has recently written his autobiography, *Twice Seven,* in which he gives an interesting account of his memories of Rolfe, and a number of characteristic letters.

really quite useless for brain work, or even for ordinary conversation, from the time I get up till tea time. Of course I can chatter, or write, but the action is merely automatic, no thought inspires or directs, and the result is perisomatic simply. For this there is no cure but rest and freedom from worry. With those I could work out my own salvation. I have not a friend in the world to help me. The literary 'patron' no longer exists, or at least he never has manifested himself to me. And, even though the quality and quantity of my work are admired, and predictions daily are made of the brilliant commercial success which will attend my stuff sooner or later, no one ever yet has conceived the idea of investing money in me to keep me alive to do more work and win that commercial success. And I think on the whole that's it. Nothing but a thousand pounds, I name a sum at random, nothing but a sum, a lump sum, will brush away these cobwebs, which are stifling me, and give me *confidence,* sweet reasonableness, strength to use myself well and aptly. I have none to lean on, and that kills.

The secret lies in the lump. That is quite essential. Little bits are worse than useless, they irritate, they exasperate, they annoy, simply because they prolong my agony, but they are quite useless to do me any real good. With the lump, I could clear off my really paltry embarrassments, go to sleep for a month by some sunny sea and clean my soul of horrible dreams; and then go to work again with vigour, knowing that I had something behind me, that I need not refrain from going for a good long walk when the spirit moves me to it, just because of the necessity of saving boot leather, of saving a clean shirt and collar for the time when I am obliged to go out to see a publisher or comfort my mother and sister. This may give you a faint idea of the restrictions which make me writhe.

While he was wandering thus round London, making contacts, but not contracts, with its hard-headed publishers, an old school friend met him and took pity on the haggard and hungry author. This friend was warned against Rolfe by Kains-Jackson, to whom he wrote in reply:

You don't quite see our attitude with regard to Corvo. He is mortally frightened of all men, of all publicity, of all day-light upon himself and his deeds. Well, we decided to accept him without prejudice and give him another chance. We obliterate the last twenty years; the world refuses to do so. Therefore F. and I are the only two people in the world he believes in or can trust. We save him from himself by purposely ignoring anything amiss in him; and he responds to this attitude gallantly. The man I knew and loved twenty years ago was bound to do so. To us he is F. W. Rolfe; he assumes no other identity. Of course in thus disarming our-selves we risk something: one must risk something to work a miracle of healing. And we are bent on working one . . . He says he does not dare to meet you or any of the Gleeson White people. I suppose you know too much. . . . He is a jaundiced, bitter, persecuted pariah: that is evident; he has done badly by the world he lives in and his fellow-men, and he naturally fears it and them. He has spoiled his life. And we want to bring a ray of hope and comfort into it, even if he doesn't deserve one. He hasn't hurt us; nor will we hurt him; he has just realised this about two people out of a million . . . Do not be troubled about my renewal of friendship with Corvo; I assure you that sincere pity for his awful state is my funda-mental motive. His example, his counsel, his influence, is not going to have weight with me. I cannot afford to become a crank; I don't mind being a lever, however.

But even this good-natured friend was rebuffed after a short time, and Baron Corvo once more pursued a miserable and lonely path. The wheel of his life had made another complete circle; the new Ixion was as completely poor, friendless, prospectless and estranged from the world as when he had left Italy for England in 1890, or Holywell for London in 1898. But that desperate resolution which had already carried Rolfe alive through so much hard-ship was not exhausted; he took refuge from his disappoint-ment and regrets in his own spirit, and, accepting for the

moment the loneliness that was his lot, by an intense effort
of will, once more made a new beginning. For the fourth
time he put the past behind him to create a new career. A
new life demanded a new name; and so, 'the years of toil
which went to make the pseudonym having been annulled'
(as he wrote to his brother), the barony of Corvo was
abandoned, as it had been adopted: it had certainly brought
him no luck. Henceforth he styled himself 'Fr. Rolfe'.
The abbreviation stood truthfully enough for Frederick;
while those who misread it as 'Father' were only
recognizing, in its bearer's view, that tenaciously maintained divine call to which the powers of the Church had
been so strangely blind.

XII

INTERREGNUM

By this time my Quest for Corvo had brought me a considerable understanding of his character. The answer to half the problem I had started out to solve was in my hands. I knew, now, the links of the long repressed misery to which he gave expression and relief in *Hadrian the Seventh*, which was the first-fruit of his new life. A happy man could not write such a book: there would be no need. In that intensely personal *roman à clef* Rolfe dramatized the long misadventure of his life, and made real, on the plane of imagination, his defeated dreams and hopes. Moreover, the overwrought paranoiac was able, by this projection of himself, to satisfy his spleen against all those who had in fact or in his fancy injured him, to 'cleanse his bosom of much perilous stuff'. All the grudges which he had harboured for years, against Fr. Beauclerk, against John Holden, against Trevor Haddon, against the Scots College and its students, against the author of the Aberdeen attack, against his superiors in the Church, were, in and by this book, paid off in full. He rose refreshed, like a sinner after absolution, ready, though he did not realize it, for another revolution of the wheel of his torment. For, though he was relieved, the relief could not be lasting. In all human lives there is a recurring pattern, sometimes difficult to perceive, sometimes on the surface; and the pattern is drawn from within. By the end of these pages, Rolfe's pattern will, I hope, be sufficiently clear, if it is not so already. This is not the place for a final diagnosis of his fascinating, distorted temperament; nor need we at this point speculate as to whether or not any lasting remedy could have been found for the inward cause of his woes. For the moment, like the cat which chews grass, he had found his own cure: time was to restore his malady, and plunge him into fresh circumstances of painful friendship and strange unhappy adventures. It must be remembered, however, that, as I have shown in my first chapter, Rolfe did far more, in *Hadrian*, than pay off old scores. He expressed *himself* in that haunted book; and his Self was something beyond the ungrateful beneficiary that so many, in daily life, found him to be, something beyond the unscrupulous, egocentric, homosexual pretender of Aberdeen, Holywell, and Rome. There is greatness, genius, the true note of a vital and unique personality expressed in its intense pages. Those who feel disposed to sentence and dismiss him should re-read the prayer of his *Prooimion* before signing judgement.

*   *   *

I knew, as I have said, the answer to half that problem which had perplexed me when I first read *Hadrian* and Millard's letters—how Rolfe's masterpiece came to be written, and what manner of man its author was; but the rest still waited for solution—what had happened to the lost manuscripts, what train of chances took Rolfe to his death in Venice. The Quest continued.

Rolfe's relatives are not scarified with his acquaintances in *Hadrian*. Instead, he sought and reached a reconciliation. There seemed no impediment to his *vita nuova*, which opened auspiciously when his book found a publisher within a month of its completion. 'This is Fr. Rolfe's first work', he wrote to his brother; and this time he did not sell his book outright. The contract provided a royalty basis whereby the author was to receive a shilling for every copy sold after the first six hundred; and 'I have every reason to believe that Chatto and Windus are a different class of publisher to Lane and Richards', he grimly wrote, little suspecting that his new bargain was to work out even more badly than those he had previously made. But this time at least he did not permit himself the extravagant hopes which he had attached to his earlier books. 'At present I am undergoing the depression which always follows publication', he wrote to Herbert Rolfe. 'A piece of Me has been taken from me. I have the limpness of a brand-new mother. After the usual interval, Nature will enable me to replace what I have exuded. But, for a week, you may think of me as a piece of thread.' 'I look upon the whole thing as a toss-up', he adds. 'I did not go out of my way to read reviews of my other books: and knowing what I know now (from practical experience) of reviewing and of the intelligence as well as of the *bona fides* of reviewers, I am not going to seek them or worry about them or let myself be influenced by them now. I know that I have done my best; and, if that is not good enough, I'll try again.'

The one contemporary critic who gave Rolfe's master-piece its due was Henry Murray. 'This is a book for which I think it safe to predict a fairly large measure of success', he wrote, with, alas, unjustified hopefulness. 'Fr. Rolfe's book . . . is dazzlingly clever in parts, and almost consistently admirable throughout.' He gave long quotations to display the qualities of his discovery, and praised the style and the plot with courage and discernment. But despite his praises, and those of a few others, *Hadrian* is still waiting for its proper applause, and place in literature. Fr. Martindale, of that Society of Jesus which Rolfe so often feared, observes of it that 'Over much of it plays the light of a quite uncanny beauty; its crackle of epigram is continual; an under-current of white-hot personal passion is at all times discernible.' My own impression has been given in the first chapter. Another who has been dazzled by its glow is D. H. Lawrence, who wrote: 'The book remains a clear and definite book of our epoch, not to be swept aside. If it is the book of a demon, as [Rolfe's] contemporaries said, it is the book of a man demon, not of a mere poseur. And if some of it is caviare, at least it came out of the belly of a live fish.'

*   *   *

Rolfe believed devoutly in his Guardian Angel; but that overworked spirit proved inefficient to protect his protégé from new mischances. In the autumn of 1903, while finishing *Hadrian*, 'Fr. Rolfe' came into touch, by means of an advertisement, with a man whom he subsequently described as 'an obese magenta colonel of militia with a black-stubbed moustache and a Welsh-tongued proposition', Colonel Owen Thomas, subsequently Brigadier-General Sir Owen Thomas, M.P. Col. Thomas, who had served with distinction in the Boer War, was an expert adviser of the Rhodes Trustees. In that capacity he had collected, at substantial expense, a mass of evidence concerning pastoral and agricultural prospects in Rhodesia, which he was desirous of making into a report to be submitted, first to the Trustees of the Rhodes Estate, and subsequently, in book form, to the public. Unfortunately the Colonel had no gift for writing; so he sought the help of some trained hand to present his facts in acceptable shape. Rolfe seemed just the man needed; and terms were made. Not, however, precise terms. Doubtless the matter was left open until events showed how much Rolfe would be required to do. What his share of the labour actually was cannot now be discovered, but with his aid the Report was delivered, and in due course the book was published. The latter certainly bears in many places the stigmata of Rolfe's eccentric style; according to his claim he had expanded the Colonel's notes from a twenty-page pamphlet to a five-hundred-page volume. At all events, for his work, whatever it was (it certainly seems to have occupied most of eight months), he was in the end offered by Col. Thomas a sum which, coupled with previous payments, made the not very grand total of £50. However much or little Rolfe had expected from *Hadrian*, his hopes in respect of the connection with Col. Thomas were very, if vaguely, high, and this time his anger was not to be satisfied with the writing of sarcastic letters. The 'new life' demanded something more to appease his disappointment; and on the advice and introduction of the literary agent, Pinker, the affair was placed in the hands of a substantial firm of lawyers.

It was my good fortune to make the personal acquaintance of the solicitor who acted for 'Fr. Rolfe' in the ensuing complications. Mr. Churton Taylor remembered the case well: he had good cause. The most sedate men may be inflamed by certain provocations; the most cautious sometimes tempted into speculation. The latter fate befell Mr. Taylor when he met Rolfe, who must have been in his most persuasive mood on the fateful afternoon when he called to set out his claim, for the careful lawyer of Lincoln's Inn Fields was carried off his feet by the shabby stranger, the queerest man he had ever met. During nearly two hours he listened to the story of Rolfe's wrongs and hopes, his false friends and the wonderful books he could write if once he had peace and his deserts. *Hadrian*, and the more impressive reviews of it, were produced as evidence, together with the great Borgia roll, which, in appearance at least, was very valuable. What Rolfe needed, he explained, was a business agent who would receive his royalties and administer his affairs, giving him in return a small allowance to keep him free from worry while working. It may seem incredible, but after a few further meetings Rolfe secured a promise that not only would Mr. Taylor fight the case against Col. Thomas unprovided with funds, but also that he would make his client the necessary allowance to live on until the action was decided. Eloquence for once met its reward; or perhaps the Guardian Angel was in better mood that day.

But even Mr. Taylor's interest in the aggrieved man of letters could not blind him to the uncertain issue of his suit, and at Rolfe's suggestion he accepted, as security for costs and the money he was to advance, an assignment of *Hadrian*, and certain other unpublished or unfinished works, including that priest's diary shown to Mr. Haddon, and the translation of Meleager (of which last, however, Rolfe only claimed to be a third proprietor).

The writ was issued on August 6, 1904, and 'the plaintiff claims from the defendant as the balance of remuneration due to him for literary work and labour' the sum of £999 9s. 6d., made up for the most part by 'say 1050 hours at 10s. 6d. an hour' in writing and revising *Agricultural and Pastoral Prospects in South Africa,* Col. Thomas's book. Here again, as in the dispute with Fr. Beauclerk at Holywell, and in the correspondence with Grant Richards, I could not help noticing how Rolfe destroyed whatever grounds for sympathy he may have had by the extravagance of his claim. Not content, indeed, with asking nearly a thousand pounds for his literary labours, he also stated that 'Previous to October 1903 the plaintiff had, after spending a considerable amount of time and trouble thereon, prepared a skeleton history of the Borgia family in the form of an annotated genealogical tree . . . and in consideration that the plaintiff would neglect his own work and continue to do the work and labour [for which claim had already been made] the defendant . . . verbally promised and undertook that he would procure a purchaser . . . at a price which should yield the plaintiff not less than £2000 net'!!!—which sum the optimistic Rolfe also sued for in addition to his fee for writing the book!

However, whether Rolfe won or lost his case, he seemed to be a certain gainer, since even if the verdict went against him he could hardly be worse off than he was before the starting of the action; and meanwhile, pending the hearing, he was to be supported with funds on the security of books which, so far, had proved neither a gold-mine nor even a copper-mine to their indigent author. Rolfe had been lucky in his solicitor, but his luck went even further. Delay after delay prolonged the period of his action. Month followed month, and still the case was not listed for hearing. And when it was, Col. Thomas, a busy man and traveller, was forced to ask for an adjournment. It really seemed as though that care-free interval for which Rolfe had so long sighed, during which he would be able to write masterpieces untroubled by money worries, had unexpectedly been vouchsafed.

The opening of the year 1905 found him still enjoying the novel experience of a regular income; for his case still hung fire, and his allowance continued. In the peaceful interregnum so strangely secured, he was neither idle nor unhappy; he began to write a new book, and to make fresh friends. The new book, embodying a theme originally suggested by Temple Scott, was vividly described in a long letter to Herbert Rolfe:

St. Alphege, Broadstairs,
Isle of Thanet

xv Mar. 1905

Dear H:

I am not quite well. Tuning out of order: tongue like a pole-cat's pelt. Worry always affects me this way. Consequently I'm taking a morning easy; and here's a letter for you. I shall be better after lunch.

I always date my letters. Life is too short to date mere notes. *Don Tarquinio* is the book which I shewed you at Xmas. It purports to be written by Tarquinio Santacroce, a handsome daredevil young Roman Patrician, a bandit because the House of Santacroce was put under the Great Ban by Xystus IIII 12 years before. It describes every single thing which he did, on what he calls his Fortunate Day in March 1495, when he was living secretly in Rome under the protection of Cardinal Prince Ippolito d' Este (aet. 17 and a connoisseur of wrestlers, runners, acrobats, and other specimens of human physique). During these 24 hours, he made friends with Lucrezia Borgia and her brother Giaffredo; ran 26 miles, disguised, with a cypher message printed on his back, for Cæsar (called) Borgia (by which means the latter was enabled to escape from King Charles VIII of France, who held him as hostage); married Hersilia Manfredi; and won so much favour from Pope Alexander VI (Borgia) that His Holiness magnificently removed the Great Ban from Santacroce: with other incidents too numerous to mention. You read something of the plot in a sketch which I made for a play some months ago. I wrote this book in two ways. First, as the work of Don Tarquinio himself, saying in a preface that it was all nonsense to allege that the Fifteenth and the Twentieth Century had no Common Denominator and therefore couldn't speak to each other: because they have a C.D. in the shape of Human Nature. This version was very quaint in style: so quaint indeed, and besides so full of unique and hitherto unknown historical detail, that your perspicacious critic is not unlikely to discover an extremely fine mare's nest and proclaim that my so-called romance is nothing more nor less than a very valuable genuine historical document. But, secondly, I did the book as though I had Don Tarquinio's holograph before me; and, because 'the Fifteenth Century cannot possibly speak to the Twentieth', I have posed as an entirely modern rather slangy story-teller and have told the tale in my own words with just as many quotations from the 'original holograph' as suffice to give a verisimilitude. In this version, of course, I've had the opportunity of popping comments and reflections from the Twentieth Century point of view, which to my mind help the story and add piquancy. Both versions, however, are distinctly funny as well as instructive; and I make haste to assure you that they're only instructive in so far as that they deal with a kind of people, circumstances, mode of life and thought, never really described before. And I've done my describing in broad masterly touches with just enough detail to make the thing shine: so that, if my readers want to learn, they can learn, but if not they'll be amused and interested anyhow. And now comes the funny part of the business. It was the MS. of the antique version which I sent first to Chatto, keeping the modern one up my sleeve in case the first didn't please. But it did, on sight! They promptly offered to issue it on similar terms to the *Hadrian,* but the royalty to become due after sale of 500 instead of 600. I said thanks, sharp; and said that perhaps they would like to choose which of the two versions seemed most likely, in their judgment, to succeed.

And I plumped the second (and better, say I) MS. upon them.
They silkily thanked me for my courtesy; and that's how things
stand at this moment. I am rather curious to know which
they will choose.

But what I wish to remark is:— Here you have another example of the truth of my perennially-shouted contention that, when
I am in a position to write at ease, to produce my MS. in proper
form (i.e. beautifully written, on fine paper, and bound in white
buckram with one of my gorgeous black-and-white designs
drawn by my own hand on the cover) to send my so properly-
formed MS. about in proper sumptuous fashion,—I never yet
have failed to dispose of it myself at once. And I argue that the
only way to succeed is to keep on doing this, without intermission, until the cumulative effect of my work makes publishers
ask me for books.

I told you that I've started four new books: *The King of the
Wood* (a romance of Diana's grove at Nemi, which I know by
heart, where the priest (Rex Nemorensis or Flamen Dianæ) *had*
to be a runaway slave, to pick the Golden Bough (mistletoe)
from the oak in the sacred grove and to slay his predecessor);
Duchess Attendolo (the amazing courtship of Duchess Sforza and
her four legal marriages within one month to the Duke her
husband); *Rose's Records,* and *Ivory, Apes and Peacocks* (successors
to *Hadrian*).

I'm still in correspondence with Father Beauclerk (the most
congenitally dishonest and stupid man God ever made) and with
Father R. H. Benson (who has introduced another Catholic
called Eustace Virgo, who says that he not only goes all the way
with me but would rather see me Pope than even Hadrian the
Seventh!) But all these people are Catholics; and I never yet met
an honest one. The nearer you get to the Church, the more
noisome becomes the stench. You may stifle it with incense: just
as you may other stenches with Condy. But it's always there and
always some filthy porcheria or other. However if any of these
devils think that they quietly can confuse and delay and evade
and make of none effect, they'll find themselves mistaken. I am
very sweet and suave with them, but quite inexorable, and I

give them as much information as they deserve and plenty of
food for thought. It's horrid. Isn't it? I tell you because you've
got horse-sense. And yet, if I were not Catholic, I shouldn't be
anything at all. I can't explain. It's strange; and, therefore, true.
. . . Love to you all

                              Your affectionate brother

                                            Freddy

Though the four books which Rolfe mentions in this
letter as 'started' were lost or left unfinished, *Don Tarquinio*
did appear in print in the later part of 1905. On the title-
page it is styled *A Kataleptic Phantasmatic Romance;* and the
Prologue claims it to be a transcription of an original manuscript written by Don Tarquinio Santacroce, *circa* 1523–27,
for the edification of his son Prospero, 'the leisurely effort
of a man of unbounded energy anxious to express himself'.
The Don is supposed to write in a macaronic mixture of
Italian, Greek, and Latin; but the pretended translation does
not keep closely to the pedantic form of its mock-original;
to that extent it differs from *Don Renato* in Mr. Haddon's
recollection of it.

Truth is defined in the first chapter as 'that which every
man may acquire from the apprehensive nature of perfectly
cultivated senses'; history is the privilege of eye-witnesses.
Hence the Don's self-imposed task of recording his 'fortunate day', on which he secured release for his family
from the excommunication imposed on its members as a
punishment for murder.

Don Tarquinio cannot be called an example of learning
lightly borne, for Rolfe's hardly-won knowledge protrudes
from many pages in irritating footnotes; but these are flies
in the amber of a highly individual style and story, which
grows in attractiveness when it is re-examined. As an exercise in skill in writing—in saying, that is, only what one
wants to say—it might serve as a model; as also in its unsenti-
mental flavour of a period. And this 'Phantasmatic' romance
has the merit of being a picture apprehended by 'perfectly

cultivated senses'. Fr. Rolfe revels in the visible. 'Pages, in liveries resembling vermilion skins from toe to throat and wrist, bearing armorials on their tabards, displayed at the prow the double-cross, golden, and the high Estense gonfalon'. 'Youngsters, whose hair glittered like cocoons in candlelight, joined our progress.' Cardinal Ippolito d' Este purchases two acrobats yellow of skin as 'dew-kissed pumpkins gleaming in the sunlight'. In all ways the physical is emphasized. The colour of the flesh of Indian oarsmen 'resembled the colour of a field of ripe wheat when some delicate zephyr sways the stems in the sun, not more than half-revealing poppies: but their eyes were like pools of ink, fathomless, upon glittering mother-o'-pearl, very beautiful, and quite unintellectual'. The heroine's sea-blue robe is girdled by great cats'-eyes set in gold. After swimming, the hero is anointed in pure oil of olives in which violets have been macerated, and eats cocks'-combs on lettuce and quails farced with figs. The candle-reflections in the waxed oaken panels of floor and roof resembled golden stars in a brown sea. An impertinent page is said to have the 'face of a beautiful white fiend framed in a web of buttercup-coloured hair'.

What Herbert Rolfe's opinion was of this highly coloured romance of the flesh, which his brother dedicated to him, is not recorded; but the critics were reasonably appreciative of its many merits. 'An extravagant wealth of quaint conceit and irony.' 'A brilliant *tour de force* [which] might have come out of Boccaccio.' 'A novel of exceptional interest and dramatic power'. 'Altogether remarkable mastery over words.' 'The vivid verbal brilliance of the book is wonderful'. These cuttings were carefully sent by the exultant author to Mr. Churton Taylor. That anonymous writer in *The Times* mentioned in my second chapter gives higher and more reasoned praise. '[Rolfe's] desire to own a sumptuous vocabulary not degraded by vulgar use was characteristic. He loved magnificence purged from meretriciousness; and that ideal he realized in the neglected little masterpiece *Don Tarquinio,* in which the triple flame of the Renascence, bodily, intellectual and spiritual, burns with a cruel and yet magnanimous incandescence. Who can forget the culminating vision of the great Borgia Pope opening the cornucopia of his clemency with the gesture of Jove in a tiara, and withdrawing to his afternoon nap "like the lifegiving sun, who sinketh glorious, golden to his rest in the sea"?'

XIII

THE HAPPY INTERVAL

THE reader will perhaps remember that at the outset of my Quest a Mr. Pirie-Gordon had written offering to call for the purpose of talking about Baron Corvo. By a series of mischances, a long period passed before a date suitable to both of us could be arranged. But at last we met.

Was it, perhaps, his spidery, small writing that led me to expect a trim, precise, small man? My caller proved, on the contrary, a burly six-footer, with the shoulders of an athlete and the complexion of a countryman. I put his age at forty-five. He seemed preoccupied by an interior joke, which I found to derive from entertainment provoked by my unexpected lack of years (I was in the middle twenties at the time of these events) and from the resuscitation of Rolfe. I could hardly believe my ears when, in reply to my first question, 'Did you know Corvo personally?', my visitor replied 'I did indeed: I am Caliban, the last of his collaborators'. The consequence may be imagined: we talked for hours. Mr. Pirie-Gordon was the missing link between Rolfe's middle and his later years. He told me without bitterness of the strange way in which Baron Corvo had repaid the hospitality and help which the Pirie-Gordon family had been glad to give. He gave me an outline of Rolfe's intimacy with Robert Hugh Benson and its result. He explained how Fr. Rolfe had become a resident in Venice and never returned. And he left with me a bundle of Rolfe's letters, surpassing in interest any I had yet seen save the first volume belonging to Millard. With a spontaneity that I saw was characteristic, Mr. Pirie-Gordon declared that these letters should, in the fullness of time, be bequeathed to me.

In subsequent interviews, and by the study of the correspondence left for my inspection, I was able to piece the story together, to watch another rotation of that wheel to which Rolfe was bound.

The first meeting between Rolfe and Pirie-Gordon took place at Oxford late one night in the summer of 1906. Fr. Rolfe had secured a congenial occupation, and was staying at Jesus College, helping his former Grantham headmaster, Dr. Hardy, to whom he was acting as secretary. (Shortly before Dr. Hardy's death he told Shane Leslie: 'I liked and appreciated Rolfe's very attractive personality. In spite of his little foibles I always found him a good and loyal friend, and he was distinctly *persona grata* in my family. I sometimes worked him pretty hard. In the two years when I was Greats examiner he read papers to me for six or seven hours a day for more than two months on end.' On the subject of Rolfe's Latin scholarship it is worth noting that at this time, with Dr. Hardy's help, he wrote a long Ciceronian indictment of contemporary Catholics which was forwarded to Pope Leo XIII.)

Pirie-Gordon was a member of Magdalen, keeping a post-graduate year devoted to historical study. Enthusiastic for literature, the young man had read with admiration *Chronicles of the House of Borgia;* and when he learned that its author, now called Fr. Rolfe, was working in Jesus, paid a surprise visit to his rooms. For all Rolfe's desire to avoid notice, he was very willing to make amusing acquaintances; he did not rebuff this chance-sent admirer; soon a close friendship sprang up between the two. There was much to draw them together. Pirie-Gordon was, for a young man, wealthy; he was interested in Rolfe's favourite fifteenth century; had just returned from a long visit to Florence, Rome, South Italy, North Africa, and Spain. More than that, he had to a high degree the young man's love of fine clothes: his vast wardrobe much impressed the impecunious author, who had known what it was to wear the same garments winter and summer alike.

Above all, Pirie-Gordon had a great plan, very fascinating to the tired literary wanderer, for the furthering of which he eagerly invited Rolfe's cooperation.

This ambitious project was the founding of a secular semi-monastic order which, by joint studies, should, in a spirit of disinterestedness, add to the learning of the world. Nothing could have tallied more nearly with Rolfe's desires, and he entered with enthusiasm into the details of this substitute for priesthood. The fires of his artistic ambition flickered anew, and he set to work to design banners, emblems and devices for the Order. Before the newly-established friendship was a month old, Pirie-Gordon, with that spontaneity which I had noticed as surviving in him, impetuously urged Rolfe to spend a holiday in his father's house in Wales. Rolfe very naturally hesitated at returning to that country of misfortune, and urged that he had no clothes for country-house visits; but his young friend would brook no denial, and prevailed upon his mother to second the invitation in a flattering letter. After a week of indecision Rolfe assented; and so he who (as he sometimes boasted) had been the inmate of a Welsh workhouse, left Oxford to be entertained by the magisterial owner of Gwernvale.

Unexpectedly, he made a good impression on the Pirie-Gordons. It was not simply that he was the son's friend, or that in the flush of his pleasure at being comfortably housed he offered tactful phrases: he was liked for his own sake, and made more welcome than such a chance-comer could have expected. In this congenial atmosphere Rolfe expanded, and confided his hopes and troubles to his host. He told, more or less, the picturesque story of his life: his clerical ambitions, the unfair treatment which had barred him from the priesthood, the persecution of his Catholic enemies, the deceitful behaviour of Col. Thomas. He told of his still undecided lawsuit, and the meagre salary from Dr. Hardy on which he lived. The Pirie-Gordons, who admired his books, were touched by his confidences, and sympathized with his woes. Within a week he was 'Hadrian' to the entire family.

Perhaps Rolfe was never happier than during that summer month of his first stay in Gwernvale. Despite the pretended difficulty about clothes, his luggage included a mole-coloured velvet dinner jacket, so that he was able to appear as a spruce if mysterious figure at the dinner parties given by the Pirie-Gordons and their neighbours. At these he was a great success. He had a flow of conversation on unusual subjects which astonished all his listeners. One of his topics centred round a strange ring on his right hand, in which a small spur was mounted on a bezel. This, he explained, was for the purpose of protecting himself from kidnapping attempts, and he wore it in consequence of an assault on his person made years before by the Jesuits. When they essayed, as he fully expected, a further abduction, he would sweep with his armed hand at the brow of his assailant. A line would thus be scored in the flesh which would draw blood; and his blinded enemy (blinded by the dripping blood) would be at the mercy of the intended victim. This ring, and his others, some of which he wore strung round his neck, were made of silver; and at night they were carefully placed in powdered sulphur to preserve the right shade of tarnished darkness. He asserted, also, that he understood in part the language of the cats; and events so far bore out his claim that when, in the moonlight, he muttered his incantations on the lawn, strange cats as well as those of the household abandoned their prowls to rub purringly against his legs.

The days were hardly less delightful. They were spent, for the most part, in driving about the countryside, or in bathing in the river Usk, or in sunbathing in a walled orchard while revising the Rule of that projected Order, which finally took shape thus:

In the belief that it is desirable to revive the virtues of that period of the World's history commonly called the Middle Ages, and to practise them, in the hope that We may thereby the better pursue wisdom; and being convinced that the practice of the Catholic Faith is compatible with the pursuit of Wisdom as comprised in the human Letters and Arts; and

Being persuaded that some Individuals can aspire to Wisdom the better when associated with other Individuals having similar desires and abilities;

Therefore, We the Founders, having in Our Minds the Mediæval Ideal of a Monastic Military Order devoted to God-service,—independent inasmuch as it tolerates no interference,—but law abiding, inasmuch as it submits to the supremacy of the Monarch in whose Dominions it is located, Do Now and Hereby Institute and Found

THE ORDER OF SANCTISSIMA SOPHIA

constituted, organised and devoted in the manner of the Middle Ages to God-service in the pursuit of Wisdom by way of the Human Letters and Arts.

And to this end We intend Ourselves to provide an Establishment or Establishments where the Rule of this Our Order shall displace the existing Laws of the Land, acquiring an Island, or other Territory, over which this Our Order may exercise such supremacy as shall be necessary for the achievement of its Object.

And until such time when this may be accomplished, We intend Ourselves to maintain a convenient centre wherein the Rule of this Our Order may be prosecuted so far as is consistent with Our Religious obligations and Our loyalty to the Reigning Monarch; and We place this Our Order under the protection of the Ever Blessed and Most Glorious Trinity, of Saint Mary the Virgin, of Saint Peter the Apostle, and of Saint George the Patron of Chivalry.

Over and beyond these general objects, an elaborate scheme of government for the Order was worked out in detail. Beautiful notepaper, with headings designed by Rolfe, was printed, and orders given for a special dress, designed by Pirie-Gordon. Pending the acquisition of the desired island, Gwernvale was settled on as temporary headquarters.

But other, and more practical, plans were made by the two friends. Young Pirie-Gordon had made and laid by various abortive beginnings of books; and these, in an expansive moment, he showed to Rolfe. They included a vague romance, conceived at Harrow, of a modern man who was to relive his past, in which he was to identify himself with Odysseus; and an unsuccessful Arnold Prize essay on the life and times of Innocent the Great. Both of these beginnings were pronounced by Rolfe to have elements of excellence; and he half-hinted, half-proposed collaboration. The Pirie-Gordons were delighted at the thought that their son's vague projects might be given a useful form; Harry himself, like all beginners in letters, burned for print. Work was begun on both these books, and also on a third, more remarkable than either, a reconstruction of history 'as it ought to have been, and easily might have been, but in fact was not'. The name of this romance, I learned with the prospective joy of a discoverer, was *Hubert's Arthur!* Rolfe, I learned further, was left to do the major part of it, while Pirie-Gordon made himself mainly responsible for the re-incarnation story (called *The Weird of the Wanderer*) and, almost entirely, for the study of Innocent, which he had written originally in Rome and Amalfi for the Arnold Prize.

Months passed by. Rolfe returned to Oxford, still as temporary secretary to Dr. Hardy; Pirie-Gordon toured abroad; the collaboration was continued by post; the lawsuit was postponed once more.

But there is an end to all things, even to the law's delays. After more than two years, the action against Col. Thomas was heard in the King's Bench Court on December 17, 1906, and following a brief hearing, in which Rolfe was cross-examined severely concerning his past life, and broke down, a verdict was given for the defendant on all points with costs.

I feel exactly as though I had been beaten with beetroots and mangold wurzels all over, especially on my face, neck and hands

the unsuccessful litigant wrote to his friends,

quite sore and bruised by the court full of eyes which banged on me all Wednesday. It appears to me that I was a great fool. Not such a fool as my advisers: but a fool. Several things were omitted which ought to have been put in:—there were some of Thomas's 'rough drafts' which, when compared with my MS. and the printed book, would have shewed *How* MUCH of the work was his and how much mine—that 'Schedule' ought to have been shewn, to prove what the original £25 Report was to have been and how the Book grew out of it. . . .

And so on. That unsuccessful lawsuit was Rolfe's Moscow, though he did not know it.

*   *   *

Fr. Rolfe returned to Oxford, not yet dispirited. And, since man must rest his hopes on something, he began to have hopes of *Hubert's Arthur*.

(It) is an awful piece of work (he wrote). But it will be unlike any book ever written. And it will pay. I go on very slowly and keep on rewriting. I'm just beginning to know the people in it: but I alter so radically as the thing grows that I shan't let it be seen till it's done. And I am not going to do any one single thing beside till it is done. Mark me well.

Some of his postcards are very funny:

Have you any objection to Lady Maud de Braose being shut up in a dungeon, and fed with the tails of haddocks, two a day, till she, saltish, perishes of pure displeasure? They can sing her requiem on the eleventh day.

Of Oxford itself (which by this time he must have come to know better than any other city) he wrote to another correspondent:

This Examination (the Honour School of Literæ Humaniores) is an experience. We are doing Ancient History, Logick, Roman History, Translation. The papers are perfectly appalling. The vilest, vulgarest scripts, the silliest spelling, infinitives split to the midriff. I asked Hardy what was to be done with these crimes against fair English, and he answered sedately, 'Pass them over with silent contempt'.

I find that silent system admirable altogether.

This is why.

Whatever is of good, a man must get not from a teacher, but from his own toil.

The man who wants to write good English will, ultimately, write good English, and his work will have the supreme merit of being rare.

So this mighty Alma Mater of Oxford does well not to teach the preservation of unsplit infinitives. She teaches you how to teach yourself, and that is all, and all is everything, and there is nothing more.

But what a lovely place it is. I call it the City of Eternal Youth. All that is not life is gray and ancient, gracious colleges, gardens and the sunny river. And everywhere is musick, antiphony and song. Do you know the quality of voice which I call virgin-bass? The resonant reticent bass of the boy of twenty wearing his maidenhead for one day more? I heard that last Tuesday and recorded a new emotion. Its exceeding rarity, its evanishing bloom is as precious as carved chrusoprase. I could live here very well and do good work in the divine peace.

The friendship continued. In the following Easter, Rolfe visited Gwernvale again. His appointment with Hardy had ended, and as he had nowhere to go, he was invited to remain as a more or less permanent guest. The 'family' was abroad, travelling; and when Harry returned to Oxford, Rolfe was left alone, with the servants, as deputy master of the house. *Innocent the Great* was finished. Was Rolfe slightly vexed when Messrs. Longmans, Green and Co. accepted his young protégé's book without demur? He consoled himself, rather unkindly, by christening Pirie-Gordon 'Caliban', in reference to that passage in *The Tempest* when Prospero says:

> . . . I pitied thee,
> Took pains to make thee speak, taught thee each hour
> One thing or other: when thou didst not (savage)
> Know thine own meaning, but wouldst gabble like
> A thing most brutish, I informed thy purposes
> With words.

His envy might almost be pardoned, for publishers were once more showing an unaccountable (so he reasonably thought it) indifference to his work. Even Mr. Grant Richards (to whom he had once promised 'ruthless and persequent enmity') was approached, yet missed his chance:

Dear Mr. Grant Richards:

If you should wish to have a book or books of mine, I do hope that you will not hesitate about asking. I should be glad indeed to repeat my last offer to you, if I knew that you desired it. Pray do not misunderstand me any more. I mean you nothing but well.

Faithfully yours

Fr. Rolfe

and in a later letter this olive branch was followed up:

I have the typescript of two novels, and the manuscript of a poetry-book, ready for the printer; and I shall have two more novels ready in the course of this year. They are at the disposal of any publisher (and I feel that Fate would do admirably and suitably in making you mine) who would give me a 15 per cent royalty on the first thousand, and a rising royalty thereafter.

I was able to discover what these works offered to Mr. Richards were, from a letter that Rolfe wrote to Mrs. Pirie-Gordon:

I have on my table waiting for publication *The Songs of Meleagros of Gadara,* Greek and English, the only complete collection in the world, *Reviews of Unwritten Books,* a series of 24 witty, learned, but quite easily understood essays on such delightful subjects as Cæsar's *Life of Napoleon,* a novel about Don Tarquinio's relations called *Don Renato* (or, *An Ideal Content*), and a modern novel about friendship and literary life called *Nicholas Crabbe* (or, *The One and the Many*).

Not a single one of those books was known to survive, at that period of my inquiry. It is certainly surprising that no publisher should have accepted them, for the terms which Rolfe proposed were not onerous, while his subjects and treatment (as I hope to prove to the reader's satisfaction) were far more interesting than those of most of the books which find their way into print. But luck, and the times, were against him.

Fortune had stood him in good stead, however, and found him good friends, in the Pirie-Gordons. All through the year he remained at Gwernvale. 'Here I am, living comfortably (it is true) on the hospitality of friends, writing myself blind, but not earning a penny so far', he wrote to his mother. 'Not earning a penny' was the literal truth. No royalties had accrued from *Hadrian the Seventh* or *Don Tarquinio,* and as Mr. Taylor began to be anxious about his investment, Rolfe began to be anxious about his future. He was nearing fifty. Early in 1908 he wrote from Gwernvale a long letter to Mrs. Pirie-Gordon, who was still abroad:

Dear Mrs. Pirie-Gordon:

Let me first wish you a happier New Year; and I do that from the bottom of my heart. Next, the only reason why I have not written yet to thank you for your Christmas present is that I have been waiting from day to day for news of a certain kind to send you. None has come; and I cannot wait any longer. I cannot tell you how profoundly moved I was by your gift, the silver ankh. I instantly perceived how you, and Harry, must have thought hard till you thought my thoughts. The evidence was of many kinds, the ankh itself, the size, the metal, AND above all the adornment of it, as never an ankh has been adorned before, with my sign of the crab, and my moon, and my cross-potent-elongate, all of which make it my very very own. Such interest in ME, shown by such an exactly intimate knowledge of my secret and not more than half-formed desire and taste, has never been shewn before. The effect is almost to strike me dumb. Thank you, I do: but thanks express but feebly what I feel.

On the top of the ankh came Japanese silk handkerchiefs from Miss Handley, embroidered in red with my own R. and label. And again I am stricken dumb.

And all this has made me begin to notice the hundred thousand ways, little and large, in which you all watch my words for indications of my tastes and wants in order that you may gratify them. Do you know that even a special dish of angelica was provided for my Christmas dessert?

And I can do nothing adequate in return. That makes these favours hard to bear. But what makes it harder still is the knowledge that you dear kind souls, *who have given me so long the hospitality which not a single Catholic would dream of giving,* are adding to my burdens all unconsciously. You are giving me lovely things which I like so much that it will be a most bitter wrench to me to part from them. And I believe that there is nothing else before me but to part from everything. And I know that my nature will make me fight and struggle to retain; and as each thing is torn from me I shall have a pang each time. Pray then make it *easier* and not harder by not planting in me seeds which circumstances are going to tear up by their tender roots. This is not ingratitude by any means, but the truest gratitude: for, now that I know how eager you are to please me, I can freely tell you how to please me better. So I say, do not give me luxuries at all which it will hurt me to lose, and help me to live so that I have nothing which can be taken from me.

. . . I have asked Mr. Taylor to advance me something to live on while I go on writing. If he had done so, I should have asked you to take me into your family, letting me contribute what I have to the common fund, until by uninterrupted work I could earn enough to discharge my obligations. I should beg you to let me live here, a great deal more simply than I do now, not interfering, nor even considered, a help and not a hindrance, left entirely to myself to do my work. If this could have been done, I am quite convinced that I could make good and permanent headway. But Taylor, though he has not definitely refused, has said nothing for a fortnight, and hope deferred has made me sick. I really am tired of it all. I have so many really good irons in the fire; and now that I have to leave them I don't feel a bit like beginning this fearful twenty years all over again. Besides, I can't even if I would. There is no one else who cares. And it is no good. So I am just drifting now until one thing or another happens.

But, whether anything happens or not, do please believe me that I am most thankful to you three and to Miss Handley for hospitality, generosity, forbearance, and the very truest friendship. You have made me feel no alien while I am here.

Yes: now that I have written it down I am in love with the idea, very much in love, for it seems like a clear light on a dark path: but yet never so much in love that I could persist in liking it if you (any of you) were to say that you didn't. Of course it's easy to see that it would make things jolly easy for me; and on that account it's selfish. I should have a certain and most pleasant home among the dearest people, who looked upon me as one of the family, joyful with their ups and suffering with their downs; and at present (as you're perfectly aware) I haven't got anybody really particular to care for and to care for me. And you have perhaps perceived that I *positively fester with unused and unusual human sympathy*. And of course I could go on writing like a house on fire with such certainty and such interest behind me. And if I did go on writing, and *persistently persevering at the various schemes begun,* OF COURSE I am bound to succeed rather sooner than later. And as for my Rites—I walked to Aber and back fasting, but for an orange returning, on Christmas day—I really would regularize my life. I really would scratch a bicycle from somewhere, learn to ride, and go to Mass on Sundays and holidays. How lovely it would be to be able to do that regularly without having anything at all to do with Roman Catholics. But it is not entirely selfish. If it had been that, I don't think I should have mentioned it, or indeed allowed it to occupy my mind at all. You know I really could make myself useful, and (eventually) offer (not an equivalent for the kindness which took pity on a drifter but) an equivalent for the expense involved. You see, I only want one thing in the world. And that I may not have. So I am free from what is called Ambition. I am just too old and too tired to care for Fame. The real fun, which I enjoy, is moving others. I infinitely prefer the background for my own performances. There is more room there for real gymnastics than on the top where youngsters sweat and struggle for public applause. Oh yes: I could be a jolly good deal more useful in the background as referee, as agent, as generally dependable person. Now you have thought me cold, have assured me of friendship. I presume on the latter to be suddenly quite hot. Does it please you? If Taylor will help, may I talk the business part over with Mr. Gordon with any hope of acceptance? Don't hesitate to say No. I thoroughly understand everything. But do say Yes if you possibly can.

Rolfe was not rebuffed. Mrs. Pirie-Gordon, who perhaps understood him better than he understood himself, replied that there was no need to consider 'business arrangements' or 'definite terms', since she was well content that he should remain at Gwernvale as a guest; and that in that contentment her family concurred. To the darker parts of his letter, which I quote elsewhere, she was equally tactful. There is no doubt that, had Rolfe so chosen, he might have continued to live with the Gordons for many years. But, on the horizon, there were looming new quarrels and a new friend: a combination which, within a few months, was to transport him to Italy, to Venice, and death: to the beginning of his last 'new life'. Before that, however, there befell him two minor pieces of good fortune, though he was not destined to benefit very deeply from either. The first was the acceptance, by a publisher, Francis Griffiths, of Maiden Lane, of two of those unpublished works for which he had so long sought a market: *Don Renato*, that priest's diary which so power-fully impressed Mr. Trevor Haddon, and the translation of Meleager produced in collaboration with Sholto Douglas. His second stroke of luck, based on the first, was a successful application for money to Mr. Taylor, who agreed to make a further advance of something over £100 (he had already provided £200 and the costs of the action), to be secured by these new publications and a life insurance. On the insurance proposal form the applicant gave his full name as Frederick William Serafino Austin Lewis Mary Rolfe, which he explained thus: 'I was baptized iii Jan. 1886 at St. Aloysius, Oxford, receiving the names "Frederick William". "Serafino" was conferred by Bishop Hugh Macdonald in Aberdeen Cathedral on my profession in the third order of St. Francis. "Austin Lewis Mary" were conferred by Cardinal Manning in the chapel of Archbishop's House, Westminster, at my confirmation'. Unluckily, these welcome gifts of fortune were out-weighed by his quarrel with Robert Hugh Benson, and its consequences.

XIV

ROBERT HUGH BENSON

ROLFE's friendship with Robert Hugh Benson requires a special chapter and a retrospect. It preceded that with Pirie-Gordon, for it began in February 1905, when Benson sent the author of *Hadrian the Seventh* a letter of enthusiastic praise:

Llandaff House, Cambridge

My dear Sir,

I hope you will allow a priest to tell you how grateful he is for *Hadrian the Seventh*. It is quite impossible to say how much pleasure it has given me in a hundred ways; nor now deeply I have been touched by it.

I have read it three times, and each time the impression has grown stronger of the deep loyal faith of it, its essential cleanness and its brilliance.

You say yourself that where there is no disagreement there is no activity (only you say it much better), and of course there are things that cannot appear the same to two people. It is possibly, though not certainly, impertinent of me to say that; but I hope you will forgive it for the sake of the very real admiration I feel.

You have taught me the value of loneliness, and many other lessons.

May I say how much I hope that you will be bringing out another book soon? Only I do entreat you to put the bitterness out of sight. (This also you must forgive.)

I believe you are in Italy now; I wonder if I can be of the slightest service to you here in England? I am fairly often in London; and should be delighted to do anything for which I was competent.

Believe me Yours sincerely

R. Hugh Benson

When Robert Hugh Benson wrote that letter he was thirty-four, eleven years younger than the unknown author whose work he praised. Benson had recognized much of himself, and more with which he sympathized, in the extraordinary day-dream of George Arthur Rose. His temperament corresponded at many points with Rolfe's. Both shared a feverish energy; both were converts to the Catholic faith; both possessed a many-sided interest in the arts, and a ready pen. But their lives had followed widely different courses. Rolfe, as the reader has seen, was an almost self-educated man who had painfully gathered a mass of intimate and much-prized learning, who had rubbed hard against the corners of the world, endured many privations, and constantly fulfilled the role of outcast. A streak of the sinister was mixed in his composition with many good qualities; he was nevertheless a man of strong original mind, with very various and developed talents. Benson, on the other hand, was descended from 'a sound stock of Yorkshire yeomanry', which had gathered, in the passage of generations, association with wealth and power, and an heredity of intellect. This developing stock had flowered in Hugh Benson's father, a man of imperial, perhaps imperious, nature, a great organizer, a fine scholar, who, after a career of unfaltering success, had been elevated to the Archbishopric of Canterbury. All his children became noticed or notable in the world. Arthur Christopher Benson, after an admired career as an Eton tutor, became Master of Magdalene College at Cambridge, and even better known as the editor of Queen Victoria's letters and author of numerous volumes of reflective, sentimental essays; Edward Frederick Benson starred a long career with a succession of successful novels; an authority on Victorian scandals and characters, he survived all his brethren. Margaret Benson was also a writer. Even Martin, the first born, who died during his schooldays, was marked at Winchester by 'extraordinary and precocious intelligence and spirituality'.

Robert Hugh, or Hugh, as he came to be called, was born

in 1871, the youngest son of this able family. At Eton he was distinguished by dramatic imagination, rapid temper, indifference to scholarship, and a peculiar personal vividness. After a happy career at Cambridge, where he practised mesmerism and other amusements, and aspired to the Indian Civil Service, by a characteristic swerve he became imbued with religious ardour, and took Holy Orders. Less than ten years later he felt the call of Rome. His changeover provoked much discussion and feeling in Anglican religious circles: naturally, since the convert was son to the Archbishop of Canterbury. Perhaps his most marked contradistinction from Rolfe was that whereas the latter had spent his life vainly seeking an audience, Hugh Benson at home, at school, at Cambridge, and in the Church had always commanded hearers. There was also this further difference: that Rolfe was a natural writer, who failed; while Benson, with no deep talent for letters, made a success of authorship.

In 1905, shortly after writing to Rolfe, 'Father Hugh' returned to Cambridge, where he was remembered as a student, this time to the Catholic Rectory. Very rapidly he became one of the most regarded personalities in the city. The decoration of his rooms caused much admiration (in the theological sense); so did his eloquent sermons; while his volatility, artistic temperament, and unusual attitudes of mind made him a centre among undergraduates—easily attracted by faith and by extremes. Certain Heads of Colleges feared his entry, as a walk with him was regarded as a step to Rome.

The friendship and correspondence with Rolfe that followed after Benson's reading of *Hadrian* was one of the most interesting events in the lives of either; Benson's biographer, Fr. Martindale, is frank as to the great influence Rolfe for a time exercised over the mind of the tempestuous convert. But, unfortunately, we cannot fully follow that friendship in its flow and ebb; for, when, availing myself of Mr. Leslie's introduction, I sought Fr. Martindale, he told me that all the papers he had consulted concerning

Hugh Benson had been returned, after the *Life* was written, to Mr. A. C. Benson, from whom they had been borrowed. Assiduous in my quest I applied to Mr. E. F. Benson, survivor of the literary brotherhood, only to learn that the correspondence had not been among Arthur Benson's papers at his death, and presumably, therefore, had been destroyed as of no further consequence after Hugh Benson's *Life* was written. Fortunately Fr. Martindale transcribed fragments of many in his *Life* eighteen years ago; and from that and other sources I have pieced together all that can be salved of that intense but fruitless friendship.

What, we may well wonder, was the suspicious Rolfe's reply to Fr. Benson's first letter? Knowing his distrust of Roman priests, I cannot believe that it was other than guarded and remote. One sentence survives. Commenting on Benson's remark that *Hadrian* had taught him the value of loneliness, Rolfe rejoined 'May I say that experience has taught *me* the frightful harm of it when compulsory?' But Benson's enthusiasm and frankness soon broke down the barrier of Rolfe's reserve. In May he wrote that he had put *Hadrian* among the three books from which he wished never to be separated, though he proposed to paste together certain pages upon Socialists as too wholly sordid. But Rolfe demurred, and Benson agreed to leave the novel that had brought them together 'unbowdlerized'. Now began a correspondence described by Fr. Martindale (probably the only man living who has read it) as 'somewhat labouredly humorous at first, but afterwards terribly stripped of affectations, especially on Benson's harassed side', full of 'resentments, reconciliations, explanations and confidences'. For once Rolfe had met his match as a correspondent. Letters passed to or fro almost daily, in itself a sign of the importance attached by Benson to this new connection, for he warned even his intimates that he had no time to write more than once a month. He confessed to Rolfe that he was always quarrelling with his best friends; in return Rolfe cast his horoscope, and

ascribed the pugnacity of both to the influence of their
stars.

It is doubtful if anyone now knows the circumstances
of the first meeting of these two queer men. Both were
reluctant to risk a personal encounter for fear of disappointment. The fear seems to have been a vain one, for in August
(1905) they set out on a walking tour together, each
equipped 'with a shirt or so, a toothbrush, and a breviary',
intending not to enter large towns but to seek small
country inns. No record exists of their itinerary, but
imagination is free to invent endless conversations on
literature and liturgy, Rolfe's recitals of his wrongs and
hopes, Benson's talk of his plans. The friendship survived,
even seemed cemented by, this ordeal of juxtaposition.
Benson's friends were astonished, and some, indeed, dismayed, at the ascendancy acquired by his strange new
acquaintance. Mr. Vyvyan Holland, the witty translator
of Julian Green, writes:

As an undergraduate at Cambridge in 1906 I enjoyed, for a short
time, a close acquaintanceship with Father Hugh Benson, and
quite the most vivid recollection I have of him is of the influence
that a mysterious Mr. Rolfe seemed to have over him. Father
Benson's description of Rolfe was of a quiet gentle man of great
intellectual attainments who spent most of his life in obscure
study at Oxford. They were in constant communication with
one another.

At that time Father Benson was deeply absorbed in all questions
concerning magic, necromancy and spiritualism, and spent a
good deal of his time in reviewing books on these subjects. He
had been deeply impressed with Rolfe's casting of horoscopes.
According to Benson, if Rolfe knew the exact place, and the
time to the minute, of anyone's birth, he could lay down a
scheme for the conduct of his life, in such matters as when it
would be wise to go on a journey, or invest money. Father
Benson admitted that he himself had paid a good deal of attention
to the rules laid down for himself in his own horoscope. He

said that Rolfe had evidently devoted a vast amount of time to the study of the stars, had found a number of very obscure books on the subject, including one quite unknown book by Albertus Magnus, and that he probably knew more about astrology than any living man.

The most interesting story, by far, that Father Benson told me was of an experiment in 'White Magic' which he had carried out at Rolfe's request. Rolfe wrote to him one day in a great state of excitement and told him that he had discovered, either in his Albertus Magnus book or in some mediæval manuscript, instructions as to how to bring about a certain event. He would not, at that juncture, reveal what that event was, but he implored Father Benson to make the experiment.

As the experiment consisted mainly in the repetition of certain prayers and in certain periods of religious contemplation, Father Benson saw no harm in carrying it out. Certain rules were also laid down concerning hours of rising and retiring and the avoiding of certain foods and drink. I remember that no alcohol of any sort was allowed! The period for this régime was to be from ten days to a fortnight.

At the end of the period stated, Father Benson told me that he distinctly saw a white figure whose features were quite indistinguishable, mounted on a horse, ride slowly into the middle of his room and there halt for about half a minute, after which it slowly faded away. He immediately sat down and wrote his impression to Rolfe, who replied by return enclosing what purported to be a transcription of the passage from the book containing the instructions. This said that, if the instructions were faithfully carried out, at the end of ten days or a fortnight the experimenter would see 'riding towards him the White Knight with visor down'. Benson showed me this at the time and was deeply impressed by the last words, which seemed to explain why he could not distinguish the features of his horseman.

I give this story as it was told to me. Father Benson had, I think, been delving a little too deeply into mysticism at that time, and struck me as being in a very nervous state. But he undoubtedly believed that he had seen the horseman and that

Rolfe's transcription was honest and genuine. If the story shows nothing else, it undoubtedly shows how great an influence Rolfe then had over Father Benson.

Some time later, it was agreed that the two should collaborate in a book. Benson had already suggested that they should live together in adjacent cottages, not meeting till 2.30 p.m., the hour when he became tolerant and tolerable. The subject decided upon for collaboration was St. Thomas of Canterbury, who was to be the theme of a romantic history contrived by Rolfe's favourite artifice of transcribing from a pretended contemporary chronicler. The proposal promised several advantages to Rolfe. First, Benson's name was already well known; his novels commanded a far larger sale than Rolfe's could hope for. Secondly, and more important, Rolfe's name bracketed with Benson's on a title-page would do much to restore him to the goodwill of the authorities of his Church, who viewed with distrust the outcast subject of the newspaper attack, the hero (or villain) of the Holywell scandal, and the author of *Hadrian the Seventh*. Thirdly, it would fix by a visible bond his relationship with a priest who might easily become a Bishop,—in which event Benson had laughingly promised that one of his first acts would be to ordain Fr. Rolfe. In recognition of these advantages, Rolfe refused to take the half-share which Benson equitably offered, and would accept only one-third of the profits which it was hoped were to spring from *St. Thomas*.

The understanding seems to have been that Benson would do most of the actual writing, Rolfe the necessary research. Part of the never-completed romance survives, much varied from Benson's original letter of suggestions:

May 10, 1906

I propose that the story be told by the monk, in the same kind of way that Don Tarquinio and Richard Raynal do it, a purported translation from Old French. 2. That no female interest

enters into it, except in the Platonic love of the monk for a
female child of the age of ten years, whom he thinks to be like
our Lady, but who turns out to be entirely soulless (?). 3. . . . That
the book is written at the command of the King, in the old age
of the monk, resembling the other biographies. 4. . . . That the
monk has strong and vivid artistic perceptions and is occupied
by his community in some branch of handicraft. . . . 5. . . . That
we get the vignette scheme by giving extracts only from his
book, with caustic comments of our own—not many footnotes—
but a good deal of chronicle in our own words. This will enable
us to concentrate all our attention upon descriptive word-paint-
ing, and to serve up mystical reflections as we should wish to
see them done. We can write the historical interludes in a sharp
breezy way, which will be an agreeable relief from his musings.
6. My theory in all this is that the artistic object is shown up
through the coloured lights of the various personalities. In this
way we shall get at least three, the monk's, yours, and mine.
7. As to the scheme of the book, I suggest three parts.

1.

Begin with the departure of our man (Gervase?) at the age of
fifteen years to be page to the Lord Chancellor. (Fortunately
Thomas was very intimate with his servants; cf. Thomas of
Bosham.) Almost at once Thomas becomes Archbishop, and
the part ends with his consecration in 1162.

2.

Begin by description of St. Thomas's life. Gervase becomes
novice at Christ Church Convent; attached to Thomas; goes
with him to Northampton; row; flight of Thomas; Gervase
says good-bye to him at Sandwich in 1164.

3.

Six years have elapsed. Last Christmas. Arrival of Thomas.
Martyrdom. First miracles.

Please send comments some time *soon*, as I am beginning to
warm up about it. Please also remember that my method, when
once begun, is to work like lightning, and then to take a rest.
I can't plod *at all*. I shall start to read hard presently.

Agreement as to the terms of the collaboration was reached in August 1906, when Rolfe was staying with the Pirie-Gordons. For one reason and another, however, no active steps were taken immediately. Benson always had his hands more or less full, and Rolfe was occupied by his Oxford duties and his lawsuit.

When the long-protracted case was at last called, on December 17, Benson was present at the hearing, heard his friend cross-examined, and saw him break down. Hugh Benson would have been less than human, perhaps, if his feeling as to the desirability of Fr. Rolfe as a collaborator had remained unchanged by what he heard. It did not. In any event he had outlived the first flush of his admiration for the author of *Hadrian the Seventh*.

In the following year, however (1907), when Rolfe was at Gwernvale with time on his hands, the project was resumed. 'You once said to me that Plot was your weak point', Benson wrote. 'I think there is truth in that. What you can do (Good Lord, how you can!) is to build up a situation when you've got it. You are a vignette-, a portrait-, not a landscape-painter, a maker of chords, not of progressions. . . . Therefore I am strongly inclined to collaboration . . . I think I may be able to make a plot sometime in the summer.' The plot was devised, Benson caught fire again, and a start was made. Rolfe set down all sorts of technical phrases and facts, vignettes of the period and notes of customs, in a small notebook which went backwards and forwards between the two romancers. He sent descriptions and sketches of dresses, maps and plans of places, details of monastic life peculiar to Canterbury, as fuel for the writing fury which possessed his partner. Some time after September 30, Benson read his beginning aloud to Fr. X, who 'laughed and shook with joy'. Rolfe, too, was writing hard at alternate chapters.

By October, *St. Thomas*, though not finished, was well under way. And then, unexpectedly, Benson wrote to

Rolfe suggesting an alteration to their agreement; or, as the latter phrased it, 'showed the cloven hoof'.

He explained that during a recent visit to London, his agent, whom he did not name, had advised him that the proposed romance would have a far greater sale if Benson's name appeared on the title-page unencumbered with that of a collaborator. Accordingly, since it was the main object of both authors to gain as much money as possible, he proposed to Rolfe that *St. Thomas* should appear as 'by Robert Hugh Benson', and that a generous acknowledgement should be made, in a note, of 'Mr. Rolfe's assistance'. The money arrangements were to stand unaltered; i.e., Rolfe was to receive a third. It cannot be gainsaid that the suggestion was a cool one; and Rolfe very naturally demurred. The point was argued. 'Benson was very upset by a further refusal', says his biographer. 'He offered to make Mr. Rolfe a present of all, absolutely, that he himself had hitherto written and discovered, with full leave to publish it as his own.' But when he did so, 'he foresaw that Rolfe would refuse this', as in fact he did. Benson would make no other terms, and finally Rolfe, unwillingly, gave way.

But though Rolfe agreed to the new terms, the alteration of the agreement revived his sense of persecution in full force. He had, it can hardly be denied, some ground for grievance, since, in fact, the gaining of money had been only a part of the advantage which he looked for from the collaboration; but, as usual, he magnified his grievance into a nightmare, and saw himself again as the priest-hunted Nowt of Holywell surrounded by foes. He expressed this point of view in a letter to Mrs. Gordon:

It is horrible to tell you what I think of Benson. So horrible that I am forcing myself not to come to any definite conclusion about him. I have only his actions before me; and I refuse to pronounce or even to form a final opinion about them. You know that we began the *Thomas* book in August 1906. It was entirely his own voluntary proposal. He said that if we wrote a book together, it would rehabilitate me publicly among Catholics, make publishers look more favourably on my own works, and get me a decent sum of money. He chose the subject; and offered me half profits. I was so grateful that I refused half and would only accept a third; and I promised to do my very best and to let him have his own way entirely in the book. Then the thing dilly-dallied till last Autumn, when he suddenly began to write in a violent spurt. I tottered after him as best I could. Then, Benson most peremptorily required me to sign a bond agreeing that his name should stand alone as author of the book. He said that his agent (whose name he refuses to give) told him that he could make more money this way, and he promised that my share should be 'several hundreds of pounds with £100 on day of publication'. This proposal was a radical difference to our agreement. The only ambition I have is to be independent. The original agreement was to help me to that. The new proposal kept me a sponger upon other people's charity. Which I detest with all my heart. . . .

You know that Benson has continually consoled me in my troubles, saying that I never need worry myself with thinking that I must go back to the workhouse or sleep out of doors any more. He has always assured me that when all else failed he would gladly take me in. I have impressed upon him that I yearn to be a help and not a hindrance: and I have shewn him heaps of ways in which I could be made not only self-supporting but profitable and only too willing to share my profits with him. And so now, finding myself quite without means, and quite without means even of continuing my work, I reluctantly fell back upon him. He tells me that to take me in will break his heart and cause him strong personal inconvenience; and in the roughest possible manner he offers me the situation of caretaker in his lonely house two miles from Buntingford at 8/- a week. There I am to be quite alone, to look after the place, do the gardening, and fowls, and be two miles walk and a train-journey from Mass for seven months. He emphasises the fact that I am not to consider myself his guest but his paid servant; and asks for a bond binding me to repay him my journey-money out of my first earnings.

Now all this has taken my breath away. It is totally unexpected. I have done nothing to deserve it. And I am quite unable to explain it excepting by an hypothesis which I am frantically refusing to entertain. Roman Catholic clergymen have behaved exactly like this several times to me before; and I believe the idea was to break me, heart and soul and body. That they have not done; and I will not let it happen. Anything rather than that. But the effect of Benson's conduct is that I am inconceivably frightened of him; and all my old distrust of the clergy is rampant and paramount. What would they do with me if I put myself completely at their mercy? I don't know. But I fear all sorts of things, especially as this occasion is caused by one whom I regarded as a true friend 'and to whom I have confided all my secrets without reserve.

Fortunately, some letters exist which give Benson's side of this unlucky squabble:

Dear Mr. Pirie-Gordon,   *Catholic Rectory, Cambridge*

May I write to you frankly about Rolfe? I don't know whether or not he has told you that we have had a row. The details in any case don't matter; but I wanted to make it clear to you what my attitude is.

My last letter to R., which reached him last Tuesday, contained an apology for having expressed things clumsily and awkwardly, and an emphatic assurance that I did not consider him a 'knave', as he seemed to suspect. It also contained a suggestion that he should come next month into a house which I have just bought and live there. I proposed to offer him the house for six months, the garden with its vegetables, fowls for eggs, and a few shillings each week for further things—also I said I would furnish a couple of rooms in it and advance necessary money for his moving expenses. It was an entirely friendly and genial letter. I asked him to answer this by yesterday, as I must look out for a caretaker at once, if he did not come. This he has not answered at all.

Now I can't go on begging him to accept this kind of thing. He is extremely angry with me, I suppose.

If it is possible for you to convey to him how extremely foolish it is to behave like this, when there is nothing but friendliness on my side—though without telling him that you have heard from me—I shall be very grateful. Would it be possible for you to talk to him about plans and then to say 'Have you written to Benson?', and if he says 'That's no good', then to say 'Very well, I will', *and to do it, whatever he says?*

It seems to me that perhaps in this way he may be brought to see how foolish it is to go on like this and think himself deserted and betrayed and all the rest of it.

Please forgive me for writing. I simply cannot wait more than three or four days more. If nothing happens by then I must engage a caretaker at once. If you can give me a hint that he is likely to wish to come, I will postpone it. . . .

Yours sincerely

R. H. Benson

Benson's account of the cause of their difference does not differ, substantially, from Rolfe's:

On proposing to a publisher that [Rolfe and myself] should cooperate, he answered that he didn't want that. He wanted a book from me alone, for which he offered me a considerable sum: saying that he could not offer nearly so much for a collaborated book. I passed this on to R., thinking of course that he would not dream of insisting on his name appearing as a collaborator. What I suggested was that his name should be fervently mentioned in the preface—'invaluable assistance' etc., and that our money arrangements should remain as before. In this way he would have received a lot more money which I imagined he wanted (I certainly do).

Benson was less than just to himself as well as to Rolfe in thus insisting on money as the essence of their disagreement; indeed, if his excuse were taken at the foot of the letter, it would be a paltry one. He had made a bargain with Rolfe; and the fact that he could make better terms for himself by altering the bargain was no ground for altering it if his collaborator preferred to leave it unchanged. No doubt it was true that the unnamed publisher offered more money if Benson's name stood alone upon the title-page; but there were other reasons for Fr. Benson's desire to drop public collaboration with Fr. Rolfe. His brother Arthur had previously warned him that this new friend was a dangerous and discreditable man; and now several of his colleagues in the Church joined in adjuring him to drop the association. Their words were given weight by that cross-examination in the Thomas case to which I have referred. So Benson decided against Rolfe. But (we may suppose) he wished, charitably, not to let his collaborator feel his decision as a personal difference, and sought to throw the onus of his withdrawal on the publisher. This is surmise, but there is much to support it.

Pirie-Gordon's good-natured efforts to reconcile the two were fruitless:

Dear Mr. Pirie-Gordon,

Many thanks. But I don't in the least see what I can do now, if he insists on treating me as a suspicious enemy. If I write in a friendly manner he does not answer, and seems to think that my friendliness is a sort of frightened sop-giving. If I write my mind he thinks me brutal. The only third alternative is that I should not write unless and until he writes to me. This seems to me my only possibility. Personally I think he has treated me in an astounding manner. . . . I won't qualify it further.

But I am perfectly ready to be friendly: and to go on with *St. Thomas as soon as I have any leisure*. Only the request for this must now come from him. I am keeping his chapters for the present, in the hope that he will propose this again.

I see dimly what he thinks. But it is so amazingly unreasonable and so extremely wounding to oneself, to be treated as a fraudulent publisher, that I can hardly see how in decency I can go on making proposals. He will only see in them new and subtle plots against him. And all the while, in reality, from the business point of view it would be vastly to my advantage not to work with him at all. I have offered him the whole book, for that reason among others, if he will take it off my hands.

I am honestly beginning to doubt, for the first time, whether he is really 'fond of me' at all. I don't see at present how suspicion and friendliness can co-exist.

As for my suffering through him—I have always been perfectly aware that Catholics dislike and distrust him. It was, largely, to rehabilitate him that I have made no secret of my liking for him (that sounds rather egotistic, but at present I am in good favour with Catholics). I don't care one straw what they think about me. . . .

It is an *absolute delusion* that anyone keeps a watch on him, or hinders him. Really, in Catholic eyes, he is practically non-existent. Certainly Catholics who do know of him suspect him—but they ignore him. It is simple egotism on his part to think that they pay him any attention.

I am frightfully sorry for him. I would do anything I could: but the 'Rose' attitude of lofty isolation is intolerable and impossible. Nobody is going to 'soar' to him with sympathy. He is simply his own enemy. I am not: I want to be his friend. But it is because I am sorry for him; not because I think he is the object of a wide-spread plot.

I will await developments, and, meanwhile, keep his chapters until he chooses to write to me decently again.

Ever yours sincerely

R. Hugh Benson

If he did, he kept them for a long time. The wheel had almost turned; once more Rolfe's affairs approached a crisis. There were several factors to provoke it. First, he owed a number of small sums in Oxford, sums which, though small, he was quite unable to pay. Second, as has been seen, he had quarrelled with his friend Benson. Thirdly, Mr. Taylor's complaisance had reached its limit. Finally, the Gordons had decided that at the following Christmas Gwernvale should be closed until they returned from a tour in the East. Rolfe saw that he had to make a move; and the means lay ready to his hand.

XV

THE VOLUNTARY EXILE

AMONG those who listened with interest, and an almost unwilling admiration, to Rolfe's monologues and diatribes at Gwernvale was Professor R. M. Dawkins, at that time Director of the British School of Archæology at Athens, now the holder of the Bywater and Sotheby chair of modern Greek at Oxford. In 1907 he returned to England to settle the affairs of a small, newly-inherited estate in Breconshire, and was duly entertained as a neighbour by the Pirie-Gordons. On one of these visits he met Rolfe; and, as he writes, 'I was immediately struck by the personality of the man; not by his learning, which was on the surface, nor his history, which was picturesque, but by his personal intensity and singularity, which roused my curiosity and interest.' Later, after the inevitable quarrel, Rolfe described Professor Dawkins in his most vivid vein of personal abuse, though he added parenthetically, 'he knew more Greek archæology than anyone else in the world, and his brains were occasionally pickable.'

Indeed, Rolfe was drawn as by a magnet to this fountain of learning (who was also a landowner, and therefore, in Rolfe's eyes, rich); while Professor Dawkins, who possessed that scientific turn of mind which often accompanies scholarship, was attracted and amused by the *outré* stranger, with his mixture of superstition and personal power, who talked of astrology as though it was an exact science, and ascribed his misfortunes to planetary influences. For, though Rolfe deceived others, he seemed also the dupe of his own spells; and this, and the other elements of his contradictory make-up, provided a stimulating problem to the sceptical professor. Perhaps it was the intensity of

Rolfe's self-deceptions which gave him his power, frequently displayed, of attracting the interest and sympathy of chance acquaintances. The present instance was no exception. In one of his first letters to Dawkins (for, after the latter's return to Athens, a correspondence followed) Rolfe wrote:

My difficulty, however, is, not to find friends as I get older, but to keep those whom the gods send me in such profusion. I find that, unless one is able to reciprocate social amoenities, one's friends sheer off; and it is quite impossible to do one's share in friendship—the share which one burns and yearns to do—as long as one is harassed and distracted and simply torn to pieces by the struggle of keeping on the cheerful mask disguising one's struggles for life. So I shall watch with much interest to see how long you and I can keep it up. Don't be afraid that I shall drop it. No. When it ends, do just tell yourself that it is the malignance of my stars which has snatched my end of the cord out of my hand. And do not be surprised: for I dance on volcanoes all the time—if you can call it dancing . . . I'm telling you all this so that if I don't answer your letters you'll know that it's not the will but the ability which is lacking. When things go quite wrong with me I've got the habit of putting on corduroy and a blue belcher and a pseudonym and running away to hide myself until benignant stars bring me out into a more ample air.

In later letters Rolfe dwelt on the homelessness impending over his head: Gwernvale was to be closed, and Benson—the whole story was retold—'has let me down with a bang'. The 'blubber-lipped Professor of Greek' was touched by these confidences: it must be remembered that he knew nothing of Rolfe and his affairs beyond what he was told by the Pirie-Gordons (who naturally set their guest in a good light, since they knew no harm of him beyond that he was poor and queer) and by Rolfe himself. Seeing an opportunity to help a 'lame dog' and secure himself amusing companionship at the same time, he suggested that Rolfe should join him in a holiday at Venice later in the year, and offered to provide the money necessary for expenses. 'He was to repay me from money to be made by descriptive writing', Professor Dawkins writes. 'I was glad enough to risk a little cash for the pleasure and interest of his company, and of course I never really expected to see it back again.'

Plans were made accordingly. Rolfe was extremely excited, and very grateful; new turrets were added to his castles in the air. There was good reason for his excitement. In an expression that used to be popular, he had an elective affinity for Italy, a fostered devotion for her sunshine, her history, and her speech. His one visit to Rome had made him a Baron in name, and tinged his nature with something more than the remembrance of Southern intensity. Now, again, he was to visit the country he had so long loved, and loved all the more by revulsion from his repeated failures in his own.

Fr. Rolfe setting out for foreign travel was a curious sight. He had changed very much from the young man with the 'handsome, sensitive face' of Oscott days who had scandalized the authorities of the Scots College by his æsthetic vagaries, and captivated the elderly Duchessa by his charm. Then, he was tonsured from choice; now, in his forty-ninth year, his skull was covered with an iron-grey stubble kept closely clipped. Then, he had treasured a silver-fitted dressing case, Heaven knows how acquired; now, on this second visit, his luggage was contained in a large laundry basket, fastened by a homely bar and padlock—a mode of carrying baggage which seemed highly suspicious to the Customs officials. But still he was the same unchanging Rolfe, who contrived to give an air of queerness to ordinary actions: as in the wearing of a silver crucifix so large and heavy that to pacify his chafed flesh he wore always beneath its foot a thickness of goldbeater's skin; or the carriage of a fountain pen at least thrice the size of those usually sold in shops. 'During the war I feel sure that the secret services of Europe would have quarrelled as to which of them should shoot Rolfe as a spy. He looked always so extremely and self-consciously odd', observes his travelling companion.

Rolfe was unchanged, too, in his propensity to incur debts, and his attitude to other people's money. Officially he had not come as Professor Dawkins's guest, but as one who had borrowed money which he would presently repay. Since it was his intention and hope to repay whatever he might spend, he saw no reason for stinting himself; and his host (in fact if not in name) soon found that Rolfe's idea of enjoyment included numerous forms of 'elaborate idleness' which were expensive, as well as more than ordinarily good food and wine. Protests he met with 'a sort of worrying bullying'. Despite the subtlety on which Rolfe prided himself, he frequently went astray over simple matters. It was so now. Professor Dawkins, far from being pleased by the pleasant ways of spending money which Rolfe was constantly discovering, was disconcerted to find that he was expected to live almost *en prince* for two. So, inventing an excuse that was reasonably true, he announced his intention of examining Greek manuscripts at Rome (an alternative to Venetian idleness which did not attract Rolfe) and departed, with expressions of goodwill that he hardly felt, leaving Rolfe enough money to enable him to stay in Venice for a time and then return home. The friends never met again; indeed, not one of his English friends ever again saw Fr. Rolfe in the flesh, though they saw and shivered at his beautiful script.

Alone in Venice, Rolfe set himself to weave new dreams. The sun shone bright in the city of canals; and the battered, homeless wanderer had always loved water and sunshine. Moreover, he had money in the bank. Not much; but to one who had lived so long on debts and credit, even thirty pounds (he can have had little more) seemed a sum. We can guess almost exactly how he spent his time. Certainly he swam a great deal, and hired a sandalo, which he learned to row in the Venetian mode—a difficult task. He talked in his faulty and academic Italian to everyone in reach, from fisher-boys to hotel secretary, though perhaps most of all to the fisher-boys. And he gratified the lust of the eye. All through his life Rolfe had shown himself strongly susceptible to outward appearances. Now, in the old Italian city, he indulged in an orgy of sightseeing where there was so much to see.

Fr. Rolfe left an account of his first impressions of Venetian life which deserves quotation:

I came to Venice in August for a six weeks' holiday; and lived and worked and slept in my *barcheta* almost always. It seemed that, by staying on, I could most virtuously and most righteously cheat autumn and winter. Such was the effect of this kind of Venetian life on me, that I felt no more than twenty-five years old, in everything excepting valueless experience and valuable disillusion. The bounding joy of vigorous health, the physical capacity for cheerful (nay, gay) endurance, the careless, untroubled mental activity, the perfectly gorgeous appetite, the prompt, delicate dreamless nights of sleep, which betoken healthy youth—all this (with indescribable happiness) I had triumphantly snatched from solitude with the sun and the sea. I went swimming half a dozen times a day, beginning at white dawn, and ending after sunsets which set the whole lagoon ablaze with amethyst and topaz. Between friends, I will confess that I am not guiltless of often getting up in the night and popping silently overboard to swim for an hour in the clear of a great gold moon—plenilunio—or among the waving reflections of the stars. (O my goodness me, how heavenly a spot that is!) When I wanted change of scene and anchorage, I rowed with my two gondoglieri; and there is nothing known to physiculturalists (for giving you 'poise' and the organs and figure of a slim young Diadymenos) like rowing standing in the Mode Venetian. It is jolly hard work; but no other exercise bucks you up as does springing forward from your toe-tips and stretching forward to the full in pushing the oar, or produces such exquisite lassitude at night when your work is done. And I wrote quite easily for a good seven hours each day. Could anything be more felicitous?

And, one day, I replenished my stock of provisions at Burano; and at sunset we rowed away to find a station for the night. Imagine a twilight world of cloudless sky and smoothest sea, all made of warm, liquid, limpid heliotrope and violet and lavender, with bands of burnished copper set with emeralds, melting, on the other hand, into the fathomless blue of the eyes of the prides of peacocks, where the moon rose, rosy as mother-of-pearl. Into such glory we three advanced the black *barcheta*, solemnly, silently, when the last echo of *Ave Maria* died.

Slowly we came out north of Burano into the open lagoon; and rowed eastward to meet the night, as far as the point marked by five *pali*, where the wide canal curves to the south. Slowly we went. There was something so holy—so majestically holy—in that evening silence, that I would not have it broken even by the quiet plash of oars. I was lord of time and place. No engagements cried to be kept. I could go when and where I pleased, fast or slow, far or near. And I chose the near and the slow. I did more. So unspeakably gorgeous was the peace on the lagoon just then, that it inspired me with a lust for doing nothing at all but sitting and absorbing impressions motionlessly. That way come thoughts, new, generally noble.

The wide canal, in which we drifted, is a highway. I have never seen it unspeckled by the *sandali* of Buranelli fishers. Steam-boats and tank-barges of fresh water for Burano, and the ordinary barks of carriage, disturb it, not always, but often. My wish was to find a smaller canal, away—away. We were (as I said) at the southern side, at the southward curve marked by five *pali*. Opposite, on the other bank, begins the long line of *pali* which shows the deep-water way right down to the Ricevitoria of Treporti; and there, at the beginning of the line, I spied the mouth of a canal which seemed likely to suit me. We rowed across to it, and entered. It tended north-eastward for two or three hundred metres, and then bended like an elbow north-westward. It looked quite a decent canal, perhaps forty metres in width, between sweet mud-banks clothed with sea-lavender about two-foot lengths above high-water mark in places. We pushed inshore, near to the inner bank at the elbow, stuck a couple of oars into the mud fore and aft, and moored there.

Baicolo and Caicio got out the draught board and cigarettes, and played below their breath on the *puppa;* while I sat still, bathing my soul in peace, till the night was dark and Selene high in the limpid sapphire-blue. Then they lighted the *fanali,* and put up the impermeable awning with wings and curtains to cover the whole *barcheta;* and made a parmentier soup to eat with our wine and *polenta.* And, when kapok-cushions had been arranged on the floor, and summer sleeping bags laid over them, we took our last dash overboard, said our prayers, and went to bed. Baicola at *prova* with his feet towards mine amidships, and Caicio under the *puppa* with his feet well clear of my pillowed head. So, we slept.

Soon after sunrise I awakened: it was a sunrise of opal and fire: the boys were deep in slumber. I took down the awning, and unmoored quietly, and mounted the *puppa* to row about in the dewy freshness in search of a fit place for my morning plunge. I am very particular about this. Deep water I must have—as deep as possible—I being what the Venetians call 'appassionato per l'acqua'. Beside that, I have a vehement dyspathy against getting entangled in weeds or mud, to make my toe-nails dirtier than my finger-nails. And, being con-genitally myopic, I see more clearly in deep water than in shallow, almost as clearly, in fact, as with a concave monocle on land. So I left the *barcheta* to drift with the current, while I took soundings with the long oar of the *puppa,* in several parts of the canal, near both banks as well as in the middle. Nowhere could I touch bottom; and this signified that my bathing place was more than four metres in depth. Needless to say that I gave a joyful morning yell, which dragged from sleep the luxury-loving Baicolo to make coffee, and the faithful dog Caicio to take my oar and keep the *barcheta* near me; and then I plunged overboard to revel in the limpid green water. Lord, how lovely is Thy smooth salt water flowing on flesh!

But £30 does not last for ever, even when living is cheap; and the little store of sterling slowly melted. Rolfe wrote for more money to Mr. Taylor, and the friendly Gordons of Gwernvale. They sent £25 and £12 10s. respectively; but they also asked his plans.

His plans! He had none. He wanted to live in the sun, and that savour of the past which surrounds and exhales from the city of St. Mark; he wanted to go on talking and sightseeing, to continue his excursions, to saturate himself in the atmosphere and spirit of beauty and Italy. But the question was insistent; he could not live on beautiful impressions. So he found a 'plan'. His old-time skill in photography should be his 'plan'; and he suggested that he should establish himself as a shopkeeper in Venice, selling fine photographs to the tourists, living above his business, and, in his leisure, writing books which should make him rich.

This proposal perturbed the Pirie-Gordons. They knew Rolfe's circumstances, and something, though by no means all, of his nature: enough to appreciate the hopelessness of his plan, and also to realize that a flat denunciation of it would strengthen his impracticable determination. So, in a tactful letter, Harry suggested that his collaborator should come back to England to discuss ways and means, to consider how much capital would be needed to make a start in a small way. Reluctantly Rolfe agreed. 'It is annoying to have to waste time and money coming to England to get money', he wrote, 'but, of course, I see that there is no other way. So, as you are all so very good as to have me, expect me very soon . . . then I will finish *Hubert* and write that infernal Benson book, and do what else is necessary to return here in February 1909. Only, I firmly abhor from the notion that one might "begin small". For success, one must begin as one means to continue'. And he asked for his fare back. He got it. He also got another £15 from Dawkins. But his departure for England continued to be delayed. First his excuse was that Professor

Dawkins had created so bad an impression of the English
by his niggardly treatment of the boatmen of Venice that
he had felt constrained to set the matter right at his own
expense. Then he admitted that he had used his passage
money to pay his hotel bill. Then 'I was all ready to start
last Sunday week for England, ticket taken and insurance
. . . Suddenly other unexpected liabilities to the extent of
£20 sterling odd came in. I could not pay. Wrote to the
last man I knew, begging. On Sunday he refused. So I am
another week to the bad though I live on 40 pallanche a
day all told; and fresh bills have come in making it now
impossible for me to get away under £32 sterling. I am
sure there are no more. As I said, so far, I have maintained
a singularly honoured reputation and my credit is unimpaired. To leave obscurely or in disgrace will annul
the excellent foundations which I have laid here . . . I am
unable to finish *Hubert's Arthur* until I have consulted you
on various points of heraldry (and of good taste). I fear
that I shall within the next few days find myself without
money or friends or future in this foreign country. I am
much annoyed by this.'

His friends in England were mystified by his manœuvres.
They knew that he had little or no money, and that without
money he could not stop in Venice; yet in Venice he
seemed determined to remain. Summer does not last for
ever, even in Italy; Fr. Rolfe was no longer living in a boat,
but in an hotel on credit, with a mounting bill. What was to
be done? Pirie-Gordon was anxious for his return, anxious
to complete the book in which he was collaborating; but
it seemed useless to send more money to be spent in
defeating the purpose for which it was intended. Benson,
perhaps, desired his collaborator's return less: tired of
waiting, he had used the notes on St. Thomas compiled by
himself and Rolfe as the basis of a short biography about
to be published over his own name.

Rolfe seems to have banked his hopes on Mr. Taylor,
who, since he had granted one loan on the strength of an

insurance policy, would, he supposed, grant another on
the strength of more insurance. But again Rolfe had misread the situation. Mr. Taylor had made that final loan
as a last hope; and had taken the insurance policy as cover,
faute de mieux, to set against the loss in which the whole
transaction seemed likely to involve him. The effect of
that meeting in Lincoln's Inn Fields four years before had
long ago worn off; and the solicitor, who had not received
a penny from the 'security' of *Hadrian* or *Don Tarquinio*,
had no longer any belief in the likelihood of his loans and
costs being repaid from royalties earned by Rolfe's books.
He looked (as events proved, rightly) solely to the insurance
policy for ultimate reimbursement; and, as he realized very
well, he might have to pay premiums on that for many
years. So, when faced by appeals for funds from Venice,
he naturally wrote to say that he could make no more
advances.

Even then Rolfe refused to return to the friends who
would have supported him.

Well [he wrote to Harry Pirie-Gordon] I have told Taylor in
effect that if he stops now, he loses all he has done so far. If he
doesn't mind, that's his affair. Anyhow I'm tired out of trying
to make bricks without straw. And I am not trying any more.
A friend in need is a friend indeed . . . .
I have the habit of taking the air this way. There's a small
English *Ospedale* on Giudecca—English staff, patients chiefly
sailors. I go over every afternoon in a *sandalo* and row convalescents about in the sun. They think no end of me. So does
the matron, Miss Chaffey. Now Lady Layard (Queen of
England in Venice), who adores the hospital, does so too. I
choke 'em all off. What's the good of making new friends
when you may be denounced at the *questura* for debt any day?
I don't know what my expenses at hotel are. I always burn the
bills as I can't pay them.

What was to be done? It is a proof of the sincerity of young

Pirie-Gordon's friendship that even now he did not abandon patience with his errant collaborator. 'I cannot help thinking that we ought to do something for Rolfe', he wrote to Mr. Taylor, and suggested that, through the solicitor, he, Benson and Dawkins should remit a small sum—45 lire, then nearly £2, weekly—to Rolfe's landlord, —sufficient to keep Rolfe in modest style in Venice for three more months, by which time, he hoped, his friend would return to his senses, and home.

But the suggestion proved a useless one. Rolfe's land-lord refused to consider such an arrangement until the matter of what was already owing—approximately £40— was dealt with, and warned Mr. Taylor that Rolfe's expenditure (which was 'not excessive for a gentleman of even moderate means') was double the proposed allowance. Letters of explanation went backwards and forwards, but no acceptable compromise was found, and in the end the sums subscribed for Rolfe's benefit were returned to the three subscribers, Benson, Pirie-Gordon, and Dawkins.

The wheel had turned again. Rolfe was in the process of making new friends, but his old ones were not allowed to forget him. The familiar artillery of insulting letters was called into action. If the folly of the man is obvious, it is also tragic. Once more, torn by the distortion of his biassed vision, he saw himself playing the hero's part in the drama of The One and the Many. His batteries were turned first on Benson, who received almost daily pages of abuse, in which he was called many names skilfully calculated for their wounding truth or half-truth. Prominent among them was the charge of being a 'sadi-maniac'. Another of Rolfe's grievances was that when these erstwhile friends had agreed each to return the other's letters, Benson's letters to Rolfe had been sent back to him; but (taking heed from the violence of Rolfe's tone that worse might follow) Benson had retained Rolfe's letters to himself, 'as a protection'. Hence it came about that, years later, Fr. Martindale had the advantage, denied to me, of reading both sides of the correspondence, which passed through the scale from fervent to frantic, from affection to hate.

The next object of attack was Mr. Taylor. His main offence, naturally, lay in cutting off supplies; but almost level with it in Rolfe's view was his action in writing to the Venetian landlord with the proposal for a weekly payment. 'You have had an absolutely free hand in managing my affairs', the client wrote, mild at first; 'if they are unproductive, that can only be due to your mismanagement. Badly as I managed them myself before you took them over, I did contrive to make something of them. But you seem to have done nothing . . . I have yet to learn that you have even taken any steps whatever to quicken my publishers' energies in regard to my books. . . . Your failure to keep to your agreement . . . ought to have opened my eyes to your indifference to my interests . . . I feel that my present position is entirely due to your negligence . . . Under these circumstances, I am desirous either of completely revising the nature of our connection, or of breaking it off and transferring my obligations and my assets to more capable administration. I shall therefore be glad to hear what you suggest.' Nothing was, nothing could be, suggested, and so Rolfe refused to pass the proofs of his two books in the press (*Don Renato* and *Meleager*) and registered a protest against them with the Publishers' Association.

Meanwhile Pirie-Gordon was not overlooked. He received a short note (enclosing a letter from the long suffering Venetian landlord threatening application to the Police failing payment of his bill) intimating that only a remittance by telegram could save the voluntary exile from prison. The bluff failed; no money was sent, by telegram or otherwise: so a later letter conveyed the information:

I am now simply engaged in dying as slowly and as publicly and as annoyingly to all of you professing and non-practising friends of mine as possible. Since Saturday (this is Thursday)

I have contrived to cadge two lunches Tuesday and Wednesday and afternoon tea every day. Also I have scratched up a few walnuts and oranges. I have not slept in a bed since Friday. Next Sunday I shall have exhausted these amenities. Then I shall steal the *sandalo* from the Bucintoro Club as usual, and go a little way on the lagoon, flying the two English flags, and taking an elaborate diary of my passion, with my passport, and select correspondence with all of you dastards, and play about till the end. You have made a show of me, and you shall have full value in return.

The principal drawback to this attitude was that, to give it effect, Rolfe had actually to die; and, as he knew very well, he was not of the stuff from which suicides are made. Despite his dismal expressions, and the utter penury to which he was by now reduced, he still clung to life and credit. No doubt he went 'a little way out' in the Club *sandalo;* but if so he returned. What he did in fact was to copy the letter in his letter book. It was important, in the wordy warfare which he was opening by this long-range bombardment, not to repeat himself.

Fr. Rolfe, *circa* 1908

XVI

THE VENETIAN OUTCAST

WHAT, meantime, had been happening in Venice? The letter to Pirie-Gordon proclaiming suicide is dated April 1909; Rolfe had got through his first Venetian winter by a skilful manipulation of credit and excuses. It was a remark-able feat; but his credit had several buttresses. In the first place, Rolfe had paid handsomely while he could, and was positive that he would not be long without funds. In the second, landlords of hotels in seasonal places welcome regular residents; and since 'Mr. Rolfe' had expressed his intention of remaining permanently, Signor Barbieri, pro-prietor of the Hôtel Belle Vue et de Russie, had no wish to lose this customer, unless there was good cause. Further, Rolfe received many letters from England, mostly written on thick or official paper, the more hopeful-seeming of which he showed to the landlord, who saw that this 'English' had friends who were concerned on his behalf. But what proved the most convincing demonstration to the Italian hotel-keeper of the truth of his queer guest's claim to have property in England, which would presently be profitable, was Mr. Taylor's official letter (enclosing cheque in advance) offering, on behalf of Benson, Dawkins, and Pirie-Gordon to make a regular payment in respect of Rolfe for three months. Rolfe's anger when he heard of the proposal was genuine and impressive; but the return of the money, on which he insisted, was more impressive still, and convinced Sgr. Barbieri that if he waited he would be paid. So, through the winter, he continued to allow credit for food and housing to the eccentric Englishman.

In the course of that winter, on December 28, 1908, occurred the famous Messina earthquake which left thousands homeless. As a member of the Royal Bucintoro Rowing Club, Rolfe played an energetic part in the relief measures organized by the citizens of Venice. The Club boats (one of them under Rolfe's care) went from house to shop begging for food, clothes, and building material for the sufferers. He spent a busy and happy fortnight carrying mixed cargoes, casks of semolina, flasks of wine, blankets and old clothes to the Barracks of San Zaccaria, which was converted into a temporary warehouse.

His election to the Bucintoro Club owed itself to an amusing incident arising from his passion for swimming, and rowing in the 'mode Venetian'. One day, turning a corner of the Grand Canal too sharply, he fell overboard while smoking a pipe. Swimming strongly under water, he came up unexpectedly far from his boat, looking extremely solemn, with the pipe still in his mouth. On climbing back into the *sandalo*, he calmly knocked the wet tobacco out of his pipe; refilled from his rubber pouch, which had kept its contents dry; borrowed a light; and with the single word *Avanti* went his way. Such impassivity charmed the Venetian onlookers; word went round of this incident, which, coupled with his aquatic fervour, gained him membership of the Bucintoro, a useful privilege, since he could use the Club boats and clubhouse.

During the winter, while Signor Barbieri's tolerance persisted, Rolfe became an observed figure at the Hôtel Belle Vue. Though he kept very much to himself, he was constantly to be seen armed with his vast fountain pen and oddly-shaped manuscript books (one, which survives, is twice as tall as foolscap, though no greater in width; but even those which were less extreme in dimensions were nevertheless unusual). The beauty of his script, his benevolence in rowing convalescents round Venice, and his passion for water-sports, were all remarked; he became, as at Holywell, a 'man of mystery' by his almost ostentatious reticence: and, naturally, other English residents, in and out of the hotel, became curious concerning their reserved

THE VENETIAN OUTCAST 221

fellow-countryman. Not least among the curious was Canon
Lonsdale Ragg, Anglican chaplain to the English colony.

The Canon was wintering with his wife in the Hôtel Belle
Vue, working on the final draft of a study in ecclesiastical
history, *The Church of the Apostles*. Both Canon and Mrs.
Ragg were impressed and interested by the silent author (for
such Rolfe was known to be) who for week after week
seemed at pains to avoid their society. So marked a desire
for privacy could only be broken by Rolfe himself; and
one day he broke it. He left an exquisitely written note in
the hall, asking in brief and formal phrases for an interview.

At the subsequent meeting, Rolfe gave reasons for his
stand-offishness and his note. Both, he explained, were due
to the difficulties in which he was plunged by the unscrupulous actions of his agent in England, and the perfidy of his
friends. While his affairs were entangled he had preferred
to make no new acquaintances; but they had now reached
such a pass that he felt justified by desperation in approaching
one who, though professing a different form of faith, was
nevertheless a Christian and an Englishman, and (probably)
able to diminish his abysmal ignorance of business affairs,
and advise concerning the best action to be taken. Like the
Wedding-Guest, the Canon could not 'choose but hear'.

Rolfe then disclosed those circumstances of which the
reader is aware, but set them in a very different light. His
troubles began, in this account, when he lost his lawsuit
against Col. Thomas. In order to meet the costs of that case,
he told the interested Canon, he had been forced to pledge
his present and future work in favour of his solicitor, who
had undertaken to collect the royalties earned by the various
books so assigned, and make the author a modest allowance
on which to live. Letters from Mr. Taylor supporting these
statements were produced. But now Mr. Taylor, moved
by his own cupidity and by the malevolent counsels of the
Rev. Robert Hugh Benson and Mr. Pirie-Gordon (who
wished to force him to write books for them) had ceased to
pay what he had promised, or to deliver any accounts

showing the position. For months, Rolfe said, he had withstood this tyranny, refusing to return to England to act as
'ghost' so that others should get fame, determined to remain
in Venice, where he felt well and able to do good work. To
resist the coercion to which he was subjected he had pawned
all that he could pawn, and overdrawn at the bank. Yet,
notwithstanding, he had been unable, for some time, to pay
his bill, and now he was threatened with ejection from the
hotel. What should he do?

Canon Ragg, though flattered by this appeal to his
business sense, was (not surprisingly) at a loss for a ready
answer. Rolfe, however, supplied his own. What was
required, he pointed out, was a new agent who would extri-
cate his affairs from the malfeasance of his present one,
administer them as they should be administered, and make
him that small allowance for lack of which he was now in
need. The Canon agreed that such a solution would be
excellent if it could be attained, and promised to think the
matter over.

How much of his distorted version of the facts did Rolfe
believe? In a way, the whole. The psychology of *paranoia*
is now well documented, if not well understood. It is in
part an exaggeration of the normal human power to believe
what is known to be untrue. Who is there who does not
reject and conceal from himself certain disagreeable facts
which, if accepted consciously, would unfavourably affect
the course of life? The coward who performs acts of hero-
ism rather than admit to himself the fact of cowardice is a
well-worn example of the process at one end of the scale, as
the thief who retains his own self-respect and sense of
honesty is of the other. This ability to suppress what it is
undesirable for the mind to dwell upon is part of the basis
of personality, and expresses itself in those unreasonable (but
satisfactory) prejudices which we retain even after they have
been logically disproved. Within limits it is a beneficent
gift. But there are those in whom early circumstances or
later misfortune unduly widen the limits within which this

power can safely operate; and then arises a 'fixed idea' which, despite all evidence to the contrary, becomes the point from which reasoning proceeds. Whatever conflicts with this 'fixed idea' and the (perfectly logical) consequences which would necessarily follow, is flatly regarded by the sufferer as non-existent or untrue.

We may see a perfect working of this mental weakness in Rolfe's confidences to Canon Ragg. He had, it is true, more than one delusional 'fixed idea'; but that which at this period of his life dominated him (for which subsequently I hope to show the cause) was that his books *must* be successful, and that if they were not, any failure was due to 'the malignant spite of his foes'. The whole of his dealings with Mr. Taylor were conditioned by this belief. While he received the much-discussed 'allowance', he regarded the solicitor as assured of repayment, since he held an assignment of these (certain-to-be-successful) books. When payments ceased, largely for the reason that the expected royalties did not accrue, Rolfe sought an explanation of the fact (which could not be denied) in some human agency; and soon found one. If his books did not sell as they ought to do, it was in the first instance the fault of the publisher, who (ever-ready suspicion prompted) had, doubtless, sinister reasons for not pushing and promoting sales. In the same way, if his agent did not harass the publisher into performing his duty, it was again because, from sinister reasons, he did not choose to do so. The more Rolfe pondered the behaviour of Fr. Benson and Mr. Taylor, the more certain he was that he was right.

Such self-conviction gave him force when relating his wrongs to his new benefactor. For Canon Ragg became his benefactor. Whatever doubts he may have had of some details of Rolfe's story, he accepted it as substantially true. He was so far convinced, indeed, that he took the venturesome step of assuring the hotel-keeper of his confidence in Rolfe's bona-fides; and so the impending eviction was postponed. When it loomed again, the Canon, who meanwhile had become fascinated by the intense, solitary exile, himself guaranteed Rolfe's board for a time. 'There was something extremely attractive about him, as well as something repellent', Canon Ragg wrote to me from Bordighera, whither my letter of inquiry had pursued him; 'and the attraction was dominant when he would allow it to be. He struck me as a man of genius, or very near it. We became friends and talked literature for hours at a time. He pressed me to accept for a book on which I was then engaged the system of punctuation which he claimed to have derived from Addison. A short time after he left the hotel, and I saw nothing more of him for a time'.

To say that Rolfe 'left the hotel' was a polite euphemism: he was thrust forth. By the end of April his indebtedness was over £100; and Signor Barbieri would wait no longer. Nor would he allow the defaulter to take his 'effects' away. Now began a purgatory during which Rolfe, deprived even of his letter books, tramped or rowed idly about by day, and slept at night in a boat borrowed from the Bucintoro Club. The Club became, in fact, his head-quarters. Luckily (for literature, if not for himself) during his stay at the Hôtel Belle Vue he had finished *Hubert's Arthur*.

That much-discussed work had continued to be the subject of acid correspondence between the collaborators. Even Rolfe found difficulty in regarding Harry Pirie-Gordon as an 'enemy': he preferred to think of him as having been misled by the wicked Benson. 'Oh, what a feeble person you are to let yourself be blown about by people who have other interests, instead of sticking loyally to your spontaneously-chosen partner', he wrote, and it expressed his attitude. Nevertheless, the completed *Arthur* was sent to Pirie-Gordon in England, on the assumption that he would immediately be able to publish it; Rolfe was desperate. But no welcome cheque arrived by return, or any, post; instead, he learned that the romance on which he set so much store was being corrected by a Quaker critic, to enhance its chance of finding a market. At once a stormy letter protested against 'Your Quaker . . . rooting and snouting in my lovely Catholic garden'. 'The notion of your intermittent playing with the *magnum opus* of a starving man is more than I can stand', he added. More letters went backwards and forwards. No arrangement had been made as to the division of any moneys that might be produced by the two books written by Rolfe and Pirie-Gordon, and now all proposals for an agreement drove Rolfe to fury. He would not take a half-share, he would not take the whole, he would not allow his name to appear on the books, he would not say what he wanted. 'I have not slept in a bed nor changed my clothes for fifteen nights', he wrote; 'God knows where I shall sleep to-night. The weather is cold and wet. In this fortnight I have had 5 lunches, 2 dinners, 3 breakfasts, and afternoon teas only. I have been 39 clear hours with nothing to eat or drink. I do not stand it quite so well as I stood my last Roman Catholic persecution. I was 12 years younger then. But I am not weakening in will'. Rolfe convinced himself at last that Pirie-Gordon too was actively conspiring with Benson against his peace, and issued an incoherent ultimatum.

This is the last chance which I give you and your people of behaving straightly and treating me decently. I will treat you all most generously if you accept this offer. [Otherwise] nothing will stop me, as nothing stopped me when I deliberately ruined my own Borgia book, as nothing stopped me when I deliberately went into the workhouse for similar reasons. I will be quite open with you. I shall circularise all the publishers concerning *Hubert's Arthur* and the other book so that they never shall be published and I will come straight back to Crickhowel workhouse and die there or give your father the pleasure of committing me to gaol. I have your threats. Now you have mine. I have not eaten since Thursday mid-day. I have no chance of eating till Sunday 8 a.m. I have no roof over my head and no bed to sleep in. From Sunday I am certain of a meal a day for three days. After that I shall act.

But, though an even more blasting letter followed to remind the recipient that the third day of grace was drawing near, a letter which declared that 'A stab in the back in the dark is what Spite invariably gives to Scorn', Fr. Rolfe never explained what he wanted, nor what (short of an instant and substantial cheque) he would have regarded as 'straight' behaviour. His fury carried him to the length of applying to the British Consul for repatriation to England, but the third day passed without his leaving Venice. As for *Hubert's Arthur*, Mr. Pirie-Gordon took the only step which he conceived to be open to him: he washed his hands of all connection with the two books he had helped to write, and returned the manuscripts to his unhinged collaborator. One of these literary curiosities, *The Weird of the Wanderer*, was, subsequently, published; but the more important of the two, *Hubert's Arthur*, he never saw nor heard of again. Naturally I asked for such details of it as he could remember; and his précis made me regret its disappearance more than ever:

46 *Addison Avenue, W.*11.
Dear Symons,

Here is the précis of *Hubert's Arthur* as it was when I last worked at it—perhaps Corvo has changed it—I expect that I have forgotten bits here and there. As being professedly 'a chronicle', Arthur marries early in the story, as he would have done in real life at that time, and does not have to wait for the heroine until the last chapter as would have been the case had it been a romance. Its style was meant to be an enriched variant upon that of the Itinerarium Regis Ricardi and of William of Tyre, and in my own case was probably influenced by that of Maurice Hewlett.

Best Salaams

Harry Pirie-Gordon

HUBERT'S ARTHUR
(As far as I remember it)

It is an essay in 'what might have been' history, carefully worked out and introducing various historical characters who are all made to behave as they might reasonably have done in the circumstances imagined to fit in with the story.

Arthur, Duke of Brittany, instead of being murdered by King John, escapes with the assistance of Hubert de Burgh and takes refuge among the Crusaders in what was then left of the Holy Land. In spite of every obstacle he marries Yolande, the heiress of the kingdom of Jerusalem (who really married the elderly John de Brienne), and becomes King of Jerusalem in her right. He recovers Jerusalem by a *coup de main* from the Saracens. His best friend is his bastard cousin Fulke, King Richard's son by Jehane de St. Pol (see Maurice Hewlett's *Richard Yea and Nay*). After many adventures Arthur returns to resume his Duchy of Brittany, and joins with the King of France against John, doing homage for Normandy, Aquitaine and Poitou as nearest heir to King Richard. There is a civil war in England on John's death—the Barons are divided into three camps: some favour Henry, son of John, some Louis, son of the King of France, some, under the influence of Hubert de Burgh, now Earl of Kent and Justiciar of England, favour Arthur. The dispute between the two English claimants is settled by a trial by combat in which Arthur and Henry (who is made a bit older than he really was at the time to make a better match of it) fight for the Crown. Arthur wins, is acclaimed King of England as well as of Jerusalem, and forthwith drives the French claimant out of the country, but is killed in so doing. That I think is how I left it, but Corvo may have altered the ending. There was a lot of very carefully prepared contemporary local colour, and a good deal of heraldry. Much attention was given to the accounts of warfare in Palestine and England.

*   *   *

Rolfe's sufferings at this time were not imaginary. He frequented the Monday evening parties of Horatio Brown (biographer of John Addington Symonds, and a leader in the English colony) for the sake, as he said later, of the sandwiches on the sideboard: but took umbrage at some chance remark, and estranged himself by making an

opportunity for publicly cutting the indignant Brown.
'Now the summer is ending and the lagoon is rainy. But
I am healthy', he wrote tauntingly on a postcard to Pirie-
Gordon. The authorities of that English hospital which
he had formerly helped also fell under his displeasure,
presumably through failing to comply with his frantic
demands for assistance. He was reduced to offering his
services, in the following style, to such few British residents
as were not already at arm's length:

Reale Societa Canottieri Bucintoro

Sir:

I beg leave to apply for a situation as second gondolier. The
mismanagement of my English agent who has had charge of my
literary property, and the treachery of false friends, compels me
to seek *instant* and permanent means of livelihood. Unfortunately
I am not in a position to give references as to either my character
or my ability, though I am fairly well known in Venice. I should
therefore be willing to serve you on probation for a week; and
I assure you that I would serve you well. Requesting the favour
of an early and (if possible) an acquiescent response,

I am, Sir,

Your obedient servant

Sigr. Williamson   Fr. Rolfe

It is not known that anyone was intrepid enough to avail
themselves of his obedient services. At the height of his
desperation he was rescued by Canon Ragg.

I met him by chance and learned that he was reduced to sleeping
in the open in that rather fine 'martial cloak' in which he fancied
himself as looking like the Duke of Wellington. He was very
proud and reserved, and correspondingly difficult to help. On
some specious excuse I induced him to sup with me at a restaurant.

A visit of Mgr. Robert Hugh Benson to Venice gave me a
chance of talking over Rolfe's problem, and Benson and I spent

an evening together in a gondola, but nothing substantial came of it. Benson was afraid to touch the case.

During our last weeks in Venice, before leaving for England, we were staying in Palazzo Barbaro, and our own flat was vacant save for the luggage waiting to be transported. We then beguiled Rolfe to think he was doing us a service if he would use the flat (instead of open air) as a dormitory. Our luggage was ready labelled, and thus he became acquainted with our future address in England.

Far from being grateful, he seemed to resent all benefits. I fancy my crowning offence was introducing him to a representative of Rothschild's in Paris, a man whom all my friends admired, and who, it was thought, could unravel his financial problems if they could be unravelled at all. They met and had their talk; and for some reason Rolfe's bitterness seemed to increase from that moment.

For some time after our return to England he maintained a one-sided correspondence, mainly by the medium of insulting postcards, which he sometimes varied by unstamped letters. We refused to take the letters in, and after some months we heard no more of him.

*   *   *

Canon Ragg had, however, done Rolfe one more good turn than he knew. In March, just before the patience of Sgr. Barbieri ended, he introduced Fr. Rolfe to a friend, Dr. van Someren, settled with his young American wife in Venice. The acquaintance was not, at the time, pursued; but one evening in June, after the Raggs had returned to England, Rolfe called to see the Doctor and told him frankly that he was starving.

A knowledge of the circumstances of Rolfe's life is in itself almost sufficient to rescind any cynicism concerning human nature and its tendency to benevolence. Continually throughout his career he was aided by those on whom he had no call beyond that of obvious misery and suffering, and the impression of brilliant ability in distress. It was

so now. The charitable Dr. van Someren listened with
horror to Rolfe's story of his wanderings and homelessness, and instantly decided that it was his duty to relieve
both; accordingly, he insisted that, a few days later, when
a room had been prepared for him, the outcast author
should come to live in his house. Actually, such an arrangement was more than normally inconvenient, since Mrs. van
Someren was in child-bed at that time, with attendant
nurses who strained the accommodation available to the
limit. Rolfe was given the large first floor landing of the
marble staircase which had been partitioned in by a previous
tenant; and here, though his room had no fireplace, and
could only be heated by *scaldino,* Rolfe was made more
comfortable than, perhaps, he had ever expected to be again.

Reassured by a roof over his head, indeed, the outcast
became charming: Dr. and Mrs. van Someren found his
company a continual source of pleasure. Time had added
new strings to his conversational bow. 'Have you ever
seen serpents sliding out of the eye-holes of skulls?' was
one of his openings, derived from his explorations among
the islands, one of which he had found to be littered with
the whitening bones of Austrians heaped there at the end
of the war of liberation. He talked of the violet evenings
and rapid dawns which he had observed from his boat, and
had many stories of the quaint behaviour of his young
gondoliers, one of whom he frequently described as 'a
tiger with a simper'. There was a story, too, of a dark
night when his miserable meditations had been interrupted
by arrest as a spy. But these conversational flights were, in
the main, confined to mealtimes. Otherwise he remained
for hours on end quietly in his room, working busily on
a new book, the subject of which he preferred not to
disclose till it was finished. Though still fastidious in little
things, he gave no trouble; and when, after the birth of
Dr. van Someren's daughter, it was thought wise for the
mother to be taken for a holiday change of scene, Rolfe
was left behind with the servants.

Alone in this unexpected apartment of the vast Palazzo Mocenigo-Corner, whose walls of rusticated stone three feet thick recalled its condottiere-builder and the days of the Borgia, Rolfe picked up again the threads of his life; that is to say, his quarrels, and his incessant search for a financial partner. So far as he could, he made his 'enemies' suffer. Benson was denounced to his bishop, Mr. Taylor to the Law Society, Pirie-Gordon to the Publishers' Association. But simple denunciations did not satisfy his rage for long, and heavier weapons were called into action. All those friendly neighbours he had met at Gwernvale, for instance, were astonished by letters of which this is a specimen.

Private and Personal   *Palazza Mocenigo–Corner*
                                                          Venice

Dear Mr. Somerset,

I can't claim to know you well enough to justify me in asking your friendly intervention: but I should be more than grateful if you could see your way to cough efficaciously at your church-warden, E. Pirie-Gordon, and his son, regarding their question-able conduct towards me. E. P. G. is fully cognisant of his son's behaviour; and apparently consents to it. C. H. Pirie-Gordon arbitrarily embroiled me with my agents in England a year ago, so that they stopped communications and with-held my pub-lishers' accounts of the last three years. Consequently I became stranded here. I have had no change of clothes since August 1908. I live and sleep in the open landing of a stair in this barrack of a palace. I have walked the city many nights, wet and fine, before I found this refuge—have been six consecutive days without food, half-starved for weeks together on two rolls (at three centesimi each) a day, and endured all extremes of penury short of prison and the Asili dei Senza Tetto. All my pawn-tickets of the Monte di Pietà have expired, save one. Now and then I contrive to get a job as a private gondogliere: at present I chop and saw and carry logs, work a cream-separator, light fires, and fill boilers. My mother in England works for a living at 75: my sister has become blind; and we have not met for three years. Meanwhile, the Pirie-Gordons sulk in silence, having flatly refused to send me the things which I left at Gwernvale in August 1908 unless I pay carriage. My goods detained at Gwernvale are clothes, tools of trade, heaps of unfinished work—all I have in the world—which I might have turned into money long ago. And, considering what I have done for the Pirie-Gordons in the past—I need only mention C. H. C. P.-G.'s *Innocent the Great*, dictated from a short rejected essay, revised, edited, typed and seen through the press by me—I am utterly at a loss to understand what good reason they dare allege for (first) ruining me so that I cannot pay carriage of my goods, and (then) refusing me the use of my own life-work, manuscripts and materials, whereby I might have refunded cost of their carriage and retrieved my position long ago. I don't want to interfere between your friendly relations with the Pirie-Gordons: but, if an official word of reproof could goad them (even moderately) into a sense of decency, I should be vastly served.

Faithfully yours

Fr. Rolfe

Even this did not suffice, and he announced his intention of producing a pornographic work in Italian, French, and English, to be published at Paris for 50 francs, with the initials R. H. B. on the title-page, the Pirie-Gordon arms on the cover, and a notice within that the book was produced by the authority of that Order of Sanctissima Sophia which he had helped to found in happier days at Gwernvale. The van Somerens returned from their holiday, and found their unobtrusive guest still busy at his work; they little guessed what queer web Fr. Rolfe was quietly weaving.

It was at this period that he began that correspondence with a friend in England (now dead, who shall be nameless) which so much amazed me when Millard first introduced me to Rolfe's work. Now, when I re-read those frightening letters in the light of my later knowledge, it still seemed to me that he never sank lower than in writing them. His ingratitude to those who helped him, his objurgations against his friends, even his vindictive attempts to secure such revenge as lay in his power against those who, in his fancy, had injured him, can be explained and almost excused. He had some ground for a grudge against a world in which he found himself so misplaced, which offered such slight rewards for his gifts, and the books in which they were manifested. There was some ground for his grudge against Benson. But, if these dark letters are to be believed, he had embarked in Venice on a course of life which not even well-founded wrongs, even by his own standard, could justify. It was not only that he stood self-revealed as a patron of that homosexual underworld which exists in every city. He had become a habitual corrupter of youth, a seducer of innocence, and he asked his wealthy accomplice for money, first that he might use it as a temptation, to buy bait for the boys whom he misled, and secondly so that he might efficiently act as pander when his friend revisited Venice. Neither scruple nor remorse was expressed or implied in these long accounts of his sexual exploits and enjoyments, which were so definite in their descriptions that he was forced, in sending them by post, so to fold them that only blank paper showed through the thin foreign envelopes.

Despite that precaution, however, this side of his life was no longer completely unsuspected. Various watermen warned Mrs. van Someren that her guest bore a bad character; and rumours from other quarters reached the Doctor's ears. But Rolfe behaved with such discretion and aloofness that his hosts, disbelieving the reports, regarded him as a maligned man; Dr. van Someren even agreed to allow him a small sum weekly for stamps and tobacco. As the winter wore away Rolfe was still working indefatigably at his new book. He had taken up his residence at the Palazzo Mocenigo in the July of 1909; the spring of 1910 found him still there. And then, in an unlucky moment for himself, Rolfe was moved by natural author's vanity to satisfy Mrs. van Someren's equally natural curiosity.

She had made numerous vain efforts to persuade him into allowing her to see the manuscript on which he was working, efforts which he had politely withstood. Unexpectedly, however, one afternoon he yielded, and placed in her hands a bulky bundle of closely written sheets, the first part of his book, exacting only the condition that she would say nothing of what it contained to her husband. The condition was granted; but as Mrs. van Someren read she soon saw that it must be retracted: for, as she turned the manuscript pages written in vermilion ink, she recognized first one and then another and then another of her friends and acquaintances, pitilessly lampooned in this 'Romance of Modern Venice', *The Desire and Pursuit of the Whole*. With perverse and brilliant ingenuity, Rolfe had woven his life and letters into this story of himself (as Nicholas Crabbe, the hero) pursued and thwarted by the members of the English colony. The book was not completed; and, rancid with libel as it was, might never be published; but it was clearly impossible for the friend of Lady Layard, Canon Ragg, Horatio Brown and the rest of the English residents to share responsibility for it by sheltering the author while he finished it. So Mrs. van Someren instantly told Rolfe, adding that she must let her husband decide what action should be taken. The Doctor, when he learned how his long hospitality had been requited, issued an ultimatum: the manuscript must be abandoned, or its author must leave the house. Rolfe was equally prompt in his decision: next morning he took his few belongings and his cherished romance to the Bucintoro Club; that night he walked the streets. It was early March and bitterly cold. A month later he collapsed, and was taken to that Hospital which, in his libellous book, he had so bitterly attacked. Exposure and insufficient food had induced pneumonia. He was given the Last Sacraments; but he did not die.

XVII

THE FINAL BENEFACTOR

THE reader will probably wonder how I obtained so many details of Rolfe's life in Venice. It will perhaps be a sufficient answer that Professor Dawkins, Mrs. van Someren, Canon Ragg and others who are mentioned are still alive; and that, with greater or less difficulty, I traced them all and received, from each, fragments of the puzzle which, in the two preceding chapters, I have put together to the best of my ability. In addition, however, I had another and more important source of information.

It may be remembered that Mr. Pirie-Gordon's letter to *The Times Literary Supplement*, which had been one of the starting points of my Quest, mentioned the lost manuscript of *Hubert's Arthur* as having passed into the possession of an unnamed cleric who had befriended Rolfe; and that subsequently Messrs. Chatto and Windus had declined to show me Rolfe's Venetian romance without his authority. Even at that early date I made such efforts as I could to trace this gentleman, who was, I gathered, living. I derived his name, with some difficulty, from Mr. Herbert Rolfe, and wrote to ask for information and an interview. But, though for months I bombarded him with letters, my applications elicited no answer; and I learned from Messrs. Chatto that they too had experienced a similar silence in regard to business letters. It appeared that Rolfe's name was not a password to the attention of the Rev. Stephen Justin, and I resolved to take other measures. I wrote to announce my imminent arrival at his Rectory, a hundred and fifty miles from London; and this did bring me a response, to the effect that the day I proposed was unsuitable. Further correspondence seemed to bring us no nearer a meeting;

finally I sent a telegram, 'Arriving at noon', and left before my intention could be countermanded.

My pertinacity was richly rewarded. The Rector's reluctance to discuss Rolfe and his affairs vanished in my presence; and after lunch I assisted him to bring down from a lumber room, where they had rested undisturbed for thirteen years, the literary remains of Fr. Rolfe. It can be imagined what a breathless hour I spent in turning over the letters, notebooks, manuscripts and memoranda which my host had preserved without examination. I gathered the reasons for his indifference.

Mr. Justin met Rolfe in the autumn of 1910 in the Hôtel Belle Vue. How Rolfe had secured reinstatement under Signor Barbieri's roof was for long a problem to me; and even now I am uncertain. It seems probable, however, that after his illness a subscription was organized for his benefit and return to England, to which most of those who were pilloried in his unpublished book gladly contributed. By this account, which I do not assert with certainty, Rolfe accepted the surplus cash but declined the railway ticket, and returned to the Hôtel Belle Vue. However it was managed, there is no doubt that Rolfe's fiftieth birthday found him back at the Belle Vue, as usual deeply occupied with pen and book, and, as usual, involved in various and vitriolic correspondence. His favourite image for himself was the crab, which beneath its hard crust has a very tender core, which approaches its objective by oblique movements, and, when roused, pinches and rends with its enormous claws; but the tarantula spider seems an apter comparison for him as he watched and waited, expectant of the next benefactor. Unsuspecting, Mr. Justin walked into his web.

This time the friendship did not follow quite its usual course. Rolfe made no direct request for help. Perhaps past experience had taught him that precipitate methods failed. But he talked at length of his certainty of success if he were not hamstrung by the assignment to Mr. Taylor;

and, for perhaps the only time in his life, he was listened to without the faintest tinge of disbelief. Mr. Justin was one of those men whose acquaintance with business is *nil*, and who have not been taught by bitter experience to suspect the financial suggestions of their fellow men. If all that was needed to set Rolfe on his feet was a financial partner prepared to invest a small sum and wait a few years for an augmented return, then the problem seemed a simple one. Rolfe entirely agreed that in theory the matter was one of extreme simplicity. Complication only arose from the unchristian unwillingness of most men with money to take the slightest risk, even though by doing so they could benefit themselves and save infinite pain to a distressed fellow creature. And here he played a forcing card.

Earlier in the year, just before Rolfe's breakdown, Messrs. Rider and Co. had written offering to publish *The Weird of the Wanderer*, one of the two books written in collaboration with Pirie-Gordon, on very reasonable royalty terms. Rolfe's share was assigned to Mr. Taylor, and he therefore refused the offer. A larger one was made, and in turn refused. Thereupon the firm returned the manuscript, 'though we do so reluctantly', and suggested he should state 'the terms you would agree for us to publish [on]'. To this Rolfe, who was determined that if he could not benefit by his books no one else should, assignment or no assignment, had not replied. But, as he pointed out to Mr. Justin, what a pity that such chances should go begging!

After several conversations of this sort, Mr. Justin almost timidly suggested that as he was likely to have a spare sum for investment in the near future, he might well benefit both of them by becoming the looked-for partner. Need I say with what alacrity Rolfe accepted this happy thought? It was agreed that on his return to England Mr. Justin should see Mr. Taylor and discover what sum he would accept in discharge of Rolfe's indebtedness.

With this handsome iron in the fire, and the increased personal comfort derived from his return to the Belle Vue (which no longer exists: it was an excellent small hotel, well situated on the Piazza of St. Mark), Fr. Rolfe became less acid in his letters to England. He wrote to Mr. Taylor, who had complained of the 'tone' of his letters:

Dear and Reverend Sir,

I have just received an offer from an English publisher for immediate publication of *The Weird of the Wanderer*, which work (you will remember) stands denounced by me to the Publishers' Association, as having been stolen from me by your client, Mr. H. Pirie-Gordon. I think it right to mention this, as I know of no reason at present for the lifting of my prohibition. I sincerely trust that the 'tone' of this communication will obtain your valued approbation.

Faithfully yours

Fr. Rolfe

He also wrote a letter, remarkable even for him, to Professor Dawkins, who in answer to a previous letter had written:

Dear Rolfe,

Returning from a journey I found your last letter. The 'return' which you have made me for helping you has been to write me violent letters, and when Pirie-Gordon asked me to help you and I sent him money, you accused me of conspiring with him against you. I do not desire servility; but this 'return' is not what one expects, and the answer as to whether I have acted in cold blood, is that I have acted in anger. I have I believe received all your letters, and the camera, the return of which I thought I had acknowledged with thanks. This last letter of yours seemed a shade less hostile; if it was at all an olive-branch I take it very gladly as such. I am yours sincerely

R. M. Dawkins

Rolfe did not ignore, or could not resist, this opening; he must have felt, when he penned his answer, the joy that

John Holden noted in him at Holywell when he sat down to 'flick that gentleman with my satire':

My dear Dawkins,

I don't for the life of me know what to say to yours of the 24th ult. My pneumonia, caused by walking about frosty nights on the Lido shore last March, has done me more harm than I thought. And I have had an unspeakably awful time these last 21 months, which shows no sign of lifting. My difficulty is that I can't imagine a way of writing to you without offence, AND without seeming to ask for your friendship and your money, both of which I want, but will not touch—with tongs—unless voluntarily and spontaneously pressed on me. I am glad to know that you acted in anger. Doest thou well to be angry? I quite fail to remember that I ever asked you to help me—excepting when, face to face, I asked you to start me here as a gondogliere in Sept. 1908. As for the sums you sent between Sept. and Nov. 1908, I swear that I never imagined you to be looking for a 'return'. You see, I have always got my own pleasure out of giving; and 'return', of words, conduct, money, has been the annulment of my pleasure. I've been doing you the injustice of bringing you down to my own eccentric level; and regret it. Regarding Pirie-Gordon's petition, do try to understand the circumstances. Benson and Pirie-Gordon were supposed to be my two best friends, rich, influential, and devoted. My agent, Taylor, had assignments of all my book-rights and my life-policy of £450, in return for his promise to provide me with an income. December 1908 I wanted money. Pirie-Gordon said he'd make Taylor do his duty. Taylor knew me for a literary hack who can be plundered with impunity. Benson was using his spiritual power to coerce me to write the major part of a book (of which he was to pose as sole author) on the same terms arranged for writing a third of it in open collaboration. P.-G. possessed all my clothes, books, tools of trade, notes of a life, 4 half-finished mss., and the mss. of two collaborated books, 9/10 mine, 1/10 his. Instead of making my agent toe the line, instead of negotiating these two completed books (2 years' work of mine) he appealed to you and to Benson, without my knowledge or consent, to make me an object of charity and to keep me impotent here. And he employed my agent over my head to administer your unwelcome subscriptions. Now, do you wonder that, when I knew, I rejected the thing with the 'violence' of which you complain? I suppose I was violent: but I don't feel a bit sorry for that—though I regret hurting people's feelings, perhaps. Anyhow, the thing was impossible . . . Please, consider how I was—friendless, stripped, penniless. (You complain of the word 'conspiracy'. I'm sorry I used it. But it was Pirie-Gordon who used it first to describe your union with him and Benson and Taylor.) Well, then, I took to living in a sandalo, starving without food for 6 days at a stretch, pawning every blessed thing left, and lying like a good 'un to conceal my plight from Venetians. Do you wonder that I was, and am, in a blazing rage with all of you, who, with roofs above your heads and beds to sleep in and regular meals, could desert me and leave me to the horribly offensive torments which naturally fell to me—could, in your circumstances, pit yourselves against me, in mine. (It's a consolation to know that you, Dawkins, acted in anger. I'm glad that I've done you no harm, as I should have done if I thought that you had acted in cold blood—as Benson acted, whom I've denounced to his archbishop and prejudiced him for ever—as Pirie-Gordon acted, whose theft of my work I've denounced to the Publishers' Association, etc.,—as Taylor acted, whom I've denounced to the Law Society and the Prudential Assurance Company.)

Autumn 1909, and winter, I lived on the open landing of a servant's stair, chopping and carrying firewood and doing a fattorini's job. And I managed to write another book. This I offered to assign to Barbieri (to the amount of my debt) if he'd give me any sort of refuge where I could work. The sneers and insults I endure are indescribable. I live in a dark den on the floor of the narrow side-alley, where no sun has ever been, where I have trapped 61 rats since June, served after servants, and without a soul to speak to, and with clothes unchanged since Aug. 1908. And so on. But you act, not in cold blood, but in anger. Oh, my God! Hostile? No: I am not hostile to anyone who has not robbed me of my work, of my means of living, of my tools of trade. Olive-branch? No: if I offer olive-branches, I label myself as a conquered coward, a sucker-up, a toad-eater, the potential spunger you think me. So I wait for olive-branches to be offered to me. It's no good writing any more. I shall never make you understand. You had a chance of making an equal and a friend. And you threw it away. We were both losers. But I'm the one who suffered.

R.

Weeks and months wore away; the winter of 1910, Rolfe's third in Venice, passed; and at the end of January 1911 he was again turned out of the hotel. Again he fell ill, but recovered without hospital treatment. On the occasion of his former collapse it happened that Queen Alexandra visited Venice and the Hospital where he lay, and spoke soothing words to the apparently dying man. Moved by Rolfe's second expulsion, the Italian hotel-secretary wrote to 'beg Your Majesty to grant Her interest to the English writer, Mr. Rolfe, who after being unable to satisfy his living expenses since last Spring is now wandering homeless on the Lido island in this piercing cold'. The kind-hearted Queen sent £10 through the English consul, who thought it well not to let the haggard beneficiary know the source from whence it came. Summer returned, and he was still alive.

During the next few months he seems to have lived on pride and quarrels and sheer determination not to die. Writing from a garret or a gondola, he organized his insults, and showed himself more than ever a master of derogatory nuance. 'You must not be offended', he wrote ironically to Mr. Taylor, 'when I say that I could not have believed that a responsible firm of solicitors could have made so meek and ridiculous an admission of failure to act in their client's interests as your letter of vii June—for which I thank you'.

Later, 'This is a more formal letter than the one which
indignation at your stupidity and my sense of the ridiculous
extorted from me yesterday'. To Pirie-Gordon he wrote
indignantly, 'Have I got a job? No. AND WON'T. How can
I get a job in tatters and slippers and no pocket-handker-
chiefs? It was your business to get me a job months ago.'
Then it was Mr. Taylor's turn again: 'The line of unsup-
ported assertion and attempted bluff which you are so
misjudged as to use to me only serves to define your unfitness in more glaring colour.' Sometimes he used a more
elaborate sarcasm: 'As a blameless Erastian and the most
blameless of agents you may not know that the Doctor
Saint Alphonsus Ligorius lays down in his *Moral Theology*
this axiom . . .' What he wrote to Benson can only be
guessed! Sometimes he varied the note by trying to move
Pirie-Gordon to reconciliation:

. . . And, while these lovely things are amusing me, there you
all sit snuffling with awful and sinful pomp and dignity at him
whom you have plundered and vainly tried to crush. Why
continue to think me horrible? For Goodness' Sake do try to
get to the Height of the Comic Cosmic Viewpoint. You MUST
traverse the Valley of the Shadow. The Realm of White Light
is only reached through the Ravine of Ultra-Violet despair. Get
up on the Comic Cone; and peep at yourself in passing. View
your meaningless gyrations and senseless circumvolutions in
perspective. Stop your sulking; and come out on the blue blue
blue (turquoise, sapphire, and sometimes) indigo blue (aqua-
marine) lagoon. Squatting in your stews, you taint the light-
dowered air. And your livers get into your eyes, and your
hearts into your boots. People who can't change their minds
are in danger of losing them. It is Mirth alone which
keeps men sane. Oh yes—and, Life is Mind out for a Lark.
Well, now?

He wrote dozens of letters, all venomous and all different,
though he seldom descended to mere abuse. One began

'Quite cretinous creature'; another ended 'Bitterest execrations'. 'Your faithful enemy' was perhaps his favourite termination. Most of them were marked 'This is all without prejudice, and I reserve all rights in this and previous communications'. Meanwhile his pride remained unbroken. One day he met Dr. van Someren, who listened to his stories of new outrage and hardships. Rolfe mentioned a sum of 800 lire (about £30) as the amount necessary for his salvation. It chanced that the Doctor, who was on his way back from the bank, had in his pocket exactly the sum named. Impulsively moved by the coincidence, he handed it to Rolfe. Next day his money was returned with the message, 'I cannot give such a hypocrite the satisfaction of this theatrical gesture'.

Rescue came unexpectedly by post from England. Mr. Justin wrote that he had seen Mr. Taylor, who seemed a very reasonable man. In consequence, he was certain that the projected financial support could be arranged. Legal formalities took time; meanwhile the kindly clergyman sent his working partner an advance loan.

There ensued for Rolfe a St. Martin's Summer of prosperity. His bond to Mr. Taylor was discharged (upon, it must be said in fairness to the much maligned Mr. Taylor, terms of great generosity. He had lent over £400 to Rolfe on the security of his books, all claim on which he relinquished for less than a quarter of that sum). The way was clear at last for the man who had so long cried out that, given time and money, he would write and write and write. Both were given him, and he did nothing: it was too late. He made a few beginnings, he recopied his Venetian satire more beautifully than ever, and, since there was no longer an impediment, he accepted the offer for *The Weird of the Wanderer*. All through 1912 he received cheque after cheque from his partner (or victim) in England; and spent the money without thought of the morrow, wildly and without restraint. He, who had starved on three-centesimi

rolls, who had implored to be employed as second gondolier, now flaunted himself on the canals with a new boat
and (a privilege usually reserved for royalty) four gondoliers.
The sails of his gondola were painted by his own hand; and
he dyed his hair (what remained) red. The long days
of destitution and unchanged clothes were liberally com-
pensated now, when he became the talk of Venice by
his extravagance: it was rumoured that his bedroom
was hung with the material of cardinals' robes. His old
debts were paid and he moved freely; but his exactions and
excuses were continuous. He wrote for fifty pounds,
fifty pounds again, then again for more still; he became an
open drain upon his patron's purse.

Perhaps he knew instinctively that his time was short.
Even so, he lived too long. By the beginning of 1913 Mr.
Justin's funds were exhausted; he had parted with much
more than £1,000; not a penny was recouped from Rolfe's
books; and, reluctantly, Justin resigned himself to lose what
he had lent, and warned the spendthrift (concerning whose
spendings he was ignorant of all save the total) that he
could not go on. Can the infatuated writer have imagined
that the golden stream was unabateable? At least he seems
not to have preserved a penny against such an ending, for
now once more the story of misfortune starts. Here is his
last letter to Mr. Justin:

My dear Man:

I'm in an awful state; and I firmly believe that I'm finished if I
don't get relief *instanter*.

The last fortnight has been a chapter of misfortunes. I've
been literally fighting for life through a series of storms. Do
you realize what that means in a little boat, leaky and so coated
with weed and barnacles by a summer's use, that it is almost
too heavy to move with the oar, and behaves like an inebriate
in winds or weather? I assure you it's no joke. And storms get
up on this lagoon in ten minutes, leaving no time to make a
port. I'm frequently struggling for 50–60 hours on end. Results:

I've lost about 300 pages of my new MS. of *Hubert's Arthur*. Parts were oiled by a lamp blown over them: winds and waves carried away the rest. At every possible minute I am rewriting them: but, horrible to say, grey mists float about my eye-corners just through sheer exhaustion. The last few days I have been anchored near an empty island, Sacca Fisola, not too far away from civilization to be out of reach of fresh water, but lonely enough for dying alone in the boat if need be. Well, to shew you how worn out I am, I frankly say that I have funked it. This is my dilemma. I'll be quite plain about it. If I stay out on the lagoon, the boat will sink, I shall swim perhaps for a few hours, and then I shall be eaten alive by crabs. At low water every mudbank swarms with them. If I stay anchored near an island, I must keep continually awake: for, the moment I cease moving, I am invaded by swarms of swimming rats, who in the winter are so voracious that they attack even man who is motionless. I have tried it. And have been bitten. Oh my dear man you can't think how artful fearless ferocious they are. I rigged up two bits of chain, lying loose on my prow and poop with a string by which I could shake them when attacked. For two nights the dodge acted. The swarms came (up the anchor rope) and nuzzled me: I shook the chains: the beasts plopped overboard. Then they got used to the noise and sneered. Then they bit the strings. Then they bit my toes and woke me shrieking and shaking with fear.

Now this is what I have done. I am perfectly prepared to persevere to the end. So I have taken the boat to a 'squero' to be repaired. This will take a fortnight. When she is seaworthy again, I'll go out and face my fate in her. Meanwhile I'm running a tick at the Cavalletto, simply that I may eat and sleep to write hard at restoring the 300 odd pages of *Hubert's Arthur*. When that is done, the boat will be ready. I will assign that MS. to you and send it.

My dear man, I am so awfully lonely. And tired. Is there no chance of setting me straight?

Ever yours

R.

Were these horrors real, or invented in the hope of a further cheque? The letter is not precisely dated, and may have been written early in September 1913; it was not until the 26th of October that death superseded Mr. Justin as Fr. Rolfe's last benefactor.

The British Consul, Mr. Gerald Campbell, was called to take charge of the dead man's belongings, and wrote to his brother:

Your brother had been in good health and spirits of late, and dined at his usual restaurant, Hotel Cavaletto, on Saturday night, leaving there about 9 p.m. with a friend, Mr. Wade-Browne, who occupied rooms in his apartment. On Sunday the latter called out to him, but receiving no answer thought that he was still asleep. Towards three o'clock in the afternoon he went into his bedroom and found your brother lying dead upon the bed. He was fully dressed and it would seem that he had died in the act of undoing his boots and had fallen on the bed, knocking down the candle, which, fortunately, went out. The English doctor was called in but could do nothing beyond helping Mr. Wade-Browne to notify the authorities and summon your brother's usual medical attendant. The police came in the evening and removed the body to the Hospital Mortuary and locked up the apartment. The following morning the hospital doctor certified that the cause of death was in all probability heart failure. This diagnosis was subsequently confirmed.

Searching through the dead man's papers for the address of his relatives, the horrified Consul found letters, drawings and notebooks sufficient to cause a hundred scandals, which showed plainly enough what Fr. Rolfe's life had been. Even his business affairs were utterly disordered. Herbert Rolfe, who had journeyed from England to bury his brother, could make nothing of them; despite Mr. Justin's help, Fr. Rolfe died, as he had lived, insolvent. Horatio Brown was asked to read and advise on the value of the unpublished Venetian satire, but refused; ultimately, all the non-compromising papers were sent to the principal creditor, the unlucky Justin.

By a final irony, the *Aberdeen Free Press,* apparently forgetful of its onslaught fifteen years before, wrote Rolfe's epitaph.

AN ENGLISHMAN'S DEATH IN VENICE

MR. FREDERICK ROLFE

A Reuter telegram from Venice says that Mr. Frederick Rolfe, of London, a writer on historical subjects, has been found dead in his apartments by a friend.

Mr. Frederick Rolfe is presumably Frederick William S. A. L. M. Rolfe, the author of *Chronicles of the House of Borgia, Hadrian the Seventh,* and other works.

Mr. Rolfe was well known in Aberdeen. He studied for the priesthood at the Scots College, Rome, but did not pursue a clerical career. Through the influence of Mr. Ogilvie-Forbes he came to Aberdeenshire, and resided for a considerable time at Boyndlie. He afterwards lived in Aberdeen, where he became favourably known in literary and musical circles. Subsequently he removed to London, where he wrote extensively under the pen-name of 'Baron Corvo', and he came into considerable prominence through an article in a popular monthly, *How I was Buried Alive.* In London he was highly esteemed for his literary culture and his skill as a writer. He was a man of extraordinary genius and versatility, a clever writer, musician, and artist.

XVIII

EPITAPH

THE twisted career so sharply ended prompts questions which the wisest cannot answer. There is no easy explanation of genius or talent: they exist and we accept them as facets of creative force. Some measure of artistic power or sensibility is inherent in all humanity; 'genius' is as good a word as any other to denote those exceptional beings in whom, unaccountably, it rises to full force. And Rolfe was a defeated man of genius.

But although it is beyond the biographer's power to explain the æsthetic aptitudes and ability of his subject (if his subject possesses them), he may be able to trace and define the *character* which they accompany. And so, though the peculiar inner energy which possessed Fr. Rolfe is beyond analysis, the external events of his life, and his reactions to them, can be collated and made comprehensible. They make clear the cause of his defeat.

The starting point of his complex character is that he was sexually abnormal, that he was one of those unlucky men in whom the impulses of passion are misdirected. What the causes are of this condition, so frequently disastrous to those whom it encircles, is still debated by authorities. Luckily, it is unnecessary, for the purposes of this inquiry, to decide whether it is a congenital flaw, or an injury of the spirit, or a premature fixation in a juvenile state through which most of humanity passes and emerges unharmed. The fact that Rolfe's was a difficult birth was regarded by his family, perhaps rightly, as the origin of his eccentricities. But, though inquiry into *cause* may be neglected, it is essential, if Fr. Rolfe is to be understood, to realize that he did not *choose* his condition: that it possessed him from early years, and that he was almost powerless to alter it.

The record of ancient Greece and Renaissance Italy shows that homosexual feeling need not bar the development of personality, or stand in the way of a successful life; but Rolfe lived in Victorian England, and must perforce have realized, probably at an early age, that this tendency in himself was in opposition to the world in which he lived. At that point began the long dilemma of his life.

His temperament instinctively prompted the choice of schoolmastership as a career. By proximity he could satisfy his interest in masculine youth, which (again, probably) he did not yet recognize as a form of sexual sensitiveness. But though the nature of his feeling may not have been recognized consciously, beneath the surface his subconsciousness could not be unaware. The resulting unseen, internal conflict brought him, if not a knowledge of his own nature, a knowledge at least of his unusualness. He saw that he was not as other men.

The attractiveness of Catholic priesthood to one so circumstanced can easily be understood. Set among those who had voluntarily embraced celibacy, his abnormality became, not a possible vice, but a sign of Vocation. Hence it came about that the young student, whose unsuitability for holy orders was recognized by his fellows almost without exception, aspired to ordination. Yet, despite the disbelief of those who were well able to judge, there is no reason to suppose that Rolfe was other than sincere in his conviction that he was fitted by nature for the robe he hoped to wear. And perhaps he was. Perhaps, if he had been given the authority of orders, he would have been able (reinforced by this external prop) to dismiss all sexual feeling, and regard the dismissal as a consequence of the privilege. His early life was passed in an atmosphere of devotion which he shared. 'When I was a Protestant boy of fifteen I was very fervent. I went to confession, said the rosary, used the Garden of the Soul for a prayer-book. A few years later I became unfaithful to my Vocation, played the fool . . . but I never relinquished my Divine Gift. At twenty-four I became intensely earnest. At twenty-five I suddenly realized that I was on the wrong road . . . and Peter had the key. I realized it one Saturday morning at Oxford; and on Sunday I made my homage to Peter . . . A Jesuit received me into the Church at 24 hours notice.'

Unfortunately (or perhaps, when all is counted, fortunately) there existed in his nature, also, the talent and need for artistic expression. This need (as Vincent O'Sullivan has acutely noticed) found satisfaction in those extravagances which led him into debt, as well as in his paintings and æsthetic accomplishments. Largely in consequence of his undue indulgence of it, his superiors decided that he had no Vocation, and sent him back into the world of ordinary men.

This rejection must have been a tremendous blow to Rolfe. He knew very well his unfitness to pass unnoticed among ordinary men (since indeed he was not ordinary), and he had set his heart on the dignity and mystery of spiritual rank. What remained? Only one course, to deny the rightness of the verdict; to assert that it was the Athenians who had lost him, not he the Athenians; and this, the easiest way, he took. It was the first stage of the *paranoia* that darkened his life. On the fact of his un-ordinariness (which his subconsciousness could not ignore) he built up a phantasy picture of an abnormal Rolfe (abnormal since he had a priestly Vocation) thwarted unreasonably by those who should have known the truth. Here are his own words: 'I believe that somebody carelessly lied, that someone clumsily blundered, and that all concerned were determined not to own themselves, or anyone else but me, in the wrong. A mistake—a justifiable mistake seeing that I am an abnormal creature and my superiors about as commonplace a gaggle of fatwitted geese as this hemisphere produces—was made; and, by quibbles, intimidations, every hole and corner means conceivable, it has been perpetuated.' In this mood he

came back to England; and from it, he distilled the title
or pseudonym of Baron Corvo. That artifice disguised
the disappointing fact that he, who had left for Rome to
assume the distinguishing title of Reverend, had returned
plain Mr. Rolfe.

Had his career as a painter been crowned with success,
time might have smoothed the smart of his rejection. But
he failed, he was driven from pillar to post, from Christchurch to Aberdeen and Holywell. He could not deny to
himself the reality of this further failure; but it could be
explained if not only his Superiors, but *all* Catholics, were,
somehow, either unreasonably in league and set against
him, or likely at any moment to become so. Here again
are his own words. 'I myself am a Roman Catholick not
even on speaking terms with any other Roman Catholicks,
for I find the Faith comfortable and the Faithful intolerable.
. . . I am desperately in terror of Catholicks; never (with
one exception) having met one who was not a slanderer
(in the double sense of Herodotus) or an oppressor of the
poor (in the sense of Psalm cix, 15, A.V.) or a liar.' This
was the second stage of his *paranoia*.

Circumstances forced a life of repression on him, until
he attained that extraordinary command over his countenance and conversation remarked at Holywell by John
Holden. Were those adventures at Rhyl true, or were they
make-believe as a further disguise for his real temperament?
If Rolfe did seek out those women of the street there, it
was a desperate effort on his part to combat his abnormal
feelings, and it failed.

At last he found the true vent for his talent, and became
a writer in London. He defended his own character in
whitewashing the Borgias, but still disappointment crossed
his hopes. His work brought him neither rest nor money; he
could only exist by incurring debt. 'I sit in my bedroom
during ten months in each year. This is mitigated by
occasional plunges for pearls in the British Museum, an
hour for Mass and strolls on the Heath on holidays, an

hour a day for dumb-bells after the West Point system. And for two months I generally am at Oxford (strictly speaking more out of a boat than in at Sandford Lasher) reading exam. papers. But I have no communion with my fellow creatures. I loathe it and I crave it.'

As he grew older he became intolerably conscious of the lack of emotional satisfaction in his life. His derision of love to Temple Scott, and assertion of satiety, was, I am convinced, the disdain of the fox for the grapes out of reach. He spoke of himself more truly in *Hadrian* as a 'haggard shabby shy priestly-visaged individual', mortally afraid of his fellow men, whom he despised and envied. To attract their notice he wore his heart on his sleeve in the *Toto* stories, but failed to find 'the divine friend much-desired', in Sholto Douglas or Trevor Haddon. He strove to make a substitute for affection in collaboration as a form of intimacy. So the pattern of his life was shaped.

He sought by fresh starts to exorcise the past, not realizing that he carried the cause of his woes within. He pictured impossible situations in which ambiguous figures thawed that mail of icy reserve which 'only one dead heart ever has been warm enough to melt'. Had there been even one dead heart? He was powerless to translate such dreams into fact; but at least he could express his disappointment if not his desires. 'On these lines, he was becoming self-possessed, self-reliant, strong and potent.' His forbidden love was a source of weakness, but hate could make him strong. That was the third stage.

The friendship with Benson was of a deeper order than the rest. The lonely Rolfe had been sought out, had been praised, had been admitted as his superior, by one who had won the coveted, delusory haven of holy orders, and might be the means of bringing the never-relinquished panacea within reach of the thirsty sufferer. So at first he felt. Afterwards, as Benson recovered from his first enthusiasm, and asserted his natural dominance, Rolfe's warmth diminished; and when he was, as he felt, 'betrayed', shut off from even literary association (which, to him, meant so much more than the mere writing of a book in collaboration), his liking turned to rage for which Venice was a violent, but ineffective, carthartic.

Instead, he indulged, at last, his passion. The mask still clung, but the repression disappeared. He warmed both hands before the fire of such love as money and flattery could buy. But his delusions were still necessary to compensate his prolonged disappointment; and he retained them to the end. Yet, though he repaid succour with scorn and kindness with ingratitude, it is unjust, in reviewing his career, to withhold admiration and pity. It is very difficult to be just to Frederick William Rolfe. He had so many gifts, and industry above all; but what he had to sell found no price in the market-place. His brilliant books, expressed in prose as exquisite as the hand and as brightly coloured as the inks with which it was written, brought him trivial sums and no security. For his *Toto* stories thirty pounds, for his *Borgia* history not quite fifty, for translating *Omar* twenty-five; for the rest, nothing. He never, during his lifetime, received a penny in respect of *Hadrian the Seventh* or *Don Tarquinio,* for the publishers specified that there should be no royalties on the first six hundred copies, and so neither book had earned any money when Rolfe died. Small reward, it must be conceded; is it a wonder that he took such revenge as he could upon a world which ignored what he was, and what he offered, or that the books by which readers know him are but an earnest of what he might have written, and less than half of what he did write? Behind his fury and lack of financial scruple, behind his inconvenient insistence on the artist's right to live at the expense of others, behind the excesses into which his repressed nature tempted him, there remains an intense soul which maintained its faith, and expressed its aspirations in many excellent words and works.

*   *   *

He was capable of queer kindnesses. In 1928 I received
a letter which made me rub my eyes, for though it was
addressed to me, the handwriting was plainly Rolfe's. I
was almost frightened as I opened it.

London Hospital,
Whitechapel, E.1.

Dear Sir,

Probably it will surprise, possibly it will interest you to see that
the calligraphy of Frederick William Rolfe still lives. When I
was a little boy of 6 or 7, Rolfe was an occasional visitor to the
house. I remember him as a man of charming manners to a
child, who knew all about magic and charms, who wore strange
rings and told fascinating histories.

   He wrote me a few letters, on the occasions of my birthdays,
which were so unlike any others I ever received both in sub-
stance and in script that they were preserved in an old cupboard.
When I was about 16 I came across them. At that time my own
handwriting was almost illegible, ill-formed, very small and
ugly. I was so struck by the beauty of Rolfe's that I at once set
myself to copy the script. In two months I was fairly proficient
in the style, and in a year it had become my normal writing, but
as you can detect the fine edge of its beauty has been lost in
passing through my hand.

Yours faithfully

John Bland

It is not only the evil that men do that lives after them!
Rolfe deserves a kinder epitaph than the belated *amende* of
the *Aberdeen Free Press*. Who could improve on his own:
'Pray for the repose of his soul. He was so tired'? Or, as
he once wrote to a friend who accused him of selfishness:
'Selfish? Yes, selfish. The selfishness of a square peg in a
round hole.'

XIX

THE DESIRE AND PURSUIT
OF THE WHOLE

MR. JUSTIN very kindly allowed me to borrow the whole of his Rolfe papers. It chanced that I was called upon to deliver, at short notice, an after-dinner address to a dining club of which I was a newly-elected member. With my head full of Fr. Rolfe and the details of his life, and my study littered with his handwriting, 'Frederick Baron Corvo' was an obvious choice. Accordingly I wrote an essay of something less than five thousand words upon his work and adventures, which was duly read to a company which included Shane Leslie and other admirers of arcane literature. I mention this circumstance not for its own importance, but because it led to an estrangement, reluctant on my part, with Mr. Herbert Rolfe.

During my investigations Mr. Rolfe had remained detached, if not aloof. He had lent me a number of letters at our first meeting, as I have narrated, but in his acknowledgement of their return he observes: 'You will, I am sure, understand that, interested though I am in this matter, I can only give it fragments of time now.' In subsequent letters he commended my industry, though, I could see, with a doubt as to where it would lead me. That doubt became certainty when I sent him the draft of my address. I had said that Fr. Rolfe lived in the recollections of his contemporaries at the Scots College as an astounding romancer; that in his last years he 'fell from grace', and 'left certain letters that Aretino might have written at Casanova's dictation'; and that his financial conduct showed, at times, a 'lack of honesty'. These observations, in Mr. Rolfe's view, were 'gratuitous, unnecessary, and incongruous'. It seemed to me that I might with justice have used harder phrases, and that my literary integrity would be compromised if I said less than I believed to be the truth; and in a letter which was, perhaps, tactless, I said so. Mr. Rolfe did not agree, and finally declared:

I have no desire to be obstructive so far as a publication of the bare events of the sad life of my brother may be concerned, and, of course, I have no title to object to literary criticism. What I have endeavoured to impress upon you is that, for reasons stated, I do decidedly object to any 'publication' whatever of matter which either implicitly or explicitly imputes to my brother dishonesty or immorality. And I will add this, that, contrary to what your letters to me seem to imply, his relatives never had, and have not now, any indication, much less proof, that he was ever guilty of either. I, and they, believe him to have been the son and brother that we knew him to be and no other. He is in the hands of the Creator of all men, and in His mercy. There we would have him left. I trust you will now understand that your pamphlet, if it remained unmodified, would cause us pain and distress, and that you will, in consequence, revise what you have written. I enclose a list of the passages to which I have previously called attention. . . . Although I send you this list I am afraid that I must say that, on the whole, we would much prefer that the whole pamphlet had been confined to the bare record before mentioned—painful though that must be—and to literary criticism. This is to guard myself from any general expression of approval.

This statement of Mr. Rolfe's attitude made me feel more than ever that a principle was involved on which I could accept no compromise. I became aware, also, that he was even opposed to any later publication of *The Desire and Pursuit of the Whole;* whereas it was and is my view that posterity owes its unlucky author the tribute of reading his last book. I said so, and our correspondence ended. I was left to make what further discoveries I could from Mr. Justin's papers alone.

I had imagined, when I met Mr. Justin and learned the details of Rolfe's death, that my Quest was over. It was not. Though the laden suitcase which I carried back with me to London was full of fascinating things, letters and letter-books by which I came to know Fr. Rolfe as well as I shall ever know him, with such curiosities as his pocket-book containing carefully preserved letters from Conte Cesare Borgia, and his visiting card engraved from a florid Italian script, there were maddening omissions. After Mr. Taylor had signed the Deed of Release giving Rolfe command again over his own work, he reassigned his property to Mr. Justin, who, as I found by an examination of his documents, was the legal proprietor of all those unpublished works of which I had heard so much: *Don Renato, Hubert's Arthur, The Desire and Pursuit of the Whole, Songs of Meleager, The One and the Many.* But, though Mr. Justin owned these books (which it must be admitted he had dearly purchased), and had the right to publish them, he possessed only one unpublished manuscript— *The Desire and Pursuit of the Whole.* In respect of the other books, I was no nearer satisfying my eagerness to lay hands on them than I had been when I learned, step by step, that they had existed. I concluded that at the time of Rolfe's death they must have been scattered about the world, waiting for the verdict of publishers to whom they had been submitted, or not reclaimed, as in the case of that manuscript which had lain forgotten in Messrs. Chatto's safe for more then ten years. Did they even survive? Unreclaimed manuscripts are not kept for ever; perhaps those strange books on which poor Rolfe lavished so many pains, for which he made such extravagant claims, were lost for ever, destroyed by careless hands which did not value their uncommercial quality.

At least I had recovered that Venetian satire to which Rolfe owed his expulsion from the Palazzo Mocenigo; and since he nearly died from the subsequent sufferings, it may be said that he almost gave his life for this book. It is indeed, as Mr. Swinnerton described it, a 'beautiful and absorbing story'; and knowing, as I did, the circumstances behind its sentences, I was spellbound by its white-hot pages, as I had been by *Hadrian*. The hero, Nicholas Crabbe, is of course Rolfe himself; or, rather, Rolfe as he saw himself. 'Nicholas Crabbe, being bored (to the extent of a desire to do something violent) by the alternate screams and snarls of a carroty Professor of Greek who had let him down', 'departed from Venice at the end of November. He went alone in his topo of six tons burden; and sailed southward along the Italian coast, with no idea in his head excepting that of thoroughly enjoying his own society, while scrupulously avoiding every kind of conversation with other human beings.' How vividly the real Rolfe speaks in that opening. Crabbe, in his sturdy, deep-bosomed, flat-bottomed, blunt-nosed boat comes alive in the pages following as clearly as George Arthur Rose in *Hadrian*. Cruising at leisure, flying the ensign of England in the liberty of wide horizons, the lone adventurer sees, from the sea, the lights of Messina and Reggio extinguished in the great earthquake of 1908. A tidal wave tosses his boat like a toy, but it survives the storm. Shocked and shaken, he seeks a peaceful haven to think things over, 'perhaps for hours, perhaps for weeks, perhaps for life'. But, in the cove wherein he anchors, he finds not peace but ruin: houses thrown down, death and horror. In the wreckage only one soul lives: a young girl of exquisite, boylike beauty. Her he rescues.

But, having found her, Crabbe is baffled to know the next move. He knows nothing of women, has always treated them as goddesses in niches. Having seen that this slip of a girl has no real injuries, he sets her ashore. An hour or so later, terrified of the stricken land, friendless, having nowhere to go, she swims back to the boat, and implores, with the devotion of sixteen to its saviour, to be taken in. And when the equally lonely Nicholas refuses her offers of service and says grimly that he will put her ashore again in the morning, she suicidally slips back into the sea, to be rescued a second time.

In the morning the girl tells her master (for such she insists he is to be) her story. She is Ermenegilda Falier, an orphan, seventeen years old in three days' time, whose father, a gondolier, always treated her as a boy, always called her one, and made her expert with the oar before his death. Then she was taken by her uncle to live on his farm, still with cropped hair and boyish dress. Now, since the earthquake, which laid the farm in ruins and destroyed its occupants, she has no human tie; and with all the passionate fervour of her Italian nature she asks Crabbe to allow her to remain with him. 'What should he do with her? What, in the Name of Heaven, was he to do with her?'

Her docility, her beauty, her knowledge of boats, and above all her flat-chested boylike appearance inspire Nicholas with a notion. 'In describing the weird gymnastics in which his mind engaged during these wave-running hours of darkness, he always laid singular and particular stress upon the influence of her phenomenally perfect boyishness—not her sexlessness, nor her masculinity, but her boyishness. She looked like a boy: she could do, and did do, a boy's work, and did it well: she had been used to pass as a boy; and she preferred it: that way lay her taste and inclination: she was competent in that capacity. There was nothing in her to inspire passion, sexual or otherwise: no one could help noticing and admiring her qualities of springlikeness, of frankness, of symmetry, of cogency; but, in other respects, she was negligeable as a boy. A youth knows and asserts his uneasy virility: a girl assiduously insinuates her femininity. Ermenegilda Falier came into neither category'. Very well. Since she so intensely wished it, since she was able to support the part, she should be a boy and his servant, Zildo, not Zilda. He could trust himself, and he would trust her.

The decision made, he returns with 'Zildo' to Venice to

attend to his affairs; Crabbe becomes Rolfe. 'It must be understood that he already had been chased from two careers, and was fairly well settled in a third. Of course a man with his face and manner and taste and talent and Call ought to have been a priest. Elsewhere it is written why he was not. The fault was hardly his.' So he was not priest, but author; his circumstances are exactly those of Frederick William Rolfe. It follows, therefore, that he has two friends, Benson and Pirie-Gordon—Bonson and Peary-Buthlaw in the book. 'The Reverend Bobugo Bonson was a stuttering little Chrysostom of a priest, with the Cambridge manners of a Vaughan's Dove, the face of the Mad Hatter out of *Alice in Wonderland*, and the figure of an Etonian who insanely neglects to take any pains at all with the temple of the Holy Ghost, but wears paper collars and a black straw alpine hat. By sensational novel writing and by perfervid preaching he had made enough money to buy a country-place, where he had the ambition to found a private establishment (not a religious order) for the smashing of individualities, the pieces of which he intended to put together again . . . He did not exactly aspire to actual creation: but he certainly nourished the notion that several serious mistakes had resulted from his absence during the events described in the first chapter of Genesis.' 'I do not pretend to be dogmatic on the point; and I merely offer the hypothetical judgement that Bobugo's view was that the error in the Creation of Man consisted in endowing him with Sense.' This was, for Rolfe, an almost charitable judgement. Mr. Pirie-Gordon and Mr. Taylor are described with equal prejudice. As in a glass darkly, Rolfe in his last book mimics the details of his life, the incidents which have brought him to Italy. All those strange episodes, which I have given in their true colours, are related and distorted from the angle of the madman who endured them. Nicholas Crabbe endures the betrayal of his false friends, the agony of hope deferred, homelessness and hunger in Venice, but cheered and supported, though he does not know it, by his growing affection for Zilda, hers for him. Plot, in the formal sense, there is none; nightmare figures loom and disappear; yet the book has a shape. Into it Rolfe pours, with the frenzy and disappointment of his real life, the beauty and satisfaction which comforted his days in Venice; and behind the dust and tears of his rage there is always the changing beauty of the lagoon and the unchanging beauty of the Church. But further summary would do injustice to a book which is valuable for its texture rather than its form, its intensity more than its message, which is the testament of a tormented personality rather than a story. It was his last self-portrait: 'Nicholas Crabbe, being Nicholas Crabbe, was as hard as adamant—outside. He tolerated the most fearful revilings, humiliations, losses, without turning a hair. He had none. Even his enemies (which means all the men and women with whom he ever had been intimate) freely admit (in their less excited moments) that nothing, at any time, ruffled his cruel and pitiless and altogether abominably self-possessed serenity of gait and carriage; and they account it to him for natural naughtiness. Of course they are imbecile idiots. What is to be expected of a man cased, cap-à-pie, like a crustacean, in hard armour of proof. Such an one has no means of exhibiting his feelings, excepting with his crookedly-curving, ferociously-snapping claws and (perhaps) with his bleak rigid glaring eyes. Crabbe was detested by people who habitually showed their feelings. He couldn't show his. He never showed his real ones for that very reason. But boobies thought that he did—thought that his breakable but unbendable shell was his expression, a horrible expression because it gave no information whatever; and then, when (quite unexpectedly) the hitherto stilly-folded claws snatched and pinched and tore and tossed presumption, with a violence sudden and frightful which manifested some appalling sensibility hidden unsuspected within, the said boobies were gravely shocked or displeased and (when clerical) much pained or even deeply grieved.

Pained, indeed! What of the torments of Crabbe, which no one ever considered because no one ever saw them?' Rolfe was able to give a happier ending to his satire than destiny reserved for him, since Nicholas and Zilda realize themselves in each other, and so 'the desire and pursuit of the whole was crowned and rewarded by love'.

But, though it was satisfactory to have found the Venetian autobiography, I still longed to discover those mediæval romances in which Fr. Rolfe embodied that historical knowledge on which he so much prided himself; and my desire was all the keener from reading, in *The Desire and Pursuit of the Whole*, his description of *Hubert's Arthur*.

He read over what he had already done. It seemed to be almost as far above the ordinary as he wished it to be—history-as-it-wasn't-but-as-it-might-very-well-have-been. For example, there is no direct evidence of the mysterious murder of Arthur fitz-Geoffrey, Duke of Armorica, by or at the instance of his wicked uncle John. Young Arthur was rightful King of England, not only by primogeniture but also by will of King Richard Lionheart. Consequently it was very necessary to John (who usurped his crown) that he should disappear. And he did disappear at Rouen. And John is credited with his murder. But—suppose that he did not really disappear, that he was not murdered, that he actually escaped from his wicked uncle, the history of England (as we have it from the monkish chroniclers) might be quite another story. This was Crabbe's idea. Young Arthur was not murdered at all. By help of Hubert de Burgh, he escaped the tormentors sent to put out his eye-lights, he escaped from John when that assassin tried to drown him in the Seine, he escaped (half-crucified) from the Giwen of Bristol to whom John-Judas had sold him for thirty-thousand marks of silver. Innocent the Third, that astute steel pontiff with the eye of a squinting lambkin, though frightfully excited about the boy, didn't see his political way at the moment to depose the rich oldster John (who was in possession of the crown of the English) in favour of the poor youngster Arthur (who so far hadn't a deed to his name). Arthur, accordingly, in an access of Angevin anger, went and did deeds in the Holy Land, as the shortest cut into Innocent's valuable affections, returning (as King-Consort of Hierusalem) just in time to find the Pope bored to death with John's abominations, and only too happy (now) to do the straight thing. Armed with bulls and whatnot, and supported by Earl Hubert de Burgh, admiral and warden and regent of England, Arthur conquered England, drove John into life-sanctuary at his Cistercian Abbey of Beaulieu, fought young Henry Lackland (commonly called Henry the Third) for the crown in ordeal of battle at Oxford; and reigned with enormous glory till the year of Our Lord 1255. And the history of it all was written, on King Arthur's death, by old Hubert de Burgh, Constable of the Tower, who had been and done everything in England for a matter of sixty years or so, and (in extreme old age) fancied that he naturally knew more about facts than a certain little monk, Mr. Matthew (formerly of Paris), who only listened to gossip and spied through the keyhole of his monastery, and wrote the stuff thus gleaned as what he had the insolence to call *The Chronicle of England*. This, Hubert de Burgh's astoundingly circumstantial [narrative], bristling with personal knowledge of men famous and infamous, with statesmanlike policy, heraldry, archæology, love, wit, sorrow, humour, courage, suffering, every high and noble human interest and activity, all illumined by the insight and pathos and power of his own personality, was embodied in a manuscript written in a very individual sort of Latin which Nicholas Crabbe pretended to have discovered in the Tower of London and to be translating in collaboration with his friend [Pirie-Gordon].

A remarkable book, apparently. But where was it to be found? After it had been refused by Messrs. Chatto the manuscript was sent, by Rolfe's direction, to a friend in America; but letters sent to him were returned 'Gone Away'. For a year I tried every hole or corner which my imagination and knowledge could suggest as the hiding place of Rolfe's lost books, but without avail. At last I abandoned the pursuit. Somewhere, I was confident, they existed: I would wait until a swirl of the waters of time brought them to the shore.

*   *   *

There is one other of Rolfe's books to which I have not referred in detail: that one in which Messrs. Rider and Son manifested so timely an interest at the moment when the author first met Mr. Justin, which appeared in print as the only tangible form of that 'financial partnership' in 1912, seven years after its predecessor, *Don Tarquinio*. This collaborated work bears on the title-page the inscription *The Weird of the Wanderer, being the Papyrus records of some incidents in one of the previous lives of Mr. Nicholas Crabbe. Here produced by Prospero and Caliban* (Rolfe's gibe against his friend, mentioned in Chapter XIII, prompted the name). Despite the duality of the pseudonym, the dust cover states that the book 'is the work of a classical scholar, and an author of genius and originality, who conceals his identity under the nom-de-plume of Prospero and Caliban'; and the publisher's catalogue bound in at the end gives Rolfe's name alone as the author. There is certainly no trace of 'genius' in this undistinguished work, which narrates in the first person the adventures of Nicholas Crabbe, of Crabs Herborough, Kent, after he has acquainted himself with the magic incantations of ancient Egypt, and seeks, by their means, to commune with the dead. His command of spells fails him at a crucial point, and he is carried back through time to an earlier incarnation of himself as Odysseus. The passage describing the translation has, more than any other in the book, a touch of Rolfe's excellence: 'I saw the histories of mortal men of many different races being enacted before my eyes . . . kings and queens and emperors and republicans and patricians and plebeians swept in reverse order across my view. . . . Time rushed backward in tremendous panoramas. Great men died before they won their fame. Kings were deposed before they were crowned. Nero and the Borgias and Cromwell and Asquith and the Jesuits enjoyed eternal infamy and then began to earn it. My motherland . . . melted into barbaric Britain; Byzantion melted into Rome; Venice into Henetian Altino; Hellas into innumerable migrations. Blows fell; and then were struck.' But though there are some interesting turns of phrase, the book, as a whole, is a failure, marked by continual pedantry of expression, and by insufferably jocose footnotes. I might have concluded, from the deterioration evident in this book, that Rolfe's later years were marked by a decline in his literary powers, had not *The Desire and Pursuit of the Whole*, and those startling Venice letters, emphatically proved otherwise.

XX

THE END OF THE QUEST

In 1927 my friend Millard died. The Quest for Corvo had been almost at a standstill for months; with Millard's passing it altogether stopped. Sometimes after dinner I turned a contemplative eye to the files and papers that I had purchased from the Rev. Stephen Justin; sometimes I looked again at those painful Venice letters; I re-read *Hadrian;* more frequently I speculated whether I should ever find the lost manuscripts of the unlucky, gifted man who had occupied my mind for so long. But nothing happened; I made no progress; without having lost interest I had lost incentive to pursue a search which for the moment I could see no way to advance. Such hope as remained to me rested on the unusual beauty of Rolfe's written manuscripts, which, judging by those I had seen, were not likely to be thrown away by anyone with eyes in his head.

And then, one fine Spring morning, a message came to my room to ask if I would see a Mr. Gregory, who had called with an introduction from Shane Leslie to ask questions about Baron Corvo. Mr. Gregory (or, as he was formally announced, Mr. Maundy Gregory) proved to be a plump, rubicund, middle-sized man in the fifties, with an expensive flower in his button-hole, an air of constant good-living, an affable smile, a glittering watchchain, good clothes and (as I noticed when he sat down) very beautiful boots. His business was briefly stated. He had read the works of Baron Corvo with fanatical admiration, my own article (published by Mr. Desmond MacCarthy after my disagreement with Herbert Rolfe) with zest; and meeting Mr. Leslie by chance, had been advised by him to seek me out as the source of further knowledge. His visit was sufficiently explained; yet a certain watchfulness in his manner, an expression of worldliness far beyond mere literary curiosity, seemed to hint at something more. I felt instinctively that this resplendent personage would take a part in my Quest; I did not guess how completely, for a time, it was to be identified with him.

I produced the Corvo manuscripts, which were the motive of Mr. Gregory's call; and his admiration was undissembled and knew (apparently) no bounds. He gazed at the letters and books I produced for his inspection with that open envy which is the pleasantest form of flattery to a collector. The multi-coloured letters to Grant Richards moved him to reverence, the Venice correspondence to awe. My reserve vanished before such pertinacious and tactful amiability, like mist before the sun; I began to like Mr. Gregory.

Then, with a curious and rather attractive diffidence, my visitor asked if I would consider selling him one of my less important treasures. He could not hope, he conceded, that I would part with any of the major manuscripts; but perhaps I could spare a fragment or a duplicate? Money was no object, he added, almost regretfully, as he turned over again the leaves of *The Weird of the Wanderer* in Corvo's beautiful handwriting. Actually I had no particular wish to sell anything that morning; but something in his hint that he was immensely wealthy, a peculiar challenge in his eyes as he made it, prompted me to pass him, more in jest than in earnest, a small poem of Rolfe's composition and in his hand, and say 'You can have that for £20'. Without hesitation Mr. Maundy Gregory's hand went to his pocket; a thick gold-edged wallet appeared and was opened; four five-pound notes were taken from an impressive wad; and 'I am most grateful to you', he murmured.

I was as much astonished as I was delighted. At the rate I had charged Mr. Gregory for this single poem, my shelf of Corvo manuscripts was worth more than a thousand pounds, a pleasant reflection for a poor man. But I knew perfectly well that they were worth no such sum, and that I had grossly overcharged for the poem. I said so. To no effect: Mr. Gregory smiled mysteriously again and repeated that money was no object to him, and that he was very grateful for the chance to acquire a unique specimen of the work of his favourite writer.

We parted after more than an hour's talking, with mutual asseverations of goodwill, and an undertaking on his part to lunch with me a few days later. As I escorted him to the door a waiting taxicab drew forward from beyond, and without a word my visitor stepped in. 'Goodness', I exclaimed, 'has that cab been waiting for you all this time?' 'Oh yes', replied Mr. Gregory, 'You see, I own it'. And with a bland salutation, but no direction to the chauffeur, he drove away.

I telephoned to ask Shane Leslie what he knew of his impressive friend; but without learning much. Shane had met Maundy Gregory at a dinner-party, and, the conversation turning on Corvo, had given him my name. I waited with interest for our next meeting.

Punctually to the moment (for the only time in our acquaintance) Mr. Gregory arrived to keep his luncheon appointment. Champagne seemed the appropriate drink for so expensive an individual, and I was not surprised when he admitted a preference for it over other wines. I tried tactfully to learn something of my visitor. Did he own a fleet of taxicabs? No, he explained, only one, which even now waited without. He used it instead of a private car for the reason that a car waiting outside a door was easily recognized, whereas a taxicab passed unnoticed. But why did he need to pass unnoticed? I persisted. He gave no direct answer, but I gathered that there were important reasons why Mr. Maundy Gregory's movements should not be proclaimed.

In a dozen ways during lunch I became aware that I was talking to a very rich and influential man. It was not the gold cigarette case he produced (a gift from the King of

Greece), nor his superb sleeve links (platinum balls covered with diamonds), nor the beautiful black pearl in his tie which produced this impression of vast wealth, so much as the implication behind everything he said that whatever he wished to do or to possess was, so far as money was concerned, a settled thing. He displayed no reluctance to talk about himself. For example, he told me that he lunched every day at the Ambassador Club, never alone, and that every day at a quarter to one two bottles of champagne were put on ice for him. I learned that he possessed two yachts, a house in London, another on the river, and a flat in Brighton. Without in the least boasting he let me know that his library contained many rare books, his cellar much fine wine. Of all these things he spoke quite calmly, and with a friendly, flattering assumption that thenceforth I should share in them.

As to Corvo, he listened to my story of the missing manuscripts with close attention, and pronounced the problem a simple one. So far I had been hampered in having to rely solely on my own resources, whereas now, with unlimited support from himself, he felt confident that everything I sought would be recovered in good time. I gathered that the publication of Corvo's unissued works, the establishment of Corvo in his proper place of repute as an author, were in future to be among his major interests, and that I could draw upon him for any reasonable sum to advance these purposes. It was a memorable and delightful lunch.

A week later we met again. This time I was his guest. The place of meeting was the Ambassador Club, which I had never before visited, but now had ample opportunity of admiring, since Mr. Gregory was an hour late. He was breathlessly full of apologies, and explained that he had been detained at Buckingham Palace on urgent affairs. The lunch was certainly worth waiting for. A bevy of respectful waiters clustered round our table while costly courses appeared and disappeared. Champagne flowed, large cigars and brandy followed. While we were lunching I learned several more unexpected things. Mr. Gregory counted Lord Birkenhead among his closer friends; he held an important post in the Secret Service; he was an intimate of many royal houses, and was, indeed, actively engaged in promoting the restoration of several. His cuff-links were no less resplendent than before, though not orbicular, and this time his gold cigarette case bore an inscription, not from a King, but from the Duke of York. We talked for hours. I was hardly surprised when, at four o'clock, looking round the magnificent but now empty restaurant, he whispered confidentially, 'Of course this place belongs to me'. I was to learn that this, like most of the things he told me, was quite true.

Our next meeting was at his office in Whitehall, whither I was summoned by telephone. I noticed with interest as I went in that the premises were those of the *Whitehall Gazette*, which, as I learned, Mr. Gregory both edited and owned. The staircase and anteroom were unimpressive, but that only pointed a contrast with his extraordinary office, into which I was ushered after a long delay. I well remember the first sight of my queer acquaintance seated in a vast red chair behind a desk crowded with signed royal portraits, telephones, and indicators that buzzed or flashed with coloured lights. After I had been given a glass of Tio Pepe, the reason for my summons was explained. Mr. Gregory felt he would like to buy the Venice letters; would I sell them, and for how much?

At that moment I needed money (since I was a schoolboy my inclinations have always exceeded my income), and I was very willing to sell. The question was, what price to name. Since money was 'no object' to Mr. Gregory, I set their value at a hundred and fifty pounds, exactly six times what I had paid poor Millard for them. So far from demurring, my host questioned (without the slightest irony) if I was asking enough for such remarkable documents; and on being assured that I was, opened a drawer of his desk and from a thick packet handed me fifteen £10 notes. The packet was not noticeably diminished by the transfer; there must have been at least £5,000 on that table. More Tio Pepe, and then I was let out by a padded, bolted double door into the evening air. I was asked for no receipt; and it was not until a week later that I could find an opportunity of handing over the letters.

Then began a series of feasts (I can hardly call them lunches), to which I look back even now with astonishment. Mr. Gregory was invariably host; he was invariably late; the food and wine were invariably first-rate and ordered with no consideration whatsoever for expense. There was often company—mostly foreign secretaries or officials, sometimes as many as a dozen guests, though usually we lunched *tête à tête*. As I came to know him better (and in the end I knew him very well) I grew to like this man of mystery. Wealth in the abstract seems to me almost non-existent: a man with a vast balance at the bank who spends very little is not rich, but poor, in my eyes. Maundy Gregory seemed to share this view. He loved visible things, and the physical results of wealth, with something between the zest of the parvenu and the joy of the artist. He had at least a dozen gold cigarette cases, and never used the same one on two consecutive days; indeed, his personal jewellery of one kind and another (all very valuable and good) would have sufficed to stock a shop. Yet for all the discursiveness of his self-revelation, I could never find out his occupation nor the source of his income. He spent at a fabulous rate. The waiter who brought his hat or his cigar received two shillings by way of tip; and the rest of his life was organized on that scale. And all his payments were made in the crispest of brand-new banknotes, or else in the shiniest of brand-new money. He really seemed, by his behaviour and extravagance, to possess a private mint.

After several months, during which Mr. Gregory's hospitality appeared to be as limitless as his purse, I was asked to lunch with him at even shorter notice than usual on 'very urgent business'. He was both late and silent on arrival; I gathered that he was expecting something. It came with the coffee, when without a word he placed in my hands a bound copy of *Don Renato; or An Ideal Content*, that lost work of Fr. Rolfe's so much admired by Mr. Trevor Haddon.

It certainly deserved his praises. No more faithful reflection exists of its extraordinary author: and it could be the work of no other hand. The infallible touches of his fascinating, overladen style (the style of *Don Tarquinio*, not *Hadrian*, of Baron Crovo, not Fr. Rolfe) are prominent from the first page to the last. As this 'Historical Romance' will perhaps not be available to general readers for many years, I extract a few details from its mosaic of strange learning and language. The Dedicatory Letter (to Trevor Haddon, dignified as Apistophilis Echis) opens:

These are the words of the book which I, Frederick William, the son of James, the son of Nicholas, the son of William, the son of Robert, wrote in London and in Rome.

Because you, o painter, incessantly perturb me with inquisitions concerning the sources of my curious knowledge of matters archaick and abnormal, because you incessantly transform me with the intent regard of your Kretan brows, and molest me with entreaties that I, as man to man or (at times) as artificer to artificer, should demonstrate to you the Four Causes of my gests, especially that I should tell you how I do my deeds (and you know how many and how rare these be)— I will give you this book.

A life, as of an anachoret, as of an eremite, in severance from the world of articulately-speaking men, while rendering me inhabile in expressing thoughts, creeds, opinions, in spoken words, has made me subadept with the pen—a very detestable condition. On this account, time and human patience would be exhausted before I should be able to satisfy you by word of mouth: but, thirteen months occupied by me in writing, and seven nights or three days (when your workshop may be obscured by London fog) occupied by you in reading, will make clear to you at least one of the sources of my knowledge.

Yet, for your hypotechnical inquiry as to How the Thing is Done, I am unable to supply an apophthegm. My own consuetude, in matters of which I desire to be informed, is to place very many interrogations among experts; and, from the responses received, to respond to myself. This mode has advantages and disadvantages. On the whole it produces satisfaction; and I know no better. Indeed I doubt whether any artificer could respond to your inquiry either in spoken words or in written . . .

But, ever since you began to inquire of me, I have pondered you and your inquiry; and, because I myself from my boyhood very gravely have laboured barehanded to obtain a little knowledge, I am the more unwilling to deny to so eager and so exquisite an artificer, that counsel and assistance which have been denied to me. For men (as far as I know them) always will tell you what they think you ought to know, and always will give you what they think you ought to want: but they never will give you what you want, and they never will tell you what you want to know. Perhaps they cannot. Perchance I myself shall fail. But I will try.

Accordingly, there follow three notes concerning the Formal, Material, and Efficient Causes of the story; the first being a discussion between publishers' managers as to the form and condition of historical novels; the second an account of that English-Italian Duchess who counted for so much in Rolfe's early life ('It will be evident to you', he says 'that, when so very great and gracious a personage admits to her comity an obscure clerk, a plebeian student, unmannered, self-taught, physically and mentally altogether dyspathetick, and manifests so profound an interest in his labours as to give him the freedom of her archives, (charters, breves, diurnals, accompts, and the multifarious manuscripts which a House can accumulate in, let us say, a thousand years,) very intimate cognition of the bye-ways of literature and history is not unlikely to be attained, very curious

knowledge is not unlikely to be acquired, very prec.
excerpts are not unlikely to be collected. Grant me so much

So much having been granted, Rolfe describes, as the
Formal Cause, his discovery of a quarto volume bound in
stout white vellum surrounded by an embossed silver band
containing six hundred pages of thin opaque paper. This is
Dom Gheraldo's Diurnal, the diary of a Roman priest
attached to the house of Santacroce, written between
1528 and 1530 in that macaronic mixture of Greek, Latin
and Italian which I had already met in *Don Tarquinio*. The
priest goes further than the prince, however, in that his
entries are written in imitation of various classic and
Italian styles. The translation of this imaginary volume
forms the body of Rolfe's book.

No writer ever set himself a more difficult task. He, or
rather Dom Gheraldo in his entries, tells a story: he reveals
by slow and feline touches the character of the priest
from within; and at the same time he attempts to give an
English equivalent for the verbal mix-up of the pretended
original. And in all this he succeeds, though in retaining
Dom Gheraldo's macaronics he almost makes his book
unreadable. Fortunately, he provides a glossary, so that it
is possible to understand, without a headache, the exact
meaning that he meant to extract from such constructions
or compounds or rarities as argute, deaurate, investite, luck-
tifick, excandescence, galbanate, lecertose, insulsity, hestern,
macilent, effrenate, dicaculous, pavonine, and torose. Even
so, *Don Renato* is not a book to read at a sitting, but rather
one to be dipped into at odd hours when the mind can be
stimulated by puzzles in verbal ingenuity, by such passages as

On the insensible stone Don Lelio lay, almost inconscious, his
form wound in a ligature, marmoreal in white stillness. His
terete members but an hour ago so apt and flexuous, were
distorted by incessant twitchings and cold as snow. Already his
lips were livid; they disclosed the purity of teeth clenched and
continually strident. In the pallid throat, palpitated a vein with

diminishing rhythm. Cœrulean stains appeared below the flickering lashes of the half-closed eyes. Like rose-petals in a breeze, even the nostrils quivered. Bloomed the abhominable unmistakeable pallor on the brow, where the soft cæsarial hair was humid with the dew of the breath of Death.

And the passage I have quoted is simple and lucid compared to most passages in this fantasy, wherein bright figures 'recline in the barge under the frondosity of sycamores' after an al fresco dinner 'in the umbriferous ilicet on the shore of the lake'. But when the effort has been made, and the pedantic vocabulary mastered, there is a reward. By touch after touch Fr. Rolfe (or Baron Corvo as he was when he wrote this book) builds up his central character, the comfort-loving, word-loving, superstitious yet learned priest, and shows the round of daily life in a great Renaissance family, the turn of mind of the sixteenth century. Perhaps this study in ivory and amber owes something to *The Ring and the Book;* certainly Browning would have delighted in Dom Gheraldo, with his mediæval medicines ('This day, to the odious Don Tullio Tripette, I gave a vial of the humor of spurge—Euphorbia polygonifolia—done with salt, wherewith to dismiss his warts'); who keeps a benevolent paternal eye on the morals of the pages, with whom he bathes naked by moonlight; who notes with satisfaction the good dishes of the day ('At supper, a proper dish of young cucumbers grown out of season, boiled, eviscerate, replenished with a farce of beef and herbs, and fried in new oil. Very grateful'); to whom water is not hot or cold, but gelid or calid; who frequently admonishes himself in his diary—'Gheraldo, Gheraldo, Gheraldo, take care of thy stile'. Perhaps there is no greater public now than when it was written for this humorous and human mixture of learning and *naïveté;* but posterity certainly owes Fr. Rolfe the tribute of a popular edition of *Don Renato; or An Ideal Content.*

*   *   *

Naturally I was staggered to find Mr. Gregory
where I had failed; and besought him to reveal ho
recovered Rolfe's pedantic masterpiece. It had be̶͟e̶͟ ͟͟͟ͅͅͅ,
I gathered, by one of his many 'agents', who, at considerable cost, had traced the original printer, and from the
depths of a rat-haunted cellar salved five copies, the only
survivors of the whole edition. Few modern books can
have a stranger history than *Don Renato*. It was written at
least as early as 1902, perhaps earlier, in the flush of Rolfe's
Borgian enthusiasm; indeed, if the dedicatory reference to
Rome is to be believed, earlier still. For years he kept the
manuscript by him, adding to its rich sentences and obscure
learning, showing it, quoting from it, offering it at intervals
to the blind tribe of Barabbas. It was one of those un-
developed 'assets' with which, in 1904, he tempted Mr.
Taylor into fighting Col. Thomas. Not until 1907 did he
find a publisher sufficiently intrepid to wish to bring it
before the public. The first proofs reached the author in
Venice in 1908, at the beginning of his feud with his
English friends. When the break came, this was the first
of Rolfe's books that he denounced to the Publishers'
Association; and though, since he had signed an agreement,
his ban had little legal weight, nevertheless on account of it
publication was delayed. Months passed; the printer failed;
the sheets (if more than a few proof copies were printed off,
which is uncertain) were destroyed; even the proofs
disappeared with the manuscript, and all traces of it sank
beneath the waters of time till the 'agent'-diver brought
this highly artificial pearl to the surface once more. With
great generosity Mr. Gregory presented to me one of the
five precious copies; and, whenever I am depressed, I dip
into its elaborate pages and, like Gheraldo, 'think more of
my stile'.

There can be no repetition of a surprise; but unexpected
repetition is itself a new surprise, and I confess that I was
startled again when, a week later, the terete and sensile
Gregory (as Rolfe would probably have called him)

produced the manuscript of that translation of Meleager's songs which Baron Corvo had made with Sholto Douglas over twenty years earlier. This time, indeed, he did more. It was part of Rolfe's plan for the book that its pages should be sprinkled with small Greek heads and figures from his own designs, printed in vermilion on buff paper. Pulls of these charming little 'shrieks' were pasted in their appropriate places in the manuscript; and lo! as I took my place at the table, there, nestling by my wineglass, were the actual blocks made from Rolfe's drawings. I almost regarded Maundy Gregory as a magician after this further demonstration of his powers as a discoverer, and said so; but he waved my praise away, and made his usual answer that with money one can do anything.

As for the manuscript itself, it suffers from the defect of all translations from verse, that it is a translation. Rolfe was no FitzGerald, to re-create in English a new work of art based upon an old original, but his version is expressed in a rhythmic prose which is dignified and rounded; and from a careful comparison with Mr. Aldington's later text, it seems that he did not often misconstrue the sense; for that, the credit was perhaps his collaborator's. I quote two examples:

By Timo's flood of Lover-loving curls; by Demo's Balsam-breathing, Sleep-beguiling skin; by Ilia's pretty pranks; by Slumber's Foe, the Lamp, that Drinketh of my Revels many Songs; O Love, but scanty Breath is left upon my Lips: yet speak the Word, and I will pour out even this.

A dulcet Strain, by Pan of Arcady, thou singest to thine Harp, Zenophila; a far too dulcet Strain thou strikest. Whither shall I flee from thee? Loves compass me on every Side; and grant me not one moment to regain my Breath. Thy Beauty filleth me with Desire, thy Musick too, thy Grace, thy——what shall I say? All, all of thee! I burn with Fire!

When Rolfe and Sholto Douglas made this translation,

Meleager's verses had not been extracted from the Greek Anthology and separately published with an English text; but during the twenty-five years that have passed since then, other hands have performed the task. There is, perhaps, no longer any need for a new version; nevertheless I hope that some day this carefully constructed monument to Rolfe's passionate love for Greek literature may stand on the shelf with his other works.

*   *   *

The day when Mr. Gregory revealed to me his second discovery was, I think, the high-water mark of his enthusiasm for Baron Corvo. Gradually his energetic lavishness diminished, and we met for Arabian Nights' luncheons less and less frequently, though when we did his links and cigarette-cases and tie-pins coruscated with all their old-time splendour, his conversation was as full as ever of interest and revelation. Since he left England to live abroad eight months ago, my inquiries have remained unanswered, and I have looked in vain for any letter in his sturdy square handwriting. His memory remains like that of an incandescent meteor in the sky of high finance, an acquaintance as fantastic and unlikely as the wildest passage in the books of the weird Baron whom we both admired.

Stimulated by his success, I renewed my own researches; and it was my hand and not his that retrieved the two remaining testaments of Fr. Rolfe's ill-rewarded but persistent toil. Multiplied inquiries in America traced at last that friend (Mr. Morgan Akin Jones) to whom the manuscript of *Hubert's Arthur* was sent by the direction of its author shortly before his death.

A great deal might be said concerning this long and fascinating product of the unlucky friendship of Prospero and Caliban which, when it attains its birthright of paper and ink, will add lustre to Baron Corvo's posthumous renown. On the first page is written 'Leniency is

respectfully requested for the manual work of this MS. It was
done by day and by night in a small fishing boat on the
Venetian lagoon with the natural interruptions of storms,
bad weather, and occasional overwhelming weariness.'
Yet it is written in unfaltering and faultless script on the
finest hand-made paper, crudely but stoutly bound (probably
by the author's hand) in thick vellum. That note, with its
pathetic implication, and pointed contrast with the unusual
magnificence of the manuscript (in these days of type-
writers and poor paper) was one of Fr. Rolfe's last signals
of invitation to the reluctant publishers before whom he
cast his pearls.

Hubert's Arthur, at least, is in its way a pearl; and again
I wondered why none of those to whom it was submitted
took their chance. Perhaps it was too long, or too strange,
or too full of heraldry or incident, or too arch, or too well
written; for it is all these things. It is Rolfe's one exercise
in English history, into the stream of which it will one day
itself pass. Since I have already printed the summaries of
both the authors of *Hubert's Arthur,* there is no need to say
more here concerning that queer masterpiece. John
Buchan, who read it for one publisher, wrote to Rolfe:
'the more I look at it the more I admire it, and the more
convinced I am that no publisher in Britain could make a
success of it'; Maurice Hewlett, who read it for another,
implored him to make a more usual use of his great gifts.
Their commendation came too late, when less than a year
of life was left to him, and only a holocaust of his 'enemies'
would have appeased his chronic wrath against the world
and against himself.

Last of all his works to come to light was *The One and
the Many*, which stands midway between *Hadrian the Seventh*
and *The Desire and Pursuit of the Whole* in the autobiographical trilogy wherein Rolfe recorded his adult life. If
time does bring him the fame that his temperament
merited and his temper prevented, this exercise in autobiography may join the other two in print, though it is

inferior to either as a work of art. John Lane, Grant Richards, and Henry Harland make a trio of villains drawn with Rolfe's usual brushful of acid; and the minor enemies who make up the 'many' are also recognisable. There are many brilliant passages of his saturnine irony, many beautiful paragraphs, many pages of self-revelation and utter self-deception. But the background lacks the interest of his other canvases, and the scale of his personalities is slight. Nevertheless it was a deep satisfaction to discover it in the depths of a literary agent's cupboard of unretrieved MSS. It was a deeper satisfaction still to know that every one of the works which had been left and lost in obscurity when Frederick William Serafino Austin Lewis Mary Rolfe died suddenly and alone at Venice had been collected together by sympathetic hands, and that, alone of living men, I had read every line of every one. Nothing was left to be discovered; the Quest was ended. Hail, strange tormented spirit, in whatever hell or heaven has been allotted for your everlasting rest!

INDEX